DIRECTING:
the Television Commercial

DIRECTING:
the Television
Commercial

by BEN GRADUS

An Official Publication of the
DIRECTORS GUILD OF AMERICA, Inc.

Focal Press
Boston   London

Focal Press is an imprint of Butterworth Publishers.

Library of Congress Cataloging in Publication Data

Gradus, Ben.
  Directing, the television commercial.

  (Communication arts books)
  Includes index.
  1. Television—Production and direction.   2. Tele-
vision advertising.   I. Directors Guild of America.
II. Title.   III. Title: Television commercial.   IV. Se-
ries.
PN1992.75.G7   1981   791.45′0233   81-4251
ISBN 0-240-51749-0   AACR2

Butterworth Publishers
80 Montvale Avenue
Stoneham, MA 02180

10 9 8 7 6 5 4 3 2

Printed in the United States of America

*This book is dedicated to
a producer whose memory is cherished
by the entire television commercial
industry:*

RAY FRAGASSO.

This delightful and astute young man
produced many of the most delightful
and effective commercials aired.
He rose to manage J. Walter Thompson's
production department but continued to
produce some commercials himself,
a creative experience that he loved
and in which he excelled.
His laughter, industry and human
consideration won him respect and
affection from every quarter.
While scouting locations in the
California Sierras for a Kodak
commercial, our helicopter crashed
and he perished.

RAY FRAGASSO was my friend and
I miss him. We all do.

Contents

Acknowledgment

I DID NOT WRITE this book alone. It includes an amalgam of interviews with dozens of TV commercial directors who freely gave me their time and thought and emotion. The original concept for this project was to quote each on the myriad of particulars of "spot" production. However, it turned out that we are of a basic cut, that our attitudes and approaches and even our personal viewpoints are amazingly alike. What emerged from the interviews was a great deal of parallel thought. No matter how diverse the range and level of talent, it seems that a director is a director is a director. Or perhaps the truisms are observed by all.

Whom, then, to quote on any one aspect when several had made the same statement? The only equitable approach was to name no one. The result of that approach, however, leaves an impression that all this information and advice comes from me alone. I do not know how to emphasize strongly enough that much of this book reflects the interviews, the books and articles that I have read and have remembered or referred to and—often enough—have pulled from a subconscious memory so deep that I myself assume they are original thoughts.

I, too, am a director and have been for a long time; my own contemplations of the craft run parallel with the "interviewees." Add to that list the many advertising agency producers, clients, cameramen, editors, gaffers, prop men, makeup people, casting agents and so on that I have also chatted with, eliciting from them what they look for in a director—or hate.

Let me list those people with whom I had the more formal interviews. It is a pathetically meager and inadequate token of the debt this book the Directors

Guild of America and I owe to them. But, they deserve at least this record of my deep appreciation.

Z. Cecilia-Mendez	Bob Vietro
Jay Dubin	Ralph Weisinger
Mike Elliot	Joel Weisman
Nat Eisenberg	*and*
Tony Ficalora	Al de Paul
Sol Goodnoff	Morty Dubin
Matt Harlib	Bill Evans, Jr.
Lenny Hirschfield	Sy Frolick
Peter Israelson	Ralph Galli, Jr.
Jack Kanakaris	Dejan Georgevich
Lear Levin	Art Jacks
Fred Levinson	Catherine Land
Amram Nowack	Mel Matz
Lee Rothberg	Neil Matz
Marvin Rothenberg	Al Mendelsohn
Rubin Shapiro	Armine Minassian
Bob Siegler	Ray Sader
Hal Stone	Les Sunshine

To those good people, to the executive editor of this book, George L. George, for his patience and wise guidance, and, to the many others . . . Thanks.

BEN GRADUS

Foreword

AT LEAST ONE-TENTH of television viewing time is devoted to commercials. The production of this most visible and pervasive communication is shaped by persons, unsung and anonymous, plying a particularized and impressively demanding craft: the television commercial directors.

It is for these artisans and their hopeful successors that this book is designed. We don't communicate with one another individually, we "TV spot" directors. We go our busy ways, study each other's completed works on TV and only on rare occasions find ourselves together to brag or bemoan or share our learning experiences.

Most of the active directors often find themselves "on location," away from peers and home. At one point, some startling statistics placed before me by my wife, Terry, proved that I was away from home—on a "few days" shoot or a week or two—a total of six months of the year. "Why is it," she complains, "that when a man must sacrifice for his art, the first thing he sacrifices is his wife?"

The particular clay of this most recently emerged art form, the television commercial, makes it probably the most complex medium extant. (There are those who refuse to consider the TV commercial an "art" form and their views will be presented later. This writer insists that the application of the term to the TV commercial is correct.) The director brings to each miniature movie a monumental arsenal of talents, knowledge and fortitude required *in toto* of no other artist in any other medium.

Consider every type of motion picture—whether recorded on film or video-tape or transmitted live—and the varied art forms it employs in varied groupings: photography, graphics, architecture, mime, music, dance, painting, acting, sculpture, interior decorating, writing, costuming, makeup, lighting, singing. Every director of every motion picture is involved with a rich combination of many of these forms at the same time and imposes his personal taste on every aspect.

Now, consider such forms that are unique to the motion picture: animating graphics and objects; editing; kinetic montage; optical effects; mixing sounds and more.

Understand that the TV commercial involves the creation of such a picture-in-motion using all these facets *plus* the added aspects of selling, public relations, applied mass psychology, propaganda and so forth.

The function of the director is to mold the pertinent forms into one whole that will attract—and hold—the viewer's attention, to create a production that will entertain, convince and, above all, *motivate* the viewer. This last goal is almost unique to the TV commercial. At the same time, the director must satisfy the TV station, the law, the varied pressure groups—and himself as an artist—in a limited and prescribed number of seconds.

The function of this book is to inform the reader as to what successful TV commercial directors consider their personal role to be in the amazingly gigantic effort involved in the production of a TV spot.

The problems, philosophies, tricks, shticks and methodologies of the director will be presented. We will be involved with two separate and distinct subjects:

1) How to direct a successful television commercial
2) How to be a successful tv commercial director

Are these not the same? Read on . . .

Hold it.

I am hardly a male chauvinist. There are female directors as well as male. And they are equally good. I have made no effort to point out that I am referring to man or ms. in any situation: I use only the pronoun "he." It's just that I dislike the self-conscious use of the word "person" or the slashed he/she. The English language has not yet evolved a satisfying pronoun, such as shehe, to indicate the reference to both or either gender. Whether I am speaking of directors, producers, reps, crew or varied agency folk, please, reader, understand that I am not referring to any specific anatomy.

Throughout this book, then, do read "he" as referring to a human being of either distaff or staff makeup.

DIRECTING:
the Television Commercial

1

The Attitude

ALMOST ANY VIDEOTAPE or film director can direct a television commercial. Yet only an amazingly small percentage of directors can add to the efficacy of a "spot" or become successful in this field. A prime factor of achievement in any area, of course, is the compatibility of a given personality with the specific field of endeavor. The TV commercial-production industry demands an unusual, if not unique, makeup—and an attitude—of the successful director.

This special person approaches each commercial with: enthusiasm; perseverance; a delight to be on the job; freedom from embarrassment at being a TV commercial director; intensity; calm; a feeling of security in his abilities; dedication to creating the best possible job; tolerance and understanding of the needs, problems and personalities of both client and agency personnel; the capability of dealing with criticism (whether constructive or capricious); and, in sum, the guts and gusto to end up with both client and agency happy and satisfied with the commercial as well as with his direction. That's it. It takes a schizophrenic who is both artist and solid citizen. (I got myself born on the cusp between Aquarius and Capricorn.)

Who is this funny animal and how does he come by his special attitude? What are his aspirations, his expectations, his dedications, his frustrations? Clues to his success should be found in his personal philosophies, his temporal and practical considerations. What, to begin with, are the reasons he enters this singular occupation?

Rewards to the TV Commercial Director

First—money. Not a bad reason. A reasonably busy director of TV commercials does quite well financially. I know one director who came from an immigrant Italian family of modest income. One day, as he tells the story, his mother finally asked him how much money he earned. "Mama," he allowed truthfully, "I make more money than the government pays the President of the United States!" The staid old lady gave him a strong how-dare-you-lie-to-your-mother look and replied with offended dignity, "Bull-a-shit!"

A number of years ago, a strike was called by New York directors. Picket lines were formed around certain studios there and the TV commercial directors showed up—in their Alfa-Romeos, Maserattis, Rolls-Royces and the like—got out of their coaches, donned the sandwich signs proclaiming the strike and walked the picket line in regal aplomb.

Many directors now own their own production companies, some in varied forms of partnership. However, owner or employee, the TV spot director who is in demand by the agencies realizes a substantial income.

In addition to the dollar income, his is a lifestyle led in the legendary American expense-account fashion. In the early days of TV, this living reached hedonistic proportions. Although the wild extravagance has abated, client and agency folk still expect to be taken to fine, if not the finest, hotels, restaurants and such. The costs are always included in the budget and subsequent bid; every bidder understands that the sybaritic life during a shoot is expected. Survey the imbibers at the Polo Lounge of the Beverly Hills Hotel at almost any time and they will include a number of TV commercial directors with their retinue of clients and agency personnel. Just call in for sandwiches in New York and only the Stage Delicatessen will do. Chinese food when the shoot or edit goes late? Order from the four-star restaurant across town. Everyone fusses about the cost but no one expects or tolerates any less than the best. Right or wrong, this is the way of life of the director and he helps ensure his success by sharing it with those people who are, in effect, his customers.

One technique during a shoot, in fact, is to have the production-house producer or his representative take the client and agency group out to an exceptionally fine restaurant for lunch, dining and wining them well and over a long period of time. This gives the suffering crew a period to get on with the job without constant interference and in a more relaxed atmosphere. (But, I'm jumping the gun here; there will be much to say later—including a lot of good things—about the client and advertising agency people.) The director gladly misses this expansive meal; he has had a surfeit of feasts and has a job to attend to.

The "good life" for the director extends beyond the epicurean. Most commercials depict comfortable living in delightful, sun-filled environs and the camera seeks out these special locations. Who is behind or next to that camera? The TV spot director. A blessed concomitant part of his life is spent looking for the most beautiful areas to set his scene—wherever in the world it is. In addition, the TV commercial that is to be aired in summer must usually be photographed in the preceding winter. Ergo, the director basks constantly in the sun.

One particularly nasty winter I spent several weeks at agency/client request traversing the entire United States and Caribbean to find the most exciting stretches of wind-swept, sun-filled landscapes. The running acknowledgment then was: "If you gotta make a living, this is the way to do it."

Once I was asked by Coca-Cola where we should shoot some beach and sailing commercials. It had to be filmed outside the United States because it was for their International Division. I thought of Argentina, which has summer when the U.S. of A. slushes through winter. I had never been in Argentina but I am an avid—and purposeful—reader and collector of *National Geographic* magazines and have an impressive, dog-eared, collection of travel books and photographs to which I have had to refer time and again. Well, the Rio de la Plata looked darned good for the need. I went first to scout and choose specific locations; everyone else was to follow a week later. When I got to Buenos Aires, I was aghast. What the books did not mention was that the water of the Rio de la Plata (River of Silver) turns brown during those summer months because of the silt it carries down. Brown water was not exactly the delectable background required by Coca-Cola.

I had to find another location—in Argentina, you can be sure. It was vacation time there and neither I nor the advertising agency could get me an airline reservation to scout Iguazu Falls up-country. Time was short and I chartered a plane. A girl was assigned from the agency to go along as guide and interpreter; my Spanish then was too halting. We flew to Iguazu, a wildly gorgeous falls different from, but they say larger than, Niagara. The six- to twelve-inch butterflies were breathtaking and the falls incomparable. The water cascaded mightily—and brown. All the photos I had seen showed crystal blue. We flew back to Buenos Aires. Almost. At seven thousand feet, the carburetor started to choke and we headed down for a forced landing. I remember looking down and thinking that, young as I was, I had already packed more excitement and beauty into my life than a dozen normal existences and death, now, would be fair enough. Curiously, I felt no fear but a terrible chagrin on one point: I could see the little headline in Spanish saying "U.S. Film Director Crashes to Death with Young Argentinian Secretary." Wasn't that a rotten legacy to leave my wife and two children!

Well, fortunately, we had passed the mountains and landed okay. I spent the night with the girl—and the pilot—in the fleabag hotel of a tiny town in the Pampas and we went on in another plane to an idyllic spot up in the Andes: Bariloche. There I found the perfect racing waterfall and gemlike lake. We had to transport the entire crew, cast, agency and client personnel and three catamaran sailing boats six hundred miles each way in two chartered planes. No, this was not a cost-plus production; it was a firm bid.

Travel for the TV commercial director is not always that fearsome. First experiences are usually the most impressive and my maiden overseas flight was to Belgium on Sabena Airlines. We were always flown first-class then and when they rolled the gourmet roast cart up to this young chubby fella, I began to forgive myself for choosing the career of TV commercial director.

But let us continue on the positive aspects of his life. What other values exist for the director? Many.

The remarkable, endless variety of locations are an exciting factor in the director's life. Travel for him becomes an adventure that no tourist can buy. Wherever he goes, he becomes involved with the natives at the location. He is invited to their homes, to their parties, to view their everyday lives. This occurs in the most unlikely places: the training camp of a professional football team; at sea with shrimp fishermen; a horse ranch in Texas; an aircraft factory; an umpire training school in Florida; the Tikal temple in the jungle of Guatemala. Any director can reel off dozens of surprising locations he has been to; those are a sample of my own. Think of any sport: scuba-diving, skiing, car-racing or sky-diving—you've seen them all in commercials. You will have seen them, too, photographed in the most photogenic locations. My Spanish has been sharpened in Puerto Rico, Spain, Argentina, Ecuador, Guatemala and Mexico—and you can include the barrios of Los Angeles, New York, Miami.

I think that any "natural-born" director is keenly interested in people and, whether or not he is a gregarious type, he tends to study their personalities, lives and actions, storing away facts, dialogues, scenes and minutiae in his memory bank. What a fascination, then, it is to work with new people with completely diverse interests and lives. One week the director will be working with or even living with a coffee grower; they will discuss the problems of farming, marketing, politics, personalities, home life, family and all other matters attendant to coffee growing and to living in a coffee-growing area. This will happen in the normal course of social amenities and is expanded by the fact that the grower is looking to the director for help in his TV debut. Since the director appears to be head honcho of the group, the personnel of the industry that he is depicting always gravitate to him for conversation. The following week, the director might well be involved with a supermarket operator, discussing his totally different problems and life. The next week, it might well be a lobster fisherman or a Wall Street stock analyst or a manufacturer of headache tablets or a distributor of feature motion pictures—ad infinitum. Steadily, and often very rapidly, new worlds open up to the director, providing a learning process and experience which can hardly be duplicated other than in the news media. One director told me that his wife refers to him as "a cesspool of human information" because of these constant contacts with other fields of endeavor.

Between setups, while the set and lights are being adjusted, the director will often chat with the subject person. This is polite and it helps keep the thread of personal, warm contact intact. The person may well be a sheepherder or he may be the chairman of the board of a giant insurance company or bank or conglomerate. The director meets people who often continue to correspond with him years afterward. It's a big deal for those people, doing a TV commercial, and they want to keep in touch. They liked the director or the crew, or the money helped them. The director has made someone feel very important, or at least the person thinks it was the director. One man, months after the shoot, sent me an excellent sketch of myself that he had made from memory.

The relationship the director has with prominent people offers a different satisfaction than the one he has with the "common" man. I am by now not especially "star-struck" or overly impressed with myself when I spend time with the big names, the VIP's. Still, these achievers are most interesting to be with and, as a television commercial director, I have spent time with a varied gamut of such people. I have dealt with newscasters and athletes, scientists and industrialists, politicians of the highest rank and even "the world's most famous pickpocket," who slipped the product *into* the victim's pocket for the commercial. I am pleased to remember that long ago I shot some commercials with the great comedian Buster Keaton, and I still boast that he used three gags that I suggested in the spot. I also brag that I beat Parnelee Jones in a car race around the Nassau, Bahamas, track. That's true only in that he followed my direction to let my camera car speed ahead of him.

They do what the director tells them, these important people. You can appreciate what an excitement it is for a TV commercial director—or any director—to be in a position to tell Lawrence Olivier or Orson Welles how to act in a certain scene. This ridiculous sense of power was talked about often in the many interviews that I had with directors as an important part of the satisfactions of the job. "The director is *boss* on the set." While there is the complication of the agency/client folk back there, the crew look to the director for instructions.

More than one director considers himself a shy person but admits to losing that shyness totally on the set. He walks onto the stage and is immediately offered coffee by the assistant director, script person and others. His comfort is a concern to almost everyone on the set—all day long! One of the best definitions of a director's job that I ever heard, and one with which any director would be amused to agree, is that "he answers questions." That's it. All through the day: "Should the source light come from the bedlamp?" "Is this color scarf okay?" "Will the first scene require darker makeup?" Or, the questions he hates to hear: "What time do you want to break for lunch?" "Will we need a driver the day after tomorrow?" "What time do you think we'll finish tonight?"—questions that try to regulate his creativity clock or that should be answered by others. The director is a kind of Force on which everyone converges. He separates the problems and reorganizes them; he keeps the production moving forward, with room left for everyone else to be creative, too.

A director said of this regal power:

It can have a corrupting influence. You really have to maintain your equilib-
rium and not believe that the shooting day is life. Too many guys really let
this go to their heads. They go off the deep end because they stop listening to
anybody. They think they're playing the lead in *Blowup* and they live accordingly.

A director's complaint:

Everybody wants to be the director. If you scratch most people who are con-
nected with film—writers, actors—they are all frustrated directors and if they
get enough power. . . . When you hear that a young actor just turned star is
gonna direct, you want to say, "Forget it." But he's got the power and the
clout to do it. So, there must be something about wanting to lead the parade.

Another director:

Many people have taste and talent but shouldn't necessarily be directors. Directing requires the ability to impart a director's strengths to others. There are
writers who are unbelievably talented and everybody knows that when they
put pen to paper they are brilliant. Shakespeare was probably the most reti-
cent, shy person who ever lived and he probably couldn't say a thing when
they gathered at the Globe Theatre in the pub . . . everybody probably
thought he was a doddering fool, but when he put his pen to paper he showed
his genius. Similarly, there are a lot of creative people in every field who
aren't especially blessed in other areas, but in the field they are talented in,
they are marvelous. The director's field, as much as anything else, is the
ability to lead, to marshal his forces, to get a concept across and make sure
that everybody is a part of it and working on a singular vision. That's not the
least of it. There is a tremendous political responsibility a director has of
making sure that his backers are always happy. In a commercial there are
different groups of people he is dealing with almost weekly who must not
only like what he is doing, but like each other.

Withal, one sobering fact that seems to amuse directors is that, once off the
set, their crowns disappear and they are instantly off the pedestal. You come
out of the studio in the rain and even a taxicab won't stop for you. Go home
and you're asked to help with the dishes—or told to.

Yet, the kids in the neighborhood continue to hold you in awe. You're the
man who did this or that commercial on TV. No matter what the age group of
the speaker, the director is given full credit, or blame, for the entire commercial, concept and all. He did it. Perhaps it is because it still is a relatively
young industry but the public, with few exceptions, does not understand the
role of the director in the production of TV spots. I'm not sure they appreciate
the difference between a producer and director in features, either.

The TV commercial director, however, has achieved a measure of respect in
the community. He is in the field termed Communications, a burgeoning industry and very competitive because of its "glamour." The director has made
it. Unlike his precursor, the social documentary film director, the spot director

seldom follows the erratic bohemian life; he lives a more stable existence, making an "honest" living.

It is not the director's fault if his job puts him into contact with some of the most beautiful girls in the world. These are the subjects he must photograph and travel with and create a friendly relationship with so that the directing will be more effective. This rather creates an uneasiness with the spouse at home but reasonable couples will be understanding and follow the old saw that, although appetites may be raised elsewhere, the meals are taken at home. I know one wife who acknowledges the problem and says, "As long as he brings the paycheck home. . . ."

Much more satisfying than these skin-deep relationships are the friends to be made within the industry. Cameramen, editors, agency producers and the like are in the main intelligent, creative, interesting people. A director finds himself spending much time with them on location, on the set or even in meetings. The rapport between us is a vital element in the realization of a successful production. We work together, think together and grow to understand each other's thought processes, problems and personalities. Many of us become quite fast friends. We bring our families together and become a close group in our social lives.

Creativity

However, all the aforementioned values of being a TV commercial director are frivolous and of little meaning when compared to the satisfaction and joy of creativity a director experiences in being involved in his work. For myself, I am never happier in my work than when I'm behind a camera. The degree of delight, of course, depends a lot on the type of scene I'm shooting, but even coaxing a flow of steam to rise in the proper direction from a cup of coffee is, to me, fun. Whether I am directing crowds of people or arranging items on a tabletop, I am calling upon the most I have to give creatively in that situation and am concentrating in full satisfaction.

What a rewarding life it is, searching for beauty and creating it! Walt Whitman said that there is a poem in a falling leaf. So there is a picture worth capturing in a bubbling hamburger or in a jar of lotion surrounded with crystal and color. One director told me—excitedly—how he had to shoot a stack of records on the piano:

> We were selling a nutty, almond-tasting wine in a brownish bottle. The director of photography put a nice russet kick in it and we had these yellow and brown and white flowers. . . . Now, I took half of those records and dumped them and replaced those albums with things in the brown tones. They were blue and white and in soft focus. . . .

Is it instinct; is it taste? Those two can be strengthened with experience—but can talent be acquired or must a director be "born with it"? What do you call the notion that comes from nowhere? Or is it from somewhere or a group of somewheres? You're shooting along a line of foods that the food-preparing machine had manipulated in different ways: sliced, ground, whipped and so on. You say, "What if the fingers that were supposed to point to the foods instead tell the story as an Hawaiian dancer would?" Having filmed the dancers in Hawaii helped trigger the idea; having shot enough food commercials and avoiding hands touching food helped. A predeliction to music, including Hawaiian, was a brain cell factor, too. All experience and thought and philosophies and tastes and the whole personality is involved in this "creative process." It is a cheerful challenge to bring it into play. While such TV commercial ideas now normally come from the advertising agency's art director and writer, the director has the obligation to supply "input" of this type himself.

One director describes his function glowingly as "choreography." The movement of his camera, the walking of his subjects, the very placing of people and objects in a scene. He speaks, too, of the choreography of transitions from one scene to another, which are planned by the director before shooting to emphasize a kinetic perception. Is there a pattern he follows, a form? As in most creativity, there are no rules. Ideas come from the guts, planted there since, or even before, the director was born, planted in a million parts.

Putting the parts together—coming up with the inspiration—is a serious business because of the need. Yet, the process is identical to a child's playing. "You be the mama and I'll be the father coming home from work. . . ." We aren't doing anything much different. Architects of fantasy, we interpret for the actor and actress the make-believe roles they are to play. We are enjoined to come up with "What if's." "What if she pretends to stifle a yawn at that point?" "What if we shoot down from the very top of the mountain to make the actor appear tiny and helpless?" "What if we overexpose the scene to give a feeling of sunny rapture?" We practically suppress a childish giggle when the idea comes that will enhance a shot or solve a problem. What nonsense, yet, what a satisfying niche we directors inhabit in the dead-serious and purposeful world of selling!

I do have a confession. There are a number of TV commercial directors who do no other kinds of production and are quite successful and excellent in their work. For myself, and I speak only for myself, I believe that a TV commercial is to a filmmaker as a crossword puzzle is to a writer. The puzzle is fun to do; it helps sharpen the craft through use of the tools of the trade; it is done with avid concentration to the best of one's ability. Yet, doing only crossword puzzles will not help a writer unless he wants to be only a puzzle-solver; likewise, doing only TV commercials for me would limit my interests and accomplishments. I prefer directing a documentary or an industrial production from time to time. I think I learn from each and bring to each form ideas and techniques from the other. The TV dramatic or comedy programs, on the other hand, are done with such speed and hard mechanics that I would by far rather do commercials.

There are many directors who enter the field of TV spots as a stepping stone toward the heights of theatrical film direction. There is no better place to learn and practice filmmaking than in TV commercial production. If a director is in demand by advertising agencies, he can shoot 100 to 150 days a year if he wants to work that hard. He will be involved in far more shooting days, far more film actually exposed, more situations and problems encountered—difficult and easy scenes and people to direct—more varied styles of photography to use, more editing and more use of different styles of directing than he can employ in any other film area. Certainly, a number have succeeded dramatically in making the transition to feature films after using TV commercial production as a training ground.

Using the TV commercial as a vehicle toward another goal is very much like using the art of painting on canvas as a means of learning to paint murals. Each stands alone as an art and here I get a lot of argument from the purist or, rather, the elitist.

The TV Commercial as an Art Form

Is directing the TV commercial an art? One director says:

> Well, I think it has a lot to do with ego. I think anybody that's worth his salt wants to be the best or among the best in his trade. When I say we're not in an art form. . . . I'm not a painter who's creating something in my name . . . this represents my thinking, my belief. I believe we are really journeymen craftsmen. It may come as a shock to a lot of people, as the ego level in this business is a very high one, that you're really not a creator. There are filmmakers who are creative artists, but the commercial doesn't tax that. I think you're a craftsman and those of us who have houses know that all craftsmen are not shoddy operators who just want to get in and out and grab their dough.

Another states:

> Advertising is a business. It can be done with artistry. And I try to bring as much business acumen and artistry to it as I can. But I do not think of it as an art. If it was an art I would control it myself. I'd have somebody take it to the gallery for me. It's a business. You have to relate to these (agency) people and they're going to hire you again. They've lived with this concept for months, maybe for years. They know it inside out: they've asked you to bring your style to it and your input, sometimes a lot more. You have to rely on them. You have to ask their opinion and you can't side-step them. . . . I *certainly* would not classify a TV commercial as an art form. . . . I think it's a form of communication. Art, for me, is a very rare thing. I think it's a new form of communication, an amazing shorthand for communicating ideas.

Let's hear it now from the positive side (my side). The dictionaries give very loose definitions of art. In fact, under those definitions, any homemaker rearranging the furniture is an artist. My definition is not all that loose. Yet, I refuse to denigrate our talent, intensity and, in a couple of cases, genius, by this effete, unwonted derision. This deprecation is derived, I feel, from a repulsion to the ultimate use of our productions. A director who agrees:

> Unquestionably. Art is a reflection of the civilization. And through every period of civilization art reflected the time it was painted in. Ancient Greece, the Romans, all the periods—the Victorian, the Impressionist—reflect the times. They didn't have cameras at that time. I think commercials today have developed into an art form—some are very bad, some are terrible, some are very good. And I think time will prove it. The motion picture—people never thought in the thirties and twenties that what they were doing was art, but it's proven itself. It's lasted and they run it like they used to exhibit art. Time will determine what is good and what is bad, but without question it's an art form.

Another director:

> Art is communication. . . . when the caveman started to draw, it wasn't because he wanted a nice picture in the cave, he was trying to communicate. They didn't have words, so they had these pictures. The Renaissance, the Middle Ages couldn't communicate Christ—the people couldn't read—so they got in some great artists and they started painting. And the other churches wanted better artists, so they got in better artists. This went on and on and they got into the ceilings and the walls and the doors. People would come in and they would see the fantasy of Christianity up there and it would really affect them. If it didn't tell the story then I think it was useless. I feel that about our art today. . . . I think the broader the communication, the greater the art.

Still another director:

> We're an art that serves business; that's our purpose. . . . Michelangelo worked for business—the Medicis—but he was still an artist. And I think we are artists; some better than others and some worse than others. It's really an art.

We are speaking on two different subjects: the TV commercial as an entity and the work of the director within that form. Once again, the architect creates the design. Are all the others who design the particulars: the murals, the doorknobs, the statuary—are they not to be termed artist rather than artisan? The writer of the TV spot has had to operate in a remarkably strict discipline of communicating an effective message in 60 or 30 or 10 seconds. I speak not only of the words but of the entire audio and visual design. This is "storytelling" of today's civilization—like it or not—wherein the author develops a situation, characters and dialogue with an aim to convince and motivate the viewer. This exquisitely honed text has been developed by the most resourceful, articulate, inspired artists of our day. You cannot measure the form of art by the idea it is trying to communicate. If you only consider the original intent, you resemble the avid atheists who believed that religion has been the curse of civilization and deprecate the art of religious icons and paintings.

The director's part in the production of a TV commercial involves many of the tenets that the most strict definers of the word "art" demand. In a manner askin to the master painter of earlier days, the director orders the cameraman to create a specific type of lighting. He takes full charge of the final composition of the picture, he decides the manner of costuming, the colors, the style of the set, the choice of location for background—all the physical matter to be seen in the completed photograph is a result of his decisions. The army of artisans—and artists—under his direction are helping to bring to life the director's creation. Beyond the obviously visible, he brings to the final production rhythm, pacing, interpretation and choreography in its broadest sense. All are of his design, as an artist working in today's medium.

(*Author's note:* Now that the two sides of this classic argument have been fairly presented and the last words have finally been set down on the subject, I do not expect the debate to continue for more than a few more millennia.)

When TV commercials first arrived on the screen, the need to compress a story and an effective sales message into 60 audio-visual seconds presented an awesome problem. Gradually, but not too slowly, the TV spot began to assume a new filmic lexicon. The viewer was pushed farther and farther away from his ingrained understanding of how a motion picture should tell a story. The makers of the commercial, challenged by the need to squeeze many sales points and ideas into seconds, became increasingly daring. They gave the audience credit for intelligence, for an ability to think quickly. The spot makers developed a shorthand presentation.

The audience had previously been accustomed to this kind of sequence: A police car pulls up in front of a hotel. A series of cuts show the cops jumping swiftly out of the car. They go through the revolving door and race through the lobby. They press the button of the elevator, wait, then get into the elevator. The lights over the door indicate the passage of the elevator to the fourteenth floor. They get out and run down the hall to Room 1417 and start to break down the door.

Today, TV commercials have had a lot to do with the omitting of all those interim shots. Now, the police will jump out of the car and the next straight cut will be to their breaking down the door of Room 1417. The audience knows that in order to reach the fourteenth floor, the police had to go through all those other situations. The viewer today doesn't need the scenes between anymore.

Another instance where the TV commercial has influenced all types of motion pictures is the extended use of optical effects. True, there is little new on the screen, but the TV spot, with its dire need for economy of time in making a statement, started to use, for example, the split screen as a means of presenting two scenes at the same time. This proved to have a value beyond the saving of time; it had its own special impact when used correctly in any motion picture. Other optical effects—such as super-impositions, mattes—became more acceptable, even welcome to the viewer, and the makers of other movies picked up the values.

We can speak of other concentrations—if they weren't innovations, they were at least being used extensively for the first time. Shooting against the sun—with its effect of silhouettes, light aberrations and flares—has became almost an obligatory technique in today's movies. Following the same pattern, windows and doorways can now let in an overriding balance of light, almost blasting out the definition of the scene itself. Another technique—if not invented, then pioneered by TV commercials—is the use of the extremely long lens to give an illusion of slow movement and heat waves rising from the ground and razor-edged shallowness of focus. Brought to omnipresent use, too, was the romantic slow-motion scene and the comic speeded-up action.

"Hold on there!" you will say. "These were used long before TV commercials." Of course, but the point is that the TV spot has to attract attention to itself in some dramatic method. The spot has to be remembered by the viewer. Therefore, the pioneering spot maker uses whatever unusual approach he can, whether it is an idea from silent movie days or a new one or one of his own invention. If it works, then it is copied, naturally, by other TV commercial makers. Then—and this has been the influence the commercials' use of unusual effects has had on the entire art of motion picture making—the repetitive airing, and the awesome amount of viewing each airing gets, brings the technique to the immediate awareness of the future filmmaker.* He also appreciates that the general audience will accept this vocabulary.

Because there are some major talents and major intelligences in the profession of TV commercial production and because of the dire need to present something different and attention-getting, the TV spot emerged as an avant-garde aspect of filmmaking. That proclivity, that challenge and that delightful excitement attracts and keeps many outstanding artists in the field.

Achieving Impact in Seconds

The dynamism of the industry is a result, too, of the fierce competition between advertisers. At the least, these prime demands are made on a TV commercial: that it reach out from the home TV set to grasp the viewer; that it convince the viewer of the need for the product; that he is also convinced of the superiority of the product over competing brands; that the memory of the commercial message be set firmly in the forefront of the viewer's consciousness so that he is motivated and activated into buying the product at the first opportunity.

The successful commercial achieves all these goals—in 30 seconds. And, there are a number of successful spots. Each is seen by tens of millions of people over and over again. Its slogan is used as part of our daily conversation. The TV commercial will fall into place as a factor in future studies of our folklore.

In the effort to produce a successful commercial, the TV screen has lit up

---

*The term "filmmaker" refers to the person who produces any form of picture-in-motion, on film or videotape, for the screen or TV.

with some of the most entrancing entertainment. Often it is said that "the TV commercials are better than the shows." Presenting sparkling bits of comedy, the most beautiful of visuals, the TV spot searches out every emotion. I once did a commercial where the viewer was reminded to take snapshots of the children before they grew up and left home. The spot follows a couple of kids in a number of scenes as they enjoy their youthful games. Suddenly the boy and girl realize they are grown—and the girl's parents realize it, too. In the space of time of a TV commercial, the audience was exposed to the story and, when it was over, the viewer actually shed a tear, or at least had to swallow the lump in his throat.

I am not presenting an apologia for the existence of TV spots; I certainly do not say that there aren't many ugly and distasteful commercials. I do say that in music, painting, writing or in absolutely any art form, the mediocre and the bad are the norm and an occasional, singular work emerges as a piece of art. So it is in our field, and the concerned TV commercial director strives—or should strive—to produce as fine a work as he possibly can.

Directing the Dull Commercial

What if the assignment does not lend itself to the production of an award-winning commercial? This one is just to be a variation on the theme of a stand-up commercial—perhaps just a talking head and cut to the product. How does a director get to do that as well as it can be done, as well as his total concentration and effort will achieve? This is what separates the TV spot men from the directors whose field is the entertainment medium. TV commercial production companies constantly get letters and requests from entertainment directors requesting to be hired for spots. It might surprise the reader to know those important "Hollywood names" that seek such employment. It is not that they consider the TV spot a grand and exciting experience. Rather, they are immediately suspected of wanting to make some of the big bucks to be garnered for a few hours of directing, to fill in the time between shows of their own ilk.

Yet, this is not the only reason they are not accepted in the special circle. Everyone who hires a spot director knows that a TV commercial is not a production that you just "knock off" and end up with a successful product. The good commercial director takes a keen, purposeful pride in the effort. I have directed many such "little" commercials that, when completed, looked as though anyone who knew enough to say "action" and "cut" could have directed them. Yet, I know, and I hope the agency and client know, that on every one I had to overcome a myriad of problems: the actor couldn't put one word after another to make the pitch sound convincing; all the neckties he brought or were available did not portray the personality we were establishing and I insisted on the time to procure the correct one; the product supplied had visual imperfections and I demanded the time to get it repaired properly; the actor's hand shook and he could never get the right fingers in the right places on the product; his teeth smiled but his eyes didn't—and so on and on in different groups of problems for different productions.

What does a director bring to such a shoot? Primarily the insistence on meticulous perfection of detail and the knowledge of what details are important for an effective TV commercial. The entertainment director might—*might*—have the patience and the interest and the energy to work over each detail. The question is: does he have the experience and the very instinct to know what makes good advertising and what will please or displease the client and agency personalities? Too, the entertainment director, in his field, has the sole decisions on the specifics of a scene (a magic, longed-for moment to a TV spot director). Can the entertainment director handle himself—and the serious kibitzers behind him—when direction after direction is questioned and argued, often at ridiculous lengths and sometimes in rather coarse, belligerent language? This group also knows soon and full well when the director has not done his homework, has not arrived on the set fully planned, a luxury only a top star feature film—or a documentary film—director can afford betimes.

The Pigeonhole

A TV commercial director has a sample reel of his work to show to prospective clients. (Don't ask me how to gather up a sample reel of spots you have directed if no one gives you the opportunity to direct the spots to place into your sample reel). From this sample, the producer and his group in the advertising agency get a better feeling about your ability and whether you are the director who can do the type of commercial they have planned. To the director's chagrin, dismay and disbelief, he finds that he has been pigeonholed. He is considered a dialogue director, an action director, a slice-of-life director, a person (to bring out the warmth) director, a location director, a cameraman/director who does pretty pictures, a tabletop director, a high-fashion director and so on ad nauseam! He wants to shout that he has done all these successfully at one time or another but he complains to no avail. He is pigeonholed. It is true that a photographer, for example, who has had a star-studded career in high fashion and has moved into directing TV commercials will be superior to a "person" director in fashion spots. But, this is an unusual situation, and any director worth his megaphone can—and does—do varied types of directing and do them equally well. After all, in a feature film, the director is presenting a multitude of different types of scenes within one motion picture.

The entertainment director, able and famous for his abilities as he may be, is an entertainment director and, alas, that is his pigeonhole and he is squeezed in there so tightly he can never get out. He is not expected to want to "live" with the commercial. This may include a couple of weeks "just thinking about it," which happens before and after the bidding, then some days or a week of planning and meetings and location hunts and meetings and casting sessions and meetings and pre-pre-production meetings (honest) and pre-production meetings and the fierce dedication to the effort during the shoot and the hovering over the editing and the total, total concern and involvement the agency has come to expect from the pros. The time involved is an exaggeration in most cases, but not all. Agencies and production houses alike, therefore, do not hire the entertainment director for their commercials because they do not believe he will approach the spot with the proper knowledge and, more important, with the proper attitude.

Concentration on the Job

From what mysterious well does the TV commercial director draw the energy that maintains his interest and effort level throughout this ten-hour, or more, day? Perhaps he knows that this tortuous battle is more than a test of his intellectual and physical stamina. He knows that he is being carefully monitored by crew and client. He knows that he will see the spot long afterward and anguish (as he has done so often before): "What a piece of crap! If I had only. . . ." He has also long since given up allocating more intensity to a more interesting shoot than a dull one. In fact, he turns up the generator even higher to overcome any apathy to the latter.

I interviewed a producer of a production house and asked him whom he would hire as a director. He said:

> I don't like a director who looks at a commercial and says, "Ah, that stinks. I don't wanta do that." Not for me. I don't feel there is any place where a person in this business—and it *is* a business—has a right to judge other people's work. Those folks at the advertising agencies are our customers. They're doing the best work they can, given the limitations of their accounts, given the limitations of networks, the censors. We must take their work and say, okay, it's a piece of work; we must do it as well as we possibly can. Hopefully, we might like the next piece of work better than this one but we don't wear judicial robes. We're here to serve the industry that pays our bills and I would like to hear that from a director, or words to that effect.

How does a creative person manufacture all that enthusiasm that is so important in every job? The client has only one product in which he himself has become totally immersed. Every aspect of each shot becomes vital for him. On the other hand, the director may have worked that month on commercials for a cereal, a newspaper and a perfume. The client still expects him to rivet his whole person on still another product. Quoting a director: "The most difficult part of this job is getting up in the morning and getting that motor to run and getting all the juices to go, to get the interest and concentration." But, you're a pro and you're only as good as your last job. You blow the whistle on your daydreaming and fogginess to dedicate yourself to the new production. That is the major key to your success: the dedication of total effort you bring to the TV commercial. Very possibly, directing a television commercial requires more concentrated time and effort than any other type of film because it comes up so suddenly into your consciousness and must be dealt with immediately and completely. You don't let go. The spot becomes your baby for a time and it's going to reflect your ability and talent. You stay with the birth as long as you can: into the narration recording, the music session, the mix. A director said:

> You find yourself in the midst of a very intense experience. On a permanent basis it is far more intense than a minute out of a hundred and twenty or whatever in a picture. So the search for locations, for talent, for the correct lens, for certain lighting effects, or whatever it is that appears . . . is so intense . . . that it tends to satisfy the need to give the amount of personal commitment and energy to any given project. This is an energy-demanding medium. What makes an intelligent commercial visually appealing and noticed, at least for me, is the amount of energy I can put into it.

During the shoot, the director allows no distraction to minimize his effort. When the air conditioner gives out and the hot lights melt the crew, cast and the set itself; when the sound gear is picking up strange noises; when the lamps start to blow one after another; when it hardly seems to be worth it anymore to anyone—the director is the *strength* to keep it going. He has the self-discipline to drag himself out of the morass and, with even more powerful leadership, carry an enthusiastic stage full of people along with him. As one director put it: "If the director doesn't have it, nobody else will have it."

That is a glorious theory, is it not? Can only Supermen be directors? Well, a director must certainly have a good deal of physical stamina. For the rest, the brain and the emotion can raise a person's potential capabilities manyfold in an emergency. To a director, single-minded in his pursuit of the successful completion of his mission, these distractions and frustrations are emergencies. His dedication is the vital source of his energy and power.

It is the source, too, of some untoward agonizing. The successful director reflects the sober, all-consuming drive of the advertising world in his personality as well as in his mode of labor. For some directors, going onto the filming stage is akin to an actor's entrance on stage. Every director has a real concern before every job. A few, I learn, even become physically ill, no matter how often the entrance is made. "I'm paranoid until eight-thirty that morning," says one director. Another says:

> I start thinking that you get very paranoid doing this all these years; suppose something were to happen to me now, somebody's going to be looking at my dailies and I don't want them to be laughing. That could be the last thing anybody remembers about me, and that's the way I go into a job. And that brings on the intensity. The only problem with intensity is that agency people sometimes get scared because you're not smiling, your tail's not wagging, you're not happy. They get a little nervous.

Yet, the impossible must be made possible:

I think every director feels he gives more than the next guy. It's just a matter of ego. I feel I do. And when I lose a job I feel sorry that the client is not coming to me, not because he's not coming to me, but because I don't think he's gonna get as good a job elsewhere as he would with me. I'm sure it's mostly ego, but I feel if we lost that, we would lose a lot of our self-judgment of what's good. If the director does not have the ego to feel he can do better than anybody else, really inside, nobody else is gonna feel it. I think you have to feel that power inside and utilize it correctly. I'm not saying it's so—that I'm better than anybody else—but when I'm working, I really have to have that feeling.

Unhappy Aspects

The director goes on the set, then, confident and dedicated. Obviously, he also goes on the set with much concern. Let us examine more elements of the director's work, some that are not as delightful and positive as those aspects which I originally posed. Being a director of TV commercials does have some definite, consuming drawbacks.

One school of psychology holds that the prime concern and motivating force is not sex nor is it the need for basic shelter, food and family. The most vital drive in the modern person is for creditable standing in the community. How does the TV commercial director rate in the community? In wordly goods, he measures up well. He is usually intelligent, interested and able in the arts, and he is educated. He travels and is interesting, bringing back stories and fascinating show-and-tell items from all over. But, does the community have respect for a TV commercial maker? Do they accept or condemn what he does for his living?

The reply, as usual, depends on the person questioned. The dilettantes and the delicate frown mightily on the entire industry and its output. They are revolted by the intrusion of commercials into their thoughtful news, documentary and special entertainments. They do not believe that the claims made for products are true and believe that the advertisers are creating false needs and values. Special railing is directed against advertisers to children, claiming that the advertising is surreptitious and harmful brainwashing. They are concerned that the advertisers influence the presentation of news and documentary facts and argue vociferously that the air waves belong to the people and that the advertisers are usurping public property.

The detractors of TV commercial advertising have much more to say, but it is not the purview of this book to argue the case either way. What is pertinent here is that, when a person is introduced as a TV commercial director, the reaction is a cool, "Oh?" I myself confess that, when asked what my line of work is, I reply, "Documentary film director"—which I am. The discussion then goes into the inevitable "Have I seen your work?" and I name some documentaries and, since I have never cared to work for the networks, they have never seen my films, and I next say, "I also do commercials." These almost everybody has seen and I immediately become a hero or a pariah, depending on the group. There are cynics, and they anger me greatly, even among my fellow commercial directors. I have argued that I believe our work is important and good for the public. I base this on the belief that America is a strong and rich country because we are still the greatest marketplace in the world, buying from and selling to each other. The TV commercial is the most effective selling tool today and the use of the director's expertise and art is a vital factor in the comparatively high standard of American living. Without sales, there would be less manufacturing, consequently less jobs, therefore less money to live well and purchase necessities and luxuries, which create jobs, and so on.

I am happy to be a director of TV commercials despite the condemnation of my profession by much of the community. Another director has this to say:

> Frankly, there is more of a stigma attached to people who do television series than there is to commercial directors because in today's world most people are willing to believe that the visuals that go into a commercial director's work are far more interesting and far more vital than what the normal fare is on the television show. There is a far more receptive audience to (the work of) a commercial director than to a man who proved he can do hackneyed work for half an hour.

There is little argument that, measured against directors of other types of film, the director of a theatrical feature film gains the most respect in the community.

There is little question, too, that the feature director garners all the public fame. While even he can never be the household name that actors can become, the importance of the director in a feature movie is gaining strong acknowledgment by the public. An increasing group of directors' names are known now by persons beyond the traditional world of movie cognoscente. The director of TV commercials does not have any such possibility. He can be a giant among his peers, held in awe by the entire commercial industry, but his name never appears in the national magazines or newspapers. I like to tell the story of the one time when I received telephone calls from various parts of the country from friends saying, "I saw your name in the papers." No, it was not because of my achievement in the art at which I labored so long and so hard and successfully. I had bought an automobile and was called by an aide of Earl Wilson, the gossip columnist. I answered, "Yes, I had bought Elizabeth Taylor's Rolls Royce . . . Yes, I was a director at Filmways, Inc. . . . No, the ashtrays were not silver . . . Yes, Mike Todd had had each of the pull-down picnic tables inscribed 'Liz' and 'His' . . . No, I was buying it from her husband, Eddie Fisher . . . My wife, Terry? She complained, 'All I ever get is Liz's hand-me-downs.'" Well, all that was the lead story in the column, including a statement that the ashtrays *were* silver—and I then was finally famous for a day.

Little respect, no personal fame—what about the satisfaction of doing creative work? How creative is your production? You still tell a story that must have someone hold up the toothpaste or product or get into a car. You still have to fit it into 30 seconds. You do creative work—within bounds. The director, far from shaping a TV spot out of his own person and personality, is acting as an extension of the advertising agency. He is helping to create a tool that is very functional and whose use has been pre-designed. The strictures are many and sometimes strange. A scene may play delightfully if the funny lady will screw up her expressive face at the sight of the powder detergent, since she is hailing its rival liquid detergent. But, the manufacturer of the liquid detergent also manufactures powder and doesn't want to demean his other product. The director must find another approach—usually one that is not as good as the original idea—and compromise.

Compromise is the name of the game. You push as hard as you can for the direction you think is best, but the pro knows what he is there for and it is not merely to please himself. TV directors are very vocal on this subject, gnawing as it does at their vitals. According to one director:

> If we are doing it solely to satisfy ourselves and our own egos, it is entirely possible that the job at hand will become secondary and will not become good advertising. You always have to keep in mind what you're there for and hope to combine your own fantasies and your own ego with the job at hand. . . . You're an interpreter of many, many tongues going on but after all you can't lose sight of the fact you're communicating. It's a house of Babel, but you've got to remember that eventually you've got to be speaking to somebody through one tongue that everyone will understand.

Another director:

> It depends on the clients. This business has changed. I used to cut every commercial. . . . We had our own staff of editors. The agencies felt that they wanted control of the editing, so they require us to shoot up to rushes. They decide which editors they want to go in and finish the commercials. In a sense, I think they did themselves a disservice; they cut the director off from contributing. They say, "Well, we want a director's cut." But sometimes it's a very hollow statement.

About the "good old days" for the director:

> He still had to put together the subject . . . which a normal person watching television could see and understand and gain something from. However disciplined that time was, it still had to go on the air and be intelligible. . . . The directors who lose sight of that ultimately produce unusable commercials, but I don't think many directors in this business get carried away with the idea that this is a director's medium.

About his modern-day limits:

> Most pre-production meetings, as you know, are confined to minutiae: whether the .blouse should be white or yellow or pink. And that can take up

a good hour of discussion. So I don't think you go into the formulation of strategy or anything like that. You're spending most of your time going over every little last detail, so that when you get on the set, there's nothing left to chance. So very often that's like a straitjacket, too. It seems to me that the larger the agency and the larger the client, the more stratified this becomes. You begin to think you're working for Civil Service or the Pentagon. You're allowed enough creativity between A and B.

A producer in a production house had been concentrating his talk on the business of TV spots and the restricted role of the director. I asked about the creative aspect of directing. He answered:

> If you are a good director, you'll be creative. The creativity starts with the concept. The enhancing of that concept is accomplished with the tools of your trade, which is the camera, your camera moves, your lenses, your direction of talent, your choice of sets and locations, your use of light, the bringing together of all the elements in your cast so that the people relate to each other and they relate to their surroundings. Creativity is just a natural consequence of doing your job with more than just a functional attitude. If you try too hard to be creative, you're liable to trip over an elephant. . . . You want to watch out for the young creative directors who can screw up a job so badly. He's creative as hell—he just doesn't know how to make motion pictures.

Well, the young director may know very well how to make pictures. What the producer is seething about is the director who does not accept the TV commercials director's specific role in the ad game. The script and storyboard he has been given before hand is the commercial to be made. The concept has been set, the marketing area targeted and the specific words honed to a sharpness approved by each of the hierarchy in the agency in turn, by the levels of power at the client's offices, by the offices of the attorneys of agency, client and network. This is no exaggeration. It has taken months of rewrites and approvals to get the script to this point and the director is called in to record the storyboard onto film or videotape. The savvy agency appreciates that all of the personnel have been too long at the spot; they look to a competent director as a knowledgeable and tasteful professional to bring in his fresh, outside perspective to the effort. He is not sought after to make changes; he is expected to present the storyboard with the maximum effectiveness and impact possible. If a director is to accomplish this, everyone understands, he must be a "creative" person.

In each of the steps of production, the director is asked for his input, theoretically. Before production, he is asked for his reaction to specifics and for his suggestions for changes. Often, the ideas he comes up with have been proffered by others in the preceding months and have been rejected. At a recent meeting, I complained that a piece of dialogue would not sound natural or real. The writer immediately jumped in. "You see? Mr. Gradus has directed I don't know how many hundred commercials and he immediately picked that up!" Obviously, an argument had been raging over those two lines and the writer had been forced to set down what he knew was wrong. My objection did not settle the matter but it brought it out for discussion again. In most any type of production other than a TV commercial, the director's decision there would have been final.

While shooting, a string of client/agency people are looking over the shoulder, or into the videotape monitor, of the director. It's their money and their storyboard and certainly they have confidence in the director, but all the same . . . So, you shoot the same scene over and over again even though the second take was entirely to your liking. You are not shooting all those takes to attain perfection; you shoot them to make certain that as many of the hierarchy's objections, logical and nonsensical, are assuaged before you continue on. This is perhaps the most virulently negative aspect of the job of directing TV commercials.

In the editing, you can expect to hear, "Why didn't we . . . ?" The "we" is politesse when the speaker means, "Why didn't the idiotic director . . . ?" This can refer to the need for cutaways because, between the shoot and the editing, the legal department ordered a phrase or a word cut out. "Why didn't we shoot the finger of the little girl tapping. It would have been a great cutaway." "Why didn't she carry a coat?" (It had just been decided the client could air the spot on TV in the winter as well.) It doesn't matter that all this Monday-morning-quarterbacking is being done about a shoot at which all were present—the *director* should have thought about it. He is the pro to have covered all (to mix a metaphor) bases. Would you believe that an experienced director of TV commercials anticipates such after-thoughts? He *does* shoot cutaways despite the agency's objection at the shoot that he is wasting time unnecessarily. He *does* insist on wardrobe that will not indicate any season anywhere. He *does* shoot scenes (always at agency's request) two ways. A director friend once told me that he plays scenes two ways so often that when he gets home to his wife. . . .

Pre-production Involvement

Today's days are always the "good old days" of tomorrow. If some of us are nostalgic for the good old TV spot production days, it's because the director was so much more involved in the commercial. This is no judgment on that which is bad or better—some directors must be a decided help in screening talent, supervising the editing, or shooting without a storyboard or even a script. In some cases, the director must be much too costly or too intrusive to be involved in what the agencies now consider activities that should be under their sole direction. However, I cannot understand why the director is not involved in the subsequent narration. Are agency producers actually better directors in the recording studio than we film/videotape directors? I genuinely doubt it.

There is a certain amount of bitter comfort in the fact that the director is at least called into the agency to help choose one of three actors for the spot. By this time, the agency has had a casting session and videotaped a number of applicants—under someone's direction. There may well have been additional sessions and callbacks before the agency chose the three. Now a session is held where only the videotapes of the three are shown to higher agency personnel and the client. This is where the director comes in for the first time. It's a small comfort to the director. He has no idea how the talent takes direction— certainly not his. He has had no opportunity to see the others and use his intuitive director's eye and gut to know that one actor, who was not one of the chosen three, would have been perfect, if directed a certain way. Now he is faced with the videotape and the question: "Which one do you like?" The only reason for the invitation might seem to be an open opportunity for the agency people to be able to say to the director, when the talent turns out to be a horror in the shoot, "You picked him." There are times and places where the director is called in earlier, but these times are becoming more and more rare.

The completed script is, once again, the result of tens of meetings among varied types of committees. This is a fact of life: many able, professional minds explore and revise a TV spot before it emerges. The commercial, now in storyboard form, is "safe"—nothing illegal, obnoxious or negative to the intended message in any form. The pros do a good job to ensure this. The only problem left is that most often the life has been beaten out of the idea. The original concept of the writer or art director or creative director has been flattened to where the audience will not have any objections—nor will they be attracted to it or hold it memorable to a degree that the original design would have achieved. When the director enters, he is handed this limp body and now all look to him to bring it to life. He tries. He tries with all his might to convince everyone to add this, omit this, change that. They have already thought about most of his ideas and one committee or another has dismissed those very ideas prior to his joining the fray. If they have respect for the director's opinion and meet him somewhere near halfway, he will contribute much to the spot's success. If not, as one sad director put it:

> So, there is a certain point beyond which it doesn't make any sense to continue any mini-crusade. I have to get through all the pre-production to get to the part that I enjoy—which is shooting, no matter what it is, (even) if it's packaged horseshit. When I shoot, I'm king for a day and they can't take that away from me, no matter what they do.

Fear of Failing

Even under these worst of circumstances, the director will probably not fail to do a professional job. He is too afraid to fail, the TV commercial director. He is always his most fierce, insistent critic, suffering a terrible constant fear. Most directors face this fear quite consciously:

There's so much at stake. I mean, every time I go out, it's my reputation. I just take it very seriously. I take an approach to it. I think it's very important to be a leader if you're a director. It's more than just showing up and doing your job. I don't go about it that way. I want to be a leader; I want the crew to be proud of me. They don't have to like me, but I want them to have a lot of respect for me and I want them to know that I'm working harder than anybody else.

You know damn well that as soon as the electrician hits those lights you have to know where you are and where you're going. Because if you're not prepared . . . I mean, I've never been nervous except if I know that I have not done my homework. . . . Everybody else on that stage can sit and wait for you to say, "all right, now our first shot's gonna be . . ." and "Okay, I think we've got that now . . ."—seventeenth take. The first take was good, but you pleased everybody. "Let's move on." Meanwhile, you've got your eye on the clock because you know you've got ten setups left and there are four hours and you know you can't possibly do it in that time.

Yeah. I still have a form of stage fright before I shoot . . . my wife knows I'm going through what she calls a decline, which is really a kind of tuning out of things at home, the day or three days before a shoot. I'm getting into that mood and I know when I have to get into my private planning brain to make myself work properly. I'm very serious about it because I guess somewhere there's a lurking fear that I'm gonna blow it. . . . Today's gonna be the day they discover, yes, I'm ordinary. I'm just another guy, or I'm a bad director. It's better now than in the early years when I invariably got sick the night before shooting, throwing up and having diarrhea. Now, one out of four shoots I don't get that sick, but there will be some kind of symptoms the day of the shoot.

We perform, unconsciously or even consciously, for the crew—perhaps to keep them jolly so that they'll think we're terrific and maybe not charge us golden time penalty if we go fifteen minutes over lunch-break time. Keep 'em laughing, keep 'em loose, keep 'em interested. Maybe we're acting for those behind our backs, the agency/client audience. We cannot help thinking of the next gag to keep people chuckling, whether it's the tired actor or the people around us or even the stage manager, who's reluctantly bringing out wings we hadn't planned on using.

Finally, one of the most exasperating aspects of the job comes when it's all over. This probably happens to experts in any field, but it rankles nonetheless. The director has gone through his various hells to arrive at the rushes stage. He has solved the problems inherent in the original script and storyboard; he has made those who were non-actors act; he has molded beautiful pictures where none had been contemplated nor seemed possible; he has made the sluggish flow; he has overcome all the boulders and dams placed before him by budgets and laws and uncomprehending clients and their "make-it-safe" minions. An effective, artistic spot will be the result. Does he get huzzahs and champagne

and carried on shoulders for his victory? Not at all. "Good job. Thanks."
That's it. Why? Because it is *expected* of him! He is *expected* to overcome the
difficulties and bring fresh ideas for a successful and effective commercial.

On to the next storyboard.

2

Moralities

My wife has brought back from our travels an ancient Egyptian unguentarium. A noble lady thousands of years ago used it to hold her makeup, perhaps, makeup that gave her eyes the cat shape we see on their murals. It occurs to me that makeup has been used for so long that the viewer knows full well that what he is seeing is paint and not the actual skin. The red lips, shadowed eyes, rouged cheeks and even the skin base are not the real thing but a representation, a glorification of the actuality. The point is that we accept the glorification as such and do not believe that the makeup is the person.

Movie Magic

This point is the reason, and I hope not the rationalization, why in the "old days" we used representations of the product rather than the product itself. We knew that the *viewer* knew that we were glorifying the product and therefore we made it look as good as possible. Before there were TV commercials, there was movies. And, in these fictions, every photographic trick in the book was used to make something look better on the screen. For instance, if the scene called for actors sitting around talking and eating ice cream, then, during the time they were talking, the ice cream would melt to a liquid under the hot lights. So, it made sense to use mashed potatoes instead; it looked like ice cream and the audience didn't care. The cellophane covers of cigarette packs crumpled into a glass of water looked like crushed ice and didn't melt. The fire in the fireplace could come from gas jets playing over fake logs, instead of real wood.

This "movie magic" was well known to the audience and accepted without negative criticism. Then, these same movie makers started to make TV commercials. Each brought with him his bag of tricks and each invented more ways to display the product better. Beer lost its head swiftly under the lights and this created a major problem when a dozen or so actors were to hold beautiful glasses of beer at the same time in a scene. A good way to make a head that looked good and also held for a long time was to pour the correct amount of headless beer into a glass. Then beer was put into a "seltzer maker," the CO_2 capsuled syphon bottle. When the gas squirted the aerated beer, it came out as a heavy foam, a perfect-looking head that lay on the beer in the glass for a long time—through several takes! But, what about the beer itself in the glass? It looked okay, yet there were ways to make it look better. Instead of beer, use ginger ale. It was clearer and the bubbles looked and rose better. Wait, there's something better. Champagne! A champagne-filled glass topped with an aerated beer head—now that was a picture of perfect liquid with beautiful rising bubbles, a thick head—and one that held that way for a long time.

If you were selling cigarettes, the manufacturer sent in some that were especially made extra long. The actress just looked better with the longer cigarette. And so on. When color came in, a whole new bag of manipulations had to take place, since the film stock at that time did not reproduce colors exactly. In order to show a yellow product package on the TV screen, it was absolutely necessary for the manufacturer to make up some special boxes in a chartreuse. The final print then showed the package in its original yellow. Later, of course, the film stock became capable of reproducing the exact shades without the magic.

Subhuman nature being what it is, this ability to glamorize and romanticize a product was soon taken up by some venal advertisers to tell downright lies about what their products looked like or could do. Correctly, this brought the consumer and the law down on all advertisers and extremely strict limitations were enforced under the general heading of Truth in Advertising. Beer and beer heads are now real beer and real beer heads: ice cream is ice cream.

A note on the bizarre, at least to my way of thinking: the federal government, in its first determined crackdown on untruth in advertising, just happened to pick on a commercial that was not guilty. My understanding of what happened is that the commercial said that, for some people, shaving is like shaving sandpaper. Cut to a razor shaving sandpaper. Now I (yes, I) had, just before that was produced, figured out how to make a hand, held away from the face and without a razor, look like it was shaving. The advertised shaving soap moved down the face as though a razor was pushing it. ("Using this soap is like shaving without a razor"). Again, that commercial was accepted by the viewer as a joke and a trick; no one would believe that you could shave without a razor. Well, the same shaving soap company did the sandpaper commercial but were having a lot of trouble getting the sandpaper shaving shot to look real and clean. My solution: Lay brown wrapping paper on the table, cover this with a sheet of plexiglass, spread rubber cement over the plexiglass, sprinkle sand over the rubber cement; on camera, shave the cement and sand off the plexiglass. The camera looking down sees only brown.

I'm not certain today what I would have done if the commercial had actually said, "You can shave sandpaper with this shaving cream." Generally, I know that I would have tried to find some sandpaper that lent itself to this possibility as, indeed, I would do today. But, the government decided that spot did not adhere to the code of Truth in Advertising and the spot was banned.

As an interesting sequel: Immediately after the decision, we had to shoot new spots under the new restrictions. First, the actors had to grow actual beards and sign affidavits to that effect. Then, they had to actually shave the beard on camera, looking directly into the lens while doing it. Oh, the blood! The first several actors we tried (several, because only one take was possible, their beard being gone) cut themselves to a man. I stopped the slaughter when it came to me that we could put a front-faced, one-way mirror in front of the lens so they could see what they were doing.

The Bad Product

Where does the director stand in the subtle realms of what is truth and what is untruth? Where, when and how does he draw the line when offered a commercial to direct which is not true—or deleterious to the consumer? One director says:

> I wouldn't want to advertise a nifty hangman's noose. I would have some qualms about that. There are products that the public really needs and I have got a feeling that the public is wise enough to know which is better for them. They might try my product . . . but if the product turns out to be no good then they will simply not go back and buy it again no matter how good my commercials are; they will try something else. To start with, I have got to think that you are not really selling the product in the sense that someone is going to buy it forever. You are trying to get the public to try it for the first time, to walk into the store and buy it. That is part of the director's function. They get the people so interested in what they are doing that they at least walk in and plunk down for whatever it is they want to try. If the product turns out to be no good, they sure as hell are not going to buy it again.

How different from the nifty hangman's noose was cigarette advertising? According to one director:

> You see, I have a theory about cigarettes. I used to smoke. I gave it up about five or six years ago, finally, after many fits and starts. I used to have these nightmares that my children would have me on trial for my life. And I'd be in this spot. They'd be saying, "You did this advertising!" . . . and then I'd be in a cart going to the guillotine, and all these non-smokers would be yelling, "Yeah!" I used to get mortified. I smoked Lucky Strikes since I was eleven years old and liked the lot of it, too. Some of my great memories

happened with a cigarette and a drink. But I never did it (advertised cigarettes). And that's that.

For myself, again, I directed many, many cigarette commercials for a number of different clients. My only defense is that, in those days, we weren't
really sure whether smoking was bad only for laboratory mice or for people as
well. However, when the Surgeon General issued the first statement that smoking was harmful, I decided flatly that I was going to do no more cigarette
commercials. I accepted none from the day of the Surgeon General's first warn-
ing through the day, finally, when cigarette advertising was banned from the
air. In between those days, I lost, not only a lot of money, but ruffled clients
who were once my friends. Neither do I direct any out-of-the-United States
cigarette commercials.

Back to the director who never did cigarette commercials:

> I don't do pipe tobaccos and I don't do cigars. I don't do political candidates
> I don't care for or causes I don't believe in. I try to stay away from certain
> hard-sell products that I might be embarrassed to be associated with. Now,
> that's my own judgment. I do much advertising for huge corporations, multi-
> national corporations and all that and, believe me, some of the things they do
> and sell and talk about are not always things I believe in, but I just have to
> balance it. There are some things I'm firmer on than others . . . I always get
> into discussions with people, especially young people and people who are not
> in advertising. I have nothing to say to them when they accuse me of working
> for Exxon or something like that. They treat me very nice and the commercials
> I've done for them I'm very proud of, and IBM and Xerox and companies
> like that. And I'm sure they've got a lot of skeletons in their closets. But I'm
> very careful when I do their advertising and I think they're even more careful
> than I am.

Every large corporation is concerned about its "image." In fact, the larger
the corporation, the more important the salubrity of that image seems to become. The public looks to the newspapers for expose´ of the seamy sides of
big business, yet, as one director describes a commercial for a newspaper:

> . . . a speak-out campaign. We went out on the street and interviewed thou-
> sands of people. And when it got down to it, it referred to a story that ap-
> peared in the paper that said "New Yorkers Are Slobs, Dirtiest Streets in the
> World." It was a comment by a visitor. We went out on the street and this
> was an ongoing weekly campaign. And one of the comments was, "Well,
> look around: people throw newspapers, they throw junk, they throw litter, the
> garbage cans are overflowing." Anyway, the agency selected that statement
> as one of four or five statements that went into the commercial. And at the
> editing session, I said, "They're not going to like that statement at all."
> "Why? It's honest. It's this, it's that." Sure enough, we cut the spot; it was
> ready to go to air. "Hold it! How can you refer to us littering the streets when
> it's our commercial? Don't run it!"

I have directed dozens of soft-drink spots for many of the top-selling products. I know the sugar in them is not doing a lot of good for the consumer,

whether child or adult. I have heard that a spoon left overnight in a cola drink was eaten away by morning. I don't know if that's true, but I'll be damned if I'll try it and find out for certain. I'll be damned anyway, I suppose, for helping entice more people to drink the stuff. Or even the drinks that have, in the place of sugar, the artificial sweeteners that are suspected of being carcinogenic. *Mea culpa.*

I am culpable, too, of the use of the craft to present the product in as positive a light as possible. There I am doing what every director, cameraman or still photographer does. Just the use of a wide-angle lens in a host of situations can produce all kinds of misrepresentations. You can make an automobile look twice as long as it is, the seats inside look as though they can fit 12 people comfortably, the auto speeding away from camera looks as though it were rocket propelled and so on. With slow motion, the four-wheel-drive car appears to float over obstructions as comfortably as a feather wafting from place to place. All this is arguably legal. On the other hand, in these days of energy shortage, a long lens can make a long car as shallow as a compact auto. The saying "the camera never lies" is, of course, the greatest lie of them all.

Add to this artistic representation by the camera (trickery), the use of lighting. A director tells of a problem:

Director:
. . . where they required a certain amount of egg yolks to do this type of meringue filling. And even though the yellow was lighter than I like to see photographically, we couldn't do any doctoring to embellish it so that it had more appetite appeal. Within the confines of the normal recipes and the results of them, we have by lighting and by angles and by actions to make it as appetizing as possible.

Gradus:
Can you use colored lights in your situation, if you wanted the yolk to look a little lighter?

Director:
The trouble is, if you start doing that, the white of the meringue becomes yellow. It's a matter of using color and lighting in a way that you don't get an overall look of the thing and that doesn't misrepresent everything. So, I think if I were to use colored lights, I would be very selective. But, I find if we get involved with that, it looks very artificial and contrived. I'd rather do it naturally and with light and shades rather than color. I let the color of the product itself work. With the knowledge of how to use lights, I get the maximum out of them that way.

Honesty in the Demo

At the heart of a great many TV commercials is the "demo," the demonstration of how and why the product works better than its competition. Here is where the great temptation arises for the director. He wants to make it look as good as possible; he wants to present the product as the latest miracle on earth. The agency/client gallery behind him are rooting for his most astounding success. If everyone in the studio is not totally mindful of the morality of showing only and precisely what the product can do, then everyone is surely mindful of the laws governing the honesty of the presentation. One director says:

> In terms of demonstrations and any kind of trickery involved, in showing a product doing something that it normally does not do, I don't do it. It just does not happen. There are ways to cheat on a demo, as we all know. I don't do it.

The major advertisers, especially those who manufacture packaged goods, have their own departments of research and development. It is my—and other directors'—contention that the proof of the efficacy of the product be demonstrated to government and network officials in labs outside the shooting studio. It is not only that we wish to make the shooting easier for ourselves; we feel there is a terrible loss of money and time for all concerned in proving the product while shooting a commercial. The camera proof can be made at a laboratory where there is relaxed time, not at an expensive studio with an exceptionally expensive crew and talent standing by. The conditions of the test, too, can be more accurate. For instance, a lipstick is used under average temperatures, not under the hot lights of a shooting stage; an animal would eat its food in surroundings to which he has been accustomed rather than in a vast stage full of strangers to which he has been brought for the first time.

Instead, the demonstration must be made the long, hard, tortuous way. A director explains:

> I just shoot until we get it. I think when I started in the business ten years ago there was a big tendency to say, "Screw it . . . let's use a double sheet instead of a single sheet; no one will ever know the difference." But, I'm not involved in it. You just get it done. It usually will work, eventually, if you're patient enough. I think with patience and a fair amount of sense of humor and intelligence, a great many more people than are doing it could direct. I don't consider myself *that* special except in the area of patience.

When this director talks about patience, he is referring to the painstaking and meticulous preparation to be made before the test is attempted. This makes a reasonable amount of sense in terms of a moral approach. However, in the studio, the demo is shot time after time until it does work. In fact, often the only reason it works is one of pure good luck. The product may very well be able to do all it claims to be able to do; this is almost invariably the case. The problem is to get the product to deliver its proof under the most difficult of locations and surroundings: the stage.

The very techniques of proof can often be a mystery to the director. For example, Detergent A can be more efficient than Detergent B when the water is, hypothetically, 350 degrees. At any other temperature, B is more efficient than A, but we're doing the commercial for A. The instructions come down from the client's R & D (Research and Development) to make the test demo at exactly 350 degrees. Not knowing any of the legalities involved—in fact, the director might think this is a legal requirement—the test proves Detergent A is indeed better than B. This example is not hypothetical; it was actually one case. Only the temperature has been changed to protect the guilty.

It is not altogether unusual now to see someone from the legal department of the agency or client on the set. One director said, "Sometimes there are even attorneys that give us documents to sign to verify that we don't do any tampering or misrepresenting of their products." The demo might have some delicate problems or the product might have had too many legal wrist-slappings. The representative might be there to make certain that the entire diaper is shown on camera and not only the clean part; that the demo is shot in one take and not left to manipulative cuts; that there are no additives such as bleach included to make the product look better. He might be there because there have been complaints that there is an insufficient number of black people or Hispanics used as extras and wants to do his own head count. An important sales point might be that families of a certain economic level can enjoy the product and he wants to check the set itself. If children's toys are being shot, he might be there to be available for questions on the various subtleties of the special laws governing children's toys commercials. There are such rules as: the children may not react in any way to the voice of the announcer (the announcer may react to the children's dialogue); the camera may pan with a moving toy— it may not truck along with it; the toy must not be distorted in any way by the use of wide or long lenses. Later, an occasional one-second cut may be used (but no more than three) in a commercial. There should be no brutality; there should be an indication whether batteries are included and so on. I do not deprecate these laws; unconscionable knaves brought the necessity for them down on the industry, as such people generally mitigate all our innocent liberties.

Believing in the Product

There is a type of commercial wherein the value of the product is, to the greatest extent, unknown. It is the political candidate commercial. Here, it is easy for the well-meaning director to get hoodwinked as easily as the voter— perhaps more easily, since he is brought face to face with the spell-binding candidate. There's the old cliche´ that "you can return a box of soap but it's hard to return a President." Usually, the offer to direct commercials for a candidate comes from outside the director's political interests. It's a job. What do you do? As one director described his attitude toward all his commercials:

> It's like I do commercials for the *News*. It's not that I don't believe in the
> *Post*. I believe in the *Times* but I don't work for the *Times*. The point is that
> I have to pull that enthusiasm no matter what it takes. You have to create that
> excitement.

One director ruminated about his doing pitches for products he really didn't believe in:

There is a moral question to that. I think about how TV commercials chip away at the morals of our society a little bit at a time, whereas a feature film takes a big chunk out of it. We do it a little bit at a time. I could rationalize the need for advertising and the economy but I really can't. I am so involved in it that I can't sit back and say "Hey, if we didn't have advertising then we wouldn't have these products made and people in factories making these products; we wouldn't have sales people and teamsters delivering and so on," but deep inside of me, I don't think that is human nature. I don't believe it is part of our nature for what we are doing. I really can't justify what we are doing. No, I don't honestly believe in everything I am advertising and would be lying if I did. Perhaps I worked on one product with which I was very pleased. I shot a job two weeks ago for (a) peanut butter, and I am not a fan of peanut butter, but I caught *Consumer Reports* yesterday and (this one) was right on top. I said, "That is terrific that I worked on a product that they think is good." It did something good for my soul, you know. That was coincidental. I work on things that are at the bottom of the heap in *Consumer Reports,* but what's important to me is that this is a business in which I can practice my craft on a daily basis. I take great pride in that and do the best possible job I can with the knowledge and experience I've got. So I can justify the form, the content I can't. I'm not responsible for the content. With all the things I've said about keeping the economy going, there are still great gaps in our society, rich and poor, the haves and have-nots, justice and injustice, and I don't think we do anything constructive with our television commercials in that respect. I think what we've done is we've replaced motion pictures as the standard by which society wants to be judged. We have created lots of wants and desires in the audience. I don't know, maybe I'm talking myself into a corner, but maybe the changes will come about because people are reached who don't have the means to buy the things we're advertising. Maybe we'll prevent an evolution or a revolution, I don't know. It's too complicated for me; I'm a craftsman, that's what I think I am as a director.

If a man is a craftsman of furniture, say, what would he do if a customer walked in with an ugly design for a bureau? Would he refuse to do it? Would he do it for the money? Would he take on the job and try to manipulate the customer into a more acceptable design? What if the design had potentially dangerous aspects? The director of TV commercials has much the same dilemmas. Is the spot harmful to the poor—to the disadvantaged—to ethnics? Does an "action" spot of healthy youths cavorting give terrible unhappiness to the crippled shut-in whose life is spent at the TV set? Contemplating moral and aesthetic issues and values can well be disheartening in any field of endeavor. For the TV commercial director, single-minded as he must be to get the best possible production, another set of issues arise: is it fair to use this person's neat home as a location? Before the crew enters, the director knows the house will never be the same. Will this non-actor look silly on the spot and is it fair to have her sign the release before she sees the completed work? A director tells his story:

We laugh now at the things that have happened to us, not while they are happening. We had a baby shoot one time and the agency had a problem with the babies. We ended up having to utilize one baby for too much time and it just refused to stay awake. So, we had the gaffer take the baby all over the place to the props (and such) and we photographed the other side of the face. We were holding the mother outside so she wouldn't know what was going on.

Money and Morals

What's all this intensity about? What earthly difference does it make to the director if label A sells better than label B? What difference is there really between one manufacturer's aspirin and another manufacturer's aspirin? One detergent or another? What difference does it make which monolith gets richer than another? The TV commercial director, concentrating on his art and craft, is much like the singer of the song, "When I'm not near the girl I love, I love the girl I'm near." The answers lie in the list of reasons why TV commercial directors stay in the field. There are, I suppose, two reasons that stand out as most important: the satisfaction of creative impulses being given reasonable rein and—as in any other business—money.

With the quest for money—and more money—comes the normal deterioration of human morals. I rush to repeat that this goes on in every business; I really believe that there is less immorality and business hi-jinks in our artistic field than in most businesses. We read constantly about widespread graft in international industries, in government, in every situation where money passes hands for one legitimate reason or another. In no way am I saying that there is no hanky-panky in the TV spot business. Cash is paid, favors are given, every ill that business is prone to exists in TV spot production. Who is guilty? Just about everybody.

Every person seeking business from another "bribes" his prospective client. The question of morality in business seems to revolve around the extent of the "bribe." I refer to the "line" that each person draws, beyond which he will not go. You are a director and you meet an agency art director on the street. You stop for a Coca-Cola together and you reach for the change first. Of course, you would do the same with any friend, but aren't you making sure that the client doesn't consider you a cheap miser? Yet, you correctly fume against those who probably pay in cash when they are awarded jobs. What's your "line"?

When on location, do you pay for the agency person's dinner? When back in home base, do you invite him to your home? However you are trying to impress him with any kind of favor, what you are trying to do is to obligate him, to get him to feel he owes you something when the next bid comes around. Take him to a theatre, buy lunch . . .

For myself, I have my own line and, like anyone else, I would like to see that line announced publicly as morally acceptable: At home base, I pay for an evening out which includes dinner, theatre and after-dinner drinks. I invite people I like to my home. On location, I pay for everything: lunches, dinners, refreshments—all is included in my original bid.

I do *not* give brown envelopes with cash or cash in any form; I do not supply anyone with members of the opposite sex for any purpose, including mere companionship; I do not offer my gorgeous rotund body to a client for the purpose of gain; I do not offer weekends away; I do not, I feel, try to buy favor in any illegitimate manner.

To my mind, our business society accepts as moral the amount of "selling" that I do and considers excessive and illegitimate any stepping beyond the "line." I know it exists in our field. I have heard of blatant offers made, most often by sales representatives, who were willing to split their commission. I have heard of weekends and weeks in the country and on boats. I have heard of all sorts of hanky-panky. Yet, almost all my clients have respected the "line" I draw. The few who didn't did hint at a more expansive treatment. When I did not respond, the matter, naturally, was dropped, but the point is that they came back again to work with me in most cases. Because of my long experience, I repeat with the utmost assurance that there must be less bribery— much less—in our field than in any other business.

I was quite interested to find that, among TV commercial directors, the business aspect of the art looms quite importantly. I think it was George Bernard Shaw who said, during his discussions with Samuel Goldwyn, "Businessmen always talk about art; artists talk about money" (or something like that). I challenged each director on two points. First, "If your satisfaction comes mainly from the creative aspect of your work, how do you get to put so much diligence and enthusiasm into a stand-up hard-sell commercial?" Here are a few representative answers to that one:

> Sometimes there are things we love to do and other times there are things we don't find as exciting to do. The most challenging things are the most mundane, that you don't have the excitement you wish you were working on. But then you have to extend yourself to find something that will make it more interesting, more desirable, more appetizing as far as the finished commercial is concerned. I have to feel motivated to do something that at least will contribute to it. . . . If you're working on something you don't like, the worst thing is to know you don't like it and to do it and get it over with because then obviously it's gonna reflect you. If you make a commitment to do something and you don't like it, then you have to be honest with yourself and do it the best way you possibly can.

> Yeah. Sometimes you have to remind yourself not to look down on this one when it's just a hard sell . . . just do it for the money. But I think there has to be a certain amount of honesty on your part. You deal with that one as well as you can deal with the other one. It's like dancing. I remember Alexandra Danilova, who I took classes with, when people used to go on tours to Wich-

ita. The audience there might have been three people—then, what should a dancer do? Just do it here in New York with a full house? You owe it to your audience, even if it's only one person. If somebody wants your talent for a stand-up commercial, well, do your best because that's what it's all about.

The other question that I posed to directors was whether they had qualms about directing a spot for a product they knew was not very good. One reply:

Well, I'm thinking it ought to bother me and I'm also trying to think of situations where it really applies and I can't really come up with anything. I've done a thousand different products, all of them okay, nothing I would take a moral position on. . . . . Is Wyler's soft drink better than Kool Aid? They're both sugar products and I suppose I could take a position that sugar is bad for your health, but I really don't believe that, being a junk-food freak myself. . . . . I think unconsciously a director of commercials makes some sort of peace with himself about the immorality of commercials, period. . . . . I think that one has wrestled with (it) unconsciously over the years and put (it) to rest, very likely conveniently, for the pleasures (to be gotten) out of it, not only the creative pleasures but the financial pleasures. So I can't get up on a white charger about the morality of it.

3

The Product

THE STORYBOARD AND SCRIPT given to the director usually starts with a playlet to attract the viewer, includes a scene of the product in use in the center, and ends with a "beauty shot" of the product to assure identification, memorability and the like.

As one director put it:

> Yeah, that's usually the offer of a solution, a way out. Instead of offering religion, we offer Anacin or Instant Maxwell House or something like that.

When the director or his assistant schedules the progression of scenes in the order they will be shot, he invariably leaves the product shot for the last of the day, and this is correct. This is correct because the sound crew can be dismissed and the balance of the crew can be striking the set and wrapping the props while that confined little scene is set up and filmed. The danger lies in forgetting that, while last, this shot is the *most!* The client has spent tens, if not hundreds, of thousands of dollars up to this moment to get a commercial produced so that he can sell more of his product. The playlet, the little drama, on which the director has spent his time, energies and creative talent was only a gimmick, a trick to get the TV viewer to pay attention to the product. The client may spend hundreds of thousands, if not millions, of additional dollars for the buying of the time on the air. This product shot, to him—to the man spending all that money—is what it's all about. The tragedy—and it's nothing short of a tragedy to the client—is that the attitude of the big-city, highly paid director to the product shot is reflected too often in the statement that goes: "Okay, we're done; let's knock off the product shot and wrap it up."

36

The Director and the Product

I was once assistant director to Josef von Sternberg, the fascinating and fierce director. He said, "You need a director even if you're going to photograph the head of the Statue of Liberty." The director is there for his taste: choosing the angle; deciding on the use of possible foreground pieces; choreographing the camera movement during the shot; resolving how much sky or land to see in the background; choosing the mood he is reaching for in the exposure, lighting, effect filters and so on. He plans all these aspects of the shot to conform correctly to the flow of images and scenes of the production that come before and after. Therefore, if the cameraman is not the genuine director, and there are many competent hyphenated director-cameramen, then I agree that a director is quite necessary for every shot in a production. The "product shot" needs a director. But does the weary director need the product shot? I asked them:

> I get totally involved in it. I had a tendency earlier—when I thought I was hot shit—to let the cameraman do a lot of that. I don't do that anymore. I realize now that I'm not as hot shit as I thought I was early on. I know what the game is about and it's about the product as much as the performance. I'm totally involved through the product shots as much as any other part. I end up doing a lot of the prop work myself and a lot of the hand stuff—I'll be the on-camera hand frequently. In many cases I can do it better, (more) simply, than whoever is doing it.

> Oh, I like to do that. I like to compose it. I don't like to walk away and say, "You do the product shot." Early days, ten years ago, I did a lot of food work on videotape . . . which won awards . . . and I consider myself as good a composer or composition man as the guy who went to art school for four years.

> It's part of the commercial. If you do a bad shot—whether it's a product shot or a closeup of somebody's face or an insert of a fingernail—that shot could be put into your work. And you could destroy an otherwise good sample or something that you see on television. And I hate to have to look at my stuff on television and go, "Oh God!" So, if I've got to set up ninety little shiny cards and one big light, I'll do it. If there's a piece of lint and I've got to redo it, I'll redo it. I just try to give it as much. It's tedious. I mean I hate a steady diet of product shots. I sort of like to work outdoors when I can because a stage floor is gonna hurt my feet. The cement floor once killed me. I like outdoors and like to have a suntan and things like that. . . . But, von Stroheim used to spend hours lighting a telephone or a silver service in his movies and if a fine feature director like that—one of the geniuses of all time—can do that, I can do it. . . . Why can't I do that? I get more dough than they did. I mean, I'm not as good as they are, but I've got more time, I can go places faster. Why shouldn't I?

> It's difficult to maintain the concentration up to the last moment. I don't find it difficult at all; I'm on a constant "high." With the product shot I'm more

free to do experimental stuff with the lighting than with anything else. I think that photographing a product in the most complimentary way is essential, in a way that you can immediately recognize it, see it very clearly for what it is, understand it, read it if you have to, display it in the best possible manner. There may be situations where you can put it on a table, put glass under it and have nice reflections, nice colors around it. Sometimes that may be completely out of the question. It may be a box where there is so much going on that you want nothing around it. But it's challenging because every product is different and there are so many things you can do with each one.

An agency producer told me of one director who worked for her. He couldn't be bothered with the product shot and left while it was being set up. He never directed for her again. Once again, the *attitude* of the director to the shoot is the key to success, both in producing a successful commercial and in being a successful TV commercial director. A director says:

> I think the approach has to be a positive one, of getting out as much character and style and quality, relative to the spot. Everything, of course, is developed to the concept and the usage. The general feeling, whether it be with talent or with food, or with a product package at the end, should be compatible to the total spot.

Importance of the Product Shot

What is the client—and therefore the advertising agency and its personnel—looking for? Simply, they want the public to bring forth a picture in their minds of the product every time they have a need for that type of ware. The picture in the mind, too, should have positive "vibrations," the mental image titillating, acceptable and desirable. But, according to one director:

> The agency has other things in mind. They will give up a good performance for a shorter take which allows the product to be on longer at the end. I've fought that battle long enough, too, to know "you ain't gonna win." Very rarely will you win, very rarely will an agency producer or a creative team listen to you and say, "You're right. That performance does elevate it four percent and maybe we can add our product on for three-and-a-half instead of four seconds." It's almost non-existent (nowadays). They will invariably opt for the four-second product shot to the exclusion of the better take.

One man who became a director later on tells me of his first visit to a shooting stage, where they happened to be filming a TV commercial:

> . . . and I see these guys. I can't see what they're looking at but I see ten people in suits ohhing and ahhing and when they finally break away what I see is a glass of beer. They were just shooting a product shot. But I realized from that moment that motion is to get somebody to want to drink their beer. It's like anything else, whether you want to make them cry over a social issue, laugh over something, learn something. The input is affecting someone and, apart from making any moral judgments about effect, the elements are there.

When you shoot the product in closeup, the background can give it
class. . .

It's as much filmmaking as any other kind of filmmaking, but it's a little more
specialized. . . . Their client, he has a vested interest and you as a director
have a vested interest. You can balance all these things. I remember being
taken by the fact that they were trying to make somebody thirsty, and thirsty
for that particular beer.

Among the many reasons for producing a powerful product shot is the long
lapse of time between exposure to the product shot on TV and the moment
when the viewer is in a situation where he will need and buy. The client trusts
that the viewer will *remember* the product and its appearance. Again, positively.

Specifically, how is this accomplished? The director, of course, has no hand
in the designing of the package. He must, however, ascertain that the advertising agency has given him a specific package to shoot that is as perfect as
human hands or machine can deliver. If it is necessary to shoot a package that
is, in effect, from the shelves as it is sold, then he must demand many—I have
gone through several gross, one by one—so he can choose one that has no

nicks, scratches, specks or scratched lettering. This may sound tiresomely exaggerated to the novice, but any professional TV commercial director will confirm the need to choose that perfect one. And, we all do it. Seriously and intently. A New York director recounts:

> Actually, we shot that out on the coast. We shot it in California, believe it or not. The company that makes those pies has a factory out on the coast and they wanted us to go out there and work, rather than send the pies out here. . . . We ended up shooting *only one pie* anyway and we went all the way out to the coast to do it. The company supplied our home economist from the factory. She really did know the pies and she was very, very good.

The Look of the Product

One pie. I shudder to think of the chance that was taken. Even when shooting videotape, wherein the client and all relevant personnel can see the final shot immediately, there have been times when a flaw went undetected all the way up the line and then, weeks later, someone saw that, perhaps, the fluting on the pie was no longer being used—that it was the old style. I'm joshing, but let me tell you of one traumatic experience with a "product." It was an automobile. The spot called for the next year's model to be shot in autumn foliage. It was a hand-built prototype, which is always used in "announcement" commercial and photographic production. We went far up into New England to catch the first color changes of the season. The locations were beautiful and we didn't stint, planting foreground bushes where necessary, rigging the camera in difficult placements, running shots, sundown shots, mirror shots, the works. We worked hard and long and came through, I must say, with a breathtakingly beautiful commercial. We showed it proudly to many huzzahs and much boisterous back-slapping. The spot was sent to Detroit and the congratulations came back. Two days later, some vice-president (in charge of skirts, I guess) asked: "Where are the skirts?" The what? The skirts are the pieces that hang under the fenders in the wheel well to hide the top part of the wheels. None of us knew that skirts came with this sport model. Reshoot.

By now, the foliage was off the trees in New England and we went out to scout locations in upper New York State. Again we came back proudly with photographs of lovely locations there and we were ready to shoot. No way. The rains came and we waited the few days until they stopped. They stopped all right, but before they did, they had washed all the leaves off the trees. Now we were racing against time. We flew to the Skyline Drive in the Carolinas and there our luck held. Beautiful scenery and good weather and perfect colors and we shot the whole spot again. With the #*:"# skirts.

For packaged products, the agency will most times supply a mock-up of the product. There is usually too much printing and over-design on a package for the swift and easy reading necessary during the seconds allotted to the shot in a TV commercial. The "corrected" package does away with all unnecessary

Choosing the perfect product for the "glamor shot" is obviously serious business. (glam'or n. Any artificial interest or association by which an object is made to appear delusively magnified or glorified; illusion; fascination; witchery.)

lettering and design to make instantly clear to the viewers what the client wants to impress into their minds. Thus, if a package for a detergent contains a list of items it will clean well, this list might be left off the "corrected" package and just the name and slogan left. (The word *"NEW"*—the omnipresent obligatory, it seems, on almost all products—will be featured, you can be sure.)

It behooves the director to discuss the appearance of the corrected package before it is made so that his creative and visually informed opinions can be considered. In this aspect of TV commercial production, too, the director takes the blame for any imperfection, no matter where the original fault lay.

The budget forms of production houses contain the item: "corrected product." (That wording is not correct, is it? You correct the package, not the product.) It is there in case the advertising agency asks the production house to get it made and I bring it up because it can be very expensive. The hand-lettering and graphics involved easily run into hundreds of dollars. Also, sev-

SOL GOODNOFF

CAN WE RAISE IT?.... JUST A HAIR!

eral must be made; some aren't made perfectly and the imperfections aren't noticed until they are magnified by the camera lens. Some, too, will get dropped or mishandled and ruined. I make it a point to take the prop products over to the prop man and hand them to him myself, making it abundantly clear that if they aren't still perfect when we go to shoot them, it's his fanny. While setting up, we use a "stand-in" for the product and then call, as it is referred to in the trade, for the "good guy," the corrected package, for the shoot.

The standard method of shooting is "in limbo": placing the product on a seamless paper, normally a light pastel shade. The paper is rolled out so that there is no sharp bend in the foreground across the flat bed and then up the vertical back, taking care that there is a soft rolling sweep from the horizontal to the vertical planes. Thus, the camera does not see any background; rather, it is just a color, the lights creating whatever pattern is desired. The ultimate effect is usually that of the product appearing to be floating in the sky. Instead of a flat bed, the studios supply a stand with the correct curved sweep built into the stand so that paper or plexiglass can be used as the base. The plexiglass is at least translucent, making it possible to create light effects from behind, giving an illusion of depth. The lighting is usually high key because most products call for a "happy," clean, positive presentation.

While the product stands out cleanly in this type of shot, there are times when the background must be tied in more firmly with the location in which the spot has been shot. In one director's experience:

> Yes, the food looked good. It was very well done. We shot in the plant manager's house, which bugged me, because the whole house was as big as this room and it made a very difficult shoot and I would like to have had my own choice of finding a house . . . we were constantly shooting like this with the back up against the wall and trying to get the shot. It wasn't too bad. We did a series of three commercials out there so it made the trip worthwhile. I always prefer to shoot on location. Now that we have a stage, we are shooting more and more on a stage but I really prefer and always have preferred to go on location. It is so much more real. Everything did look good on that thing.

The lighting should, in almost every case, present the package with definitive clarity, in addition to setting the mood. The director of photography usually greets a package of foil—silver or gold—with a sigh of despair; it is exceptionally difficult to keep the resultant flares from distorting or obliterating parts of the lettering. Such packages or products often need reflected light only, requiring a forest of white cards, small inkies as spotlights and ofttimes a gauze tent totally around the object. I mention all this because the director must know in advance what his problems are going to be when he schedules the time to "knock off the product shot." I have seen a cameraman spend eight hours trying to light a steaming cup of coffee correctly. I have spent two days lighting a wristwatch, only to have the client walk up to the screen during the rushes, point to a part of the watch and say, "You must give me more sparkle here and here." Reshoot. In the words of one director:

> That's something that no film school teaches. That it takes a guy who works in an agency and finally becomes an art director to understand that you're dealing with corporate people in companies that turn out products and work to turn out the "look". . . . To say, "This is our product" or that box of cereal or that fragrance bottle. And I don't care if that fragrance bottle is this big, I gotta tell you, that bottle better look like a million bucks.

Color

That meticulous approach to the product or package by the client extends, of course, to the color. I learned this to my horror quite early in the game when the film itself was having difficulty reproducing colors exactly. One client had a package that was basically maroon. We color-corrected the print time after time until, with a weird combination of filters, we were able to reproduce the maroon correctly in the air print. There was one devastating problem, however: when the announcer held the package up to his face, the face came up green when the package was correctly maroon. Either the package was to remain off-color or the face was to be green. Which way did we go? If you understand what I've been trying to tell you about clients and their product, you know that the green face went on the air.

SOL GOODNOFF

NOW THAT'S THE KIND OF HEAD WE WANT ON OUR BEER.

A director who does much food work says:

The approach I have is very simple. First of all, I work with a limited range of colors and by using foods from a design point of view, getting shapes of one substance, whether it be a vegetable or a fish or a dessert, to another is a matter of working with scales and with designs of each substance. The handling of the designs—whether it be peas or mashed potatoes and a steak—and arranging that compatibly in a dish is a matter of design and composition and color. The first approach is to color-key whatever I do, so that there is a continuous harmony as far as color. As I indicated, my color selections are very sure as far as range. I don't go into a spectrum of colors because I think that dilutes images. I'd rather have the color of the food come out and then be compatible and then also be a complement to that. In other words, say if I work with oranges, then I may work with little yellows or little reds or work in a monochromatic way that will complement the dish. The second thing I do is scale things so that if I start with a major thing, whether it be a fish or steak or hamburger, I scale things to that, so that if I'm shooting a hamburger, I'll select a pickle or a relish to complement it, not take away from it, and then you add colors to that, be it catsup or whatever, just to add design and color to complement that. Then you do the fringes as far as garnishing with the delicacy of little things.

Still photographers, fashion, tabletop and the like, have been attracted to the moving picture precisely for the added dimension that it offers: movement. The combination of the photograph and movement challenges their imagination. Inanimate objects are brought to exciting life for them by the moving camera, by the very editing. Now their cameras can deliver 24 different pictures each second as the camera pans along a tableful of foods; it can climb a veritable mountain of whipped cream. The "snorkel" camera can cavort around, through and in the objects which once they could only freeze in time. A whole new art form of visual kinetics opens up to them.

Handling the Product

About that tiresome, unreal shot of the product held near the face: Of course, the reason for the composition is the real need to show the product and the speaker in one shot. However, to get as close as possible to the product in this "two-shot," the speaker must hold it right next to his face, resulting in a most unnatural oversell. How do you beat the problem? First of all, decide to be conscious of the need to avoid that kind of shot. Redesign the storyboard if possible to make it a cutaway to the product in hand and then cut back to the face talking. If that can't be done, find some motivation that makes the togetherness reasonable: have the talent caress the product, kiss the thing, anything—but try to make the two-shot look natural!

Incidentally, or I should say, "of the utmost importance," during the casting sessions: we are so intent in finding the right character that, in our excitement, we may, and often do, forget to study the actor's hands. When the time for the closeup of product in hand comes up, a lot of chagrin can go flying about the studio. Remember to do it and, unless absolutely impossible, hire a hand model. (Bad fingernails should not lose the perfect character for you; they can be corrected.)

One director cautions you to listen to the agency folk very carefully when shooting the product shot:

> (He) might have read something in research that said whenever you hold (the product) that people didn't recognize the box if you held it vertical or something. Now he is on the set and he sees the director setting up the box vertical and he knows that he has got like fifty pieces of research that he spent fifty thousand dollars for saying, "Don't hold the box like that because people don't recognize it."

The director, however, should try to convince the agency folk to let the actor handle the product naturally. I have no objection myself to the holding of a product so that the fingers reveal it totally in display. But, when that scene is part of a normal life playlet and the product is picked up by one of the partic-

ipants with fingers solemnly kept off the lettering so that the display is callously obvious, I object totally. When the spot's talk has been about detergent and the actor's thumb cuts across the last "t"—let it be, let it be!

There are times when the package has to be placed in closeup into an exact spot during the scene. Often a good way to do this is to have the fingers *remove* the package from its correct final placement, running the camera in reverse. (Make certain the film has been advanced sufficiently with the shutter closed.) The scene can be shot straight this way, not running the camera in reverse; later on, print the scene in reverse. However, keep one piece of rhythm in mind. If you study the movement carefully, you will note that the hand will slow up toward the end of placing it down. Therefore, when playing the action in reverse and picking it up instead of placing it down, start the pickup slowly and then, after it is off the table a couple of inches, move it out faster. If you don't do it this way, there will be an unnatural jump of the product into place in the final straight-on version.

The scene into which the product is placed will traditionally relate to the story-line of the playlet. But, whether it is placed in arbor or armor, food or foolscap, the director again must not be carried away by the little story. The product must be the dominant item in the composition. The director will have wanted to use the final scene to cap his tiny drama, but he must rein his creative urges. When the scene is shot, the product takes precedence.

In fact, if you follow the line of the hard-sell school, you will remember to feature the product in as many scenes as possible throughout the spot. That kind of commercial will usually be a demonstration of the product in use and/or in successful competition against a rival product. (I do not decry this approach. I believe that, when the style of the playlet is in its ascendancy and the channels are airing mostly these short stories, then one product blends into another to the viewer. The most effective approach then for an advertiser is the use of a straight pitchman with a direct sell. On the other hand, the reverse is true. Too many pitchmen on the air, and the most effective spot in general is the playlet.) The point is that the director must be cognizant of the history of product use and the need of the client with respect to how he wants his product displayed, his taste and attitude. Only then can the director put up the good fight to get his own taste and attitude respected and be allowed to shoot the product his way.

The Client and the Product

Learning what's on the client's mind, I must say, can be very difficult because of the amount and caliber of the message bearers. A director's story:

> I can remember one time when a presentation was made for an automobile commercial and it was a very hurried-up presentation. Pictures were drawn by an artist. People ran out to Detroit and made the presentation in front of the client. One of the pictures that they were showing to the client had a very bad

view of the rear of the car, which was just badly drawn, and the client said, "That's an awful bad picture of the car." It was just a drawing. Out of that meeting came an edict that the rear is never supposed to be shot.

You can be reasonably sure that the word "never" was taken quite literally and the client, who had meant no such thing, may never have seen a shot of the rear of his cars after that. I hope he caught it because there would have been very few souls with sufficient fortitude to challenge that edict or even speak to the client about it. Instead, I wager that a whole rationale grew about the reasons why all automobiles should not be filmed from the rear.

You lose most, but you win some. Never forget that it is the very function of the director to inject his ideas and to fight for them. A success story:

. . . and if someone came in and said, "Now look, you have to use this phone over here and you can't pull back because the phone only looks good on closeup." It would never have gotten done. . . . The account man came in and said, "The way you do this thing is you take all these phones but try to give the impression that the telephone company has a lot of phones that they want to sell to people. Why don't we put all the phones out, all lined up, and take one big shot of that." It took a lot of tact and diplomacy to argue him out of that. I kept saying you can give the impression of a lot of phones and you don't have to put them all in one shot. Yes, you will say that there are a lot of phones—you see fifty phones in one shot—but I get the same impression that there is an infinite variety of phones by shooting each one individually. There are a lot of cuts in time to the music. I . . . see the phones better because all of them will be single phones and closeup and that is the way you have to do it. It took a lot of arguing to avoid what we were going to do: put all the phones out on a table top and light them and shoot them, which would have been nowhere as effective as it turned out to be. . . . When he saw it all finished and edited together I think he loved it because when the client came in and looked at it, his reply was that it looked fantastic. Suddenly he liked it too. . . . There is no way that I could have done something like that two ways. It took four days to shoot all those phones individually. If I was doing that on my own, I could not possibly have done that. It was very necessary to try to settle on my way of doing the thing.

Another director:

I start with an idea or work based on a sketch from the storyboard. Roughing it out doesn't work. Art directors do very fanciful kinds of sketches and frequently will create a bad frame in the sketch or a frame that is impossible to duplicate. So, I'll design it better and try to get approval on it. Occasionally (I) end up doing it two ways. I try to minimize (shooting two ways) and I'm doing less and less these days. Sometimes I'm taking a stronger stand on doing it one way.

Presenting the Product

I work with the agency art director. We contemplate presenting the product with some kind of kinetic visual fanfare: bring it out of the shadows into the spotlight during the shot; reveal it from behind an obstructing item; match-cut it in from the previous scene; bring it in through the mist, bubbles, rain, flowers, people, jewels. Make it come alive. Once, in a commercial involving flamenco dancers in the playlet, I ended the commercial with just hands, all raised in the air, clapping out the rhythm. The product was passed from hand to hand; the other hands seemed to be applauding the product.

A director recalls:

> A hand with a flower coming next to the product if it's a skin cleaner, for example, has worked very nicely. It's just a matter of selecting. Say we get a batch of peas, for example, that we are shooting. It's a matter of selecting the best of the batch then, by little techniques we have with little spurts of . . . water, or brushing it on, with a little oil. And then, of course, with the lighting. . . . Whether it be a pea, a carrot, a cucumber, a radish or an egg, we hand select each thing that we shoot and look at it visually to make sure that if it's a combination of several things then each one is going to be complementary in size scale as well as color to each other. As far as arranging, you get large peas but you have to know how to arrange it from the point of view of where the camera is—whether you get silhouettes looking straight at it from a low point of view, or if you're looking at it from a high point of view—how to arrange it so that there's a separation and a simplicity of arrangement, so that visually it comes off.

Food is the product in one type of TV commercial wherein the product stays on screen throughout the commercial. The product is the spot. Automobiles are another. Makeup, sunglasses and the like become a series of product shots. In these spots, fortunately, the product assumes a life of its own: it does things, it goes places, it has a vitality that you can maximize. But, how do you get personality into a product that just lies there? Creativity, ingenuity, tricks. You take the product out of the can and use it as did one director:

> At one time when we did food photography. . . . I believed in those days the only way to shoot spaghetti with tomato sauce was to take it out of the boiling pot, put some hot sauce on it and shoot it instantly, so that the maximum freshness was gotten out of it. But, over a period of years, I have realized you don't have to do that because there are other ways of doing it with control. As soon as we take a few shots and the spaghetti doesn't look as good as the instant of freshness, we have to devise other ways of doing it so that the freshness is sustained for a period of time to do our takes. It's so important to have a looseness of approach so that you're not doing something on a stop-and-go basis. When you work that way, it just takes longer and you don't get the real input, instinctive contributions or feel of what you want to do. So, we have devised ways of getting the maximum freshness out of everything we do. And, we try to apply all natural devices, with steam or natural juices for shine.

The work of a director of stop-motion (object animation) represents the epitome of this romance with the product. The product is going to be moved from one position to another within a specific time period. If, for instance, it is going to make a full 360 degree turn within ten seconds, then the circle has to be divided into 240 equal parts for the smoothest possible action. (The film will be projected at 24 frames per second—times ten seconds, thus we need 240 stops.) The lighting must be planned and tested so that each of the 240 frames will be correct. Then, each frame is exposed singly and the product moved 1/240th of the full circle. This is done 240 times. Of course, this would allow the smoothest possible movement, but if two or three frames or more are exposed on each stop, then there has to be that fewer stops. The fewer the frames exposed during a stop, the smoother the ultimate movement appears on the screen. Done with more frames per stop, the movements tend to be more and more jerky. One such director told me of a watchband he had to shoot that way which would twist itself into a knot and then back again. It took him 24 hours to light and then animate. He could not leave the set; the scene had to be shot continuously, because if he turned off the lights, the change in room temperature would cause some contraction of the watchband's metal. Even this slight difference would have caused a jump in the movement. And, I speak of only ten seconds. Thirty seconds of difficult object animation can seem like a decade. This is more than patience; this smacks of masochism.

I myself have shot object animation, but I did it the easier way. One scene was a rose bud opening. I lit it, then set an automatic single-frame exposure mechanism to expose so many frames per minute (I forget how many) and left the lights and the setup running all night. The rose opened on cue and the mechanism exposed the frames on the correct time basis. The shot didn't work. It seems that a flower opens slowly at first and then, at the end of the cycle, jumps to full spread suddenly. We calculated the moves from the previous take and set it up again for another night, with a lot more frames exposed toward the end. It worked. On screen, the rose opened gracefully and with consistent speed. This would not have been truth in advertising, but we weren't, fortunately, selling roses.

Another time, I wanted the sun to set prettily and smoothly behind a lake with the product in the foreground. It was to be printed in reverse to indicate sunrise. Fortunately, with the previous experience under my belt, I studied and timed a sundown the day before. I say fortunately because the same thing happens: it sinks slowly at first and swiftly at the end. We stood there and shot frame by frame while the sun went down, in a graduated series of exposure timings. On screen, the sun sank behind the horizon majestically and gracefully, in exactly the right timing. But, the shot was unusable! The water of the lake, exposed in this erratic manner, danced and jerked around as though it were boiling in hell. Next day, we shot the sun setting over solid land, avoiding even moving trees. Got it.

Just recently I was involved in a stop-motion shot of a package wrapping itself, which we did on videotape. We exposed a few seconds of each move, then, via computer editing, pulled two frames out of each move. For two-frame animation, it worked fine.

The modern museums of today are hugging the comparatively new art form

BEAT IT KID,...THIS IS A CLOSED SET!

of video "animation" to their electronic galleries. The fluid, tactile flow of color and shape changes adds to the available tools of the artist an extraordinary, surprise-filled dimension. This art form is available to the advertiser, especially in relation to the presentation of his product. With comparatively amazing ease, the picture of the product can be squeezed, distended, distorted, reshaped, pushed through tubes, keyholes, bodies and other obstructions. It can spiral, jump, back-flip, zoom, mooz, do death-defying stunts with casual ease. A color can change, brighten, flow away, add on, gravitate from background to foreground to package, be romanticized, replace itself or any part of the frame with the greatest of eclat. These factors can be achieved with a computer or with the freedom of personal manipulation. The possibilities have as yet hardly been probed in TV commercial production. The product shots should seek out that potential.

This is not to minimize the proven and traditional values of our movie animation. The animation of drawn objects offers as much creative expression as the video art; it simply has another look and envolves a totally different way of working. There is little question that film animation allows for a precision which is very important to the TV commercial maker.

Videotaping the Product

The comparative values of film *vs.* videotape have been belabored ad nauseam and in weightier tomes than this one. I must, however, mention one aspect of the subject here in relation to presenting the product in a TV commercial. One argument that cannot be countered is that videotape can produce optical effects faster than film can. When the scene calls for a product with changing background during the shot, the film optical must be created in a series of day- or week-long operations: creating a matte, or a traveling matte or even the faster method of blue matting. It still takes at least days of optical house and laboratory time. This applies also to the more complicated process of rotoscoping. Any one of these processes, moreover, too often must be re-done to get it right. With videotape, the process is immediate. The touch of a button or two and, "Hello, Chromakey!" The optical is there for all to see and approve or make changes and the optical effect is completed, ready for deliv-ery. In terms of quality and "look," you pays your money and takes your choice, but with videotape opticals, you get immediate, relief-making service.

Total relief, then, does come to client and director alike when the "beauty shot" is indeed beautiful. The talent and dedication to perfection of a TV commercial director is measured to the greatest extent by the look of the prod-uct shot. No shoot is a wrap until this vital scene, the last shot but the *most*, elicits those satisfied, congratulatory smiles from all concerned when the direc-tor calls, "Cut, print and wrap."

4

The Storyboard

I HAVE WRITTEN A POEM and want to share it with you:

SPOT

Most television
Commercials are sweet songs sung
In thirty seconds.

In answer to your question, I will tell you what kind of a poem that is. It is written within the formalized strictures of the Japanese haiku poem: three lines, the first with five syllables, the second with seven and the last with five again. I'll wait while you look back and check me out.

Counting the Seconds

For the poet, the exercise of functioning within restrictive bounds can be very fascinating. The challenge of producing a pleasing work of 30 seconds could be as equally delightful to the television commercial director, if the work did not have to be effective as well as creative. Directors refer back to the days when the one-minute spot was more prevalent, with occasional minute-and-a-halfs. The thought of directing one of the rare two-minute commercials is likened to an idyllic romantic interval. *Time!* How we directors could use the time for our part in presenting the story, the problem, the characters, the relationships, the dilemma, the hope, the promise, the expectation and finally the build to the resolving, the discovery, the explosion to the glorious climax, not to mention the time for narration, for humor, for driving home the messages. We need time to present the product in all its glory, bringing it out on its glorious float, trumpets blaring. All—all—in 30 seconds? No more time, no more.

From the director's admittedly narrow viewpoint, we argue that the one-minute commercial would often have more than double the impact, making it reasonable for the advertiser to buy twice the amount of time. In some cases, I am sure we are correct. It is true, however, that research has pointed out the ability of viewers to understand the message even when the projection of the commercial is speeded up, the 30-second spot being shown in a number of seconds less.

When the director is finally given the assignment, everyone at both the agency and the client's office has done his work. Research, legal, creative, writer, art director, accountant, brand manager, everybody. The idea has been fully discussed before the client himself. The characters of the spot have been described and the story-line told in full. The client is made to believe that all this information and mood will emerge clearly and with impact in the 30 seconds of commercial. Perhaps even the presenters believe it themselves. But, they are not worried too much that it won't happen. There it is in the storyboard, a series of sketches with the dialogue and narration under each. All the director has to do is make it work in the moving picture. The character of the heroine was delineated in the notes, but how does the director bring out the desired personality—in 30 seconds? How does he bring the static to kinetic animation? How can he build up to the laugh without diminishing the impact of the sales message? Well, that's the director's problem. The information, the sales points, the product may not be omitted or mitigated.

What happens to the director's output? He finds himself limited in style of shooting. More information has to be incorporated into each angle (e.g., the ugly three-shot with all the characters' faces to the camera abounds in commercials). Expressions on faces cannot be too subtle; the cut will not last more than a second. The camera cannot linger on what is beautiful or telling. The ultimate editing that the director is keeping in mind has the stencil "rush" stamped on each shot. The zoom works overtime and the sad dolly languishes rusting in the corner of the stage.

Pictures in a Storyboard

It especially hurts when the storyboard you are handed has page after page of sketches for the one spot. The director knows full well that this is either a case of the art director not trusting the director or a situation where the spot would be some five minutes long if the director followed those instructions. (Or, the art director is on his own political trip.) A director remarked:

> What is this storyboard? A storyboard at this point seems to me to be something that was invented to give the client a visual idea of what directors like you and I might stage in the studio. Originally, all there were were scripts with video instructions. "We open on Cookie, standing in the kitchen; it is

early morning; the chef is preparing the shrimp." Now, certainly anybody with any kind of point of view could visualize what that is. On the other hand, there were clients who couldn't visualize it, so they began to do storyboards. They show a picture of a guy preparing something on a table (with) a pot (on it) and three pots hanging down. I rarely look at the pictures, just sense what it is. And the kitchen we find, by the way, is not gonna have this counter here; that's the artist's idea. So we use this as a guide and you know that you're gonna go into a kitchen in a restaurant and therein is gonna lie the story and you're gonna shoot it with a little angle and a little move around. So the storyboard is a guide. Do we need it directorially? No. We certainly would like the script, some indication of what they want to see. On the other hand, you get much more of a challenge if they give you a script with no video. That's very rare. Then you have to be able to stage something, much like a director would do in a play. You have a two-room set, a couch, chairs, whatever the writer has given. Certainly, directorially you can position those items to give you the best movement, the best fluidity. And this is, at least, what I like to do.

A storyboard has more value than making the commercial clear to the client. It is a blueprint for all the pertinent artists, artisans and mechanics to see, if not follow. This is the most articulate manner in which the advertising agency can present its thoughts to all concerned, both in the agency and outside. The board is a guide, a direction.

Where there is no storyboard, there must be a meticulous communication between the agency and the director. There are certain directors who work for certain agencies and there are clients who trust a director to the extent of eliminating the need for the storyboard. The director is given a script, or even a concept from which he has to build. On occasion, he might be given only a still photograph of the product which is to be used in the next advertising campaign. In this case, the director truly becomes one of the creative group, improvising the shots as he feels the need. Obviously, both agency and client trust and look to him to create the basic commercial.

Good storyboards do exist. While a director would like to produce his own creative ideas, he must admit that there is a heck of a lot of talent within an agency. Its people are under the same restrictive tethers that the director is and, like a director, one or another of them occasionally finds the freedom to break out and deliver something outstanding. What a pleasure it is to pick up a storyboard and grin with delight at the reading. It's embarrassing. The director knows he should keep his own stamp off a commercial that has been perfectly boarded. However, this happens too seldom to concern us.

What do you do first with a storyboard that you've received? A director says:

> I think the first function is just to understand it, to understand what they're trying to say and who does what to whom and with what. Until you really understand what the continuity is—and very often I will say the dialogue aloud and play both parts just to hear how it sounds to my ear.

Another vital understanding is which factors are really important and which are just dressing that can be changed. There are certain essentials and they must be sought out. If the lawnmower is drawn way back in the frame with lots of green grass in the foreground, you might say that there is insufficient identification of the product and you would be right. However, in this case, the agency/client wants to emphasize the successful lawn, and this is a compromise. The storyboard is quite useful in creating a communication with the agency to determine what the sketches mean. Understand each frame with all its nuances—our business is nuances. The nuance is the director's stock in trade; that's what he's hired for, since the storyboard has the facts.

The chicken and egg proposition works here, too. If you are a director noted for your creativity, you will be given opportunities to indulge that talent. If you've hardly had the chance to work on such spots, you won't get it unless luck works with you. As one director put it:

> More opportunity has to be given to the good director for participating in the creating of the commercial—the storyboard and the bidding. Everything depends on those two things. If you get a good storyboard, you usually get a better budget to shoot it because there has been more interest from the agency; the director has more opportunities to show his style.

There is another subtle factor that a director retains in his bag of kens. The agency/client usually has been doing the same spot in varied versions over a long period of time. It's been efficacious, but the creative group and possibly the client himself is bored with its sameness. If, within the general concept, the director can add an important difference, he can be a hero. I wore the laurels after one shoot. We were filming a spot for a soft drink. The storyboard told of a disconsolate group of teenagers sitting on a beach. We see a fellow coming toward them with a six-pack and all cheer and cheer up. Okay. I suggested shooting an empty pop bottle sitting there in the sand. I wanted to shoot it against the sun to express the heat and the dryness of the kids waiting. I was told, "No." The image was bad, there was no appetite appeal in an empty bottle, the idea was too far out. I insisted that it would only take a couple of minutes. They humored me; it was my film and time. Of course, I'm telling this story because it was a success story; the client even ran an entire print campaign on the idea. I took my bonus of kudos home with me.

Painting by Numbers

I have never tried to paint by numbers. I guess I do enough of that when I am locked into a firm, unyielding storyboard. Yet, I am tempted. I think that a creative person can do with the numbered painting as we do with our storyboards. I imagine a director would use *almost* the colors called for; he would let colors slop and blend over into other numbers; he wouldn't touch some numbers and would blacken out others. The completed work would be the painting that the original creative artist envisioned but—different. I hope: better. The more creative director would, I imagine, use the numbers only as a pencil sketch on canvas is used as the start of an important work of art. I'll wager that the Directors' Guild of America could categorize and scale the creativity of directors simply by giving all of them the same numbered painting and scoring the creative urge and accomplishment. I'd better keep my mouth shut before the agencies think this is a great idea.

One director expressed this idea:

> I always assume that I try to do something to a storyboard somewhere along the way. I look at myself as a renegade director who's going to make something out of every piece that comes through, in the sense that it's gotta be the best, the greatest, the most memorable. But for the existential experience of actually getting out there and directing and doing it and it had to be the best, if you can do it, given the shit you're working with. . . . Professional doesn't mean totally hackneyed or simple journeyman work. What I mean by that is that it has to be the most vivacious, interesting, compelling piece of advertising that can be done, given the specific directions and limitations involved in that commercial.

There is often a distinct difference between the needs of the agency and the needs of the client. The client wants a commercial that will make his product look good. The agency wants this, too, but they have another distinct need: they must look good to the client. Remember that, director: you're working for the agency! This phenomenon has a distinct effect on the ideas you dream up. When you have a definite contribution to offer, the thought is presented to the agency. The agency, in turn, might take it to the client as a suggested change. This does happen. But—remember that the agency has spent all those months, dollars and strengths getting the client to approve those sensational ideas of their own. It's mighty rough for them to go back and say, "The director has a better idea." They will either go to the client with the new idea or not depending on the situation, their relationship with the client, the personality of the client, the personality of the account executive, art director, producer and so forth. The director can only assume he is there to offer his service to the agency; it is their choice whether or not to accept his suggestions. This sounds so simplistic and basic, yet it is the ulcer that eats at every director.

Changing the Storyboard

This book is obviously dedicated to the proposition that a director must give—and that successful directors do give—all they have to make the commercial better. This starts as soon as he looks at the storyboard, as articulated by one director:

> It's tough to find key words or philosophies, but if there is any one philosophy for me, from the time I see the board to the last shot of the day, through

editing, in fact, it's how can I make it better. And that's a philosophy that
strokes my own ego and hopefully will please the client. . . . How could I
make that line better, how could I make that nuance better. He's raising one
eyebrow; maybe that doesn't work. How can I make that better? Hopefully,
that's something more than the agency had expected and (it) will make them
think that I can bring something to a board that will entice them back next
time.

Each director brings his own thing. I am, myself, not very taken with the
possibilities of the validity and credibility of such studies as phrenology and
palm reading and reading tea leaves in revealing the personality of an individual. I am, however, quite certain that my little hobby of handwriting analysis
does lead me to ascertain certain personality traits in people I have never met.
(I rush to state that I accept the existence of extrasensory perception and credit
some of the personality-reading techniques to that phenomenon.) The point
here is that when a director shoots a storyboard as it is, he cannot help putting
the stamp of his own personality on it. This is what the agency looks for,
consciously or not. They hire a director for his special stamp even when the
board is to be shot as is. The director's special brain, emotions, taste and such
color the shoot. How do the agency folk choose one director over another when
the board is inviolable? ESP, perhaps, the vibrations of a certain personality of
a director which bode right for the job—who knows? It certainly could be
friendship, a past comfortable history of productions, a mother-in-law's
advice. . . .

Once on the job, the director finds it impossible not to suggest changes in
the storyboard. If the change is not drastic, if the agency/client folk are reasonable, probably most of the small changes are accepted, even sought after. But,
how much to suggest, how to suggest, how far is drastic, how much to insist?
Ah, there are the rubs:

There's pragmatism in the business. I've lost clients for pushing too hard.
Other people I've heard the opposite from, (with) people saying, "He doesn't
add anything to it; he doesn't add enough to it." These are the people who
have given me a piece of drivel, a cast that I've told them is going to do a
less than average job. There are two that stick in my mind—you always think
of the failures—that I've never worked for again. They say, "Stick with the
board—shoot the board," and that's it. Happily, that's not the average situation.

If there is one guideline in suggesting changes that will be accepted, it is to
insist on *how* the story is to play. The obvious opposite side of that coin is to
avoid suggesting any changes that will affect *what* the story is trying to say.
One director's example:

. . . a very obvious kind of thing: a commercial that has a lot of cuts in it.
We did one recently where they wanted a guy walking along the beach, coming up the steps to his beachhouse, sitting down at a typewriter. It would have
taken six setups to do. There was no justification for it. I determined that we

should do it in one take. Instead of shooting at the beach we went to the bay side, found a house right at water level. It was a very effective way of shooting the commercial, much more economical. We had a long-day bid; we didn't use it, we wrapped early.

Ordinarily, too, the visual lends itself more to accepted changes than does the audio. The dialogue and narration has been hammered out in gold leaf before the director sees the board. It is with a heart-rending longing and wishing that we hear of a commercial shot in England where a situation is set up and the actors improvise the dialogue. What a dynamic method to arrive at fresh dialogue and, more importantly, words spoken with natural cadence and emotions! What I could do with such a technique and . . . but, back to our storyboard.

Changing the Copy

A United States director has this to say about copy:

Copy is so locked in legally on so many spots that you have to try and determine in advance if they are amenable to changing any dialogue or even considering the notion of a change, even so much as adding an "um" or an "ah," because all the copy is cleared legally to start with. You determine early on, in your pre-production meetings, if any of that is going to be feasible. Those are not important words, the um's and ah's, but if something occurs to me that would make a little moment pay off better, then I'll suggest it. More often, you don't get approval on that. The attitude is generally, "Look, the client bought it this way; it's cleared through legal. Let's not start a whole new hassle." I'll push a little further, but I won't go too far.

Why does the dialogue in commercials have to be so stilted and phony? Let's be kind for a moment and consider the writer. He has a scene where a housewife says to another, "I learned that the manufacturers of the detergent BLAH have worked out a new formula. It's more economical to use." Okay, that doesn't make for a very dramatic scene, but the words could come out naturally. Hold it. The writer is told that he must indicate that the housewife has tried the detergent and is satisfied. Also, he must include the description "super-action," because that is going to be the catchword printed on every box. And, where is the word "improved"? You don't want the audience to think it's the same old product, do you? The word "new" is not enough. Besides, the sentence will take up eight seconds even now; we don't have more than six and a half. The writer is a pro and comes back with the line that is enthusiastically approved by everyone at the agency and by the client: "My new super-action detergent BLAH is more economical due to its improved formula." In time and it covers all the bases. Now the line is given to the director. It cannot be changed but—if he's a good director and wants to work with this agency again—he must make it sound like a natural dialogue between two women! #+*(:#!

I have skipped one step, a step which makes the dialogue even more difficult to change. Very often the commercial will be tested before production. If it scores well, which means the audience was happy with the spot as it was presented, then tampering with this success is nothing short of idol smashing. Appreciate, if you can, how much money is riding on this commercial by the client; he wants to be certain that he's on the right road. After all the work and testing has been done, a jaunty director enters the scene and insists that his personal advice is better than all the thinking done to date. As Jack Benny would have said: *"Well!"*

Yet, the director is often given a serious hearing and, surprisingly, his advice is often taken. That is because the field of communication is still an art rather than a science and the director is an acknowledged artist with the proper instincts for what moves men's emotions. The director must always carry this badge of unique authority with pride and assuredness; he will then continue to state his attitudes and give his advice against all horrified remonstrations of "But, we can't change that."

It's not easy. Every time a single small change is made, other changes have to follow to accommodate it. The timing of the spot is rigid; an addition here means an excision there, a word taken out may well confuse the entire rhythm, the emphases. Everyone is loath to start the revision; the director can assume that his big mouth will make him loathsome. But, we hope, even more respected.

The director, bringing up new ideas to change the storyboard which has been bid on and awarded to him, faces another problem. What is the usual answer when he suggests another way of shooting a scene? "Shoot it two ways." Shoot it the way it's in the board and then shoot it any way you like at your own time and expense. The decision between the two will be made in the editing room. Overtime costs, more film, a more tired crew and cast later on and even more nervousness on the set—these are some of the prices the director must pay for even the slightest change he would suggest. But he *should* suggest.

The director has joined the agency in providing a service to the client. Just as Michelangelo provided a service to the Church, so the director employs his art in the service of the Client. Once again, his attitude toward the production is vital. His assistants have mixed the paints, plastered the surface and stretched the canvas. In this case, the agency has done all the preparation. The director, the latter-day master artist, enters to take charge and, with precision and determined concentration, perfects this sketch called a storyboard into a work of art. It is expected of him.

The Storyboard vs the Director's Dignity

What if the attitude of the agency/client does not reflect this respect? You are a professional. Do your job. And, if you are a "superstar" director in great demand, you can say, as one did:

I just don't work with them again. It's as simple as that . . . I feel very inhibited. They wouldn't take my suggestion on the actress, they wouldn't take my suggestion on the lighting, they didn't like this, they didn't like that, and I had to put in so much time. I'd just rather not work with them again. But, I made the deal and I'll stand by it. I *hate* to be a quitter. I just hate it and I want to so much. I want to walk away, but you *can't*. I'm a grownup person, not a kid. I'm a responsible person; I can't be a schmuck.

It has been said that the only definite decision that a committee can arrive at is "it can't be done." That is what a director's suggestion is up against—a committee. The storyboard is there, in black and white—or color. How much can a director fight for his concept? Life being what it is, it depends on his stature in the industry. If he is considered "just another director," he had best have a lot of strong arguments to present. If he is turned down, it is up to his own level of pragmatism to determine how much the next job means to him. If the director feels his oats, he can take the attitude of this superstar:

But, if they lock me into a board, I won't do it. I don't need to do it. I'm fortunate. I can turn down a lot of work to take what I want to take. And, if I want to take the summer off and spend it with my kids, I'll do it. I'm just very lucky. I work hard enough and I'm in a position now where I can afford to do it. And if somebody busts my chops, I won't work with them again. I'll be perfectly civil to them on the set. I've never had any fist fights, few confrontations. But, I can usually intimidate people physically so they leave me alone. It's almost never happened.

In the case of that director, the power he describes is quite real. For him. Some directors play that part in some situations very successfully. There is a certain awe that a forceful, loud director is paid on the set. One director admits:

I've never tried to be flashy, make myself the star. There are directors who become very successful by acting the part of a director. That is an acting assignment for some people. Maybe I would have gone a lot further if I had, but that's not me, and so I guess I couldn't do it very successfully.

How often the director is given a board by the agency producer who admonishes him immediately with the caution that the board is not to be taken literally! What the producer is trying to achieve there is a production where the director will come up with as many creative ideas as possible. It is a valid ploy. However, in almost all cases, the committee moves in at the shoot and the trembling takes over and the director is crushed into shooting the board as well as his new thoughts. The clever director will convince the agency to prepare a new storyboard before the shoot which incorporates the new approaches. About such opportunities one director says:

It all depends on who you are working with. With certain agencies you are looked on as a journeyman, sort of maybe a high-class electrician or plumber. You come in and they give you the blueprint and they want six outlets. They know just where they want them. They actually do resent creative contributions. Again, I think that has a lot to do with the nervousness.

The most important factor a director can bring to the sketches on the story-board is his knowledge of editing. This, too, can be his greatest frustration. Everyone is looking at the still pictures and enjoying them at length. The director must bring to their attention that this one will last only two-and-a-half seconds on the screen, hardly enough to appreciate all the important details that reveal themselves so cleverly in a still sketch. One sketch will not "cut" into the other; this arrangement of stills won't work and so on. I recently had a storyboard where the final shot of the product was indicated by two sketches, one a long shot, the other with an explanation: "slow zoom into extreme closeup." I pointed out that there were only one-and-a-half seconds left for both those sketches; the audience would never see the product in closeup. That argument was easily won. The product shot is one the client will never fudge.

One director has his own technique. He rolls with the punches. All he ever fights for is a lot of time and film to expose. He feels that if he can get to shoot his version as well as the board, he can cut his version and sell that.

Client, Agency and Storyboard

A mixed blessing is to have the client on the set. The valuable part is that he is there to make decisions when the storyboard is to be altered. (Of the disastrous part, more later.) If the client is not there when changes are made, a real hysteria takes place. First of all, a rigidity takes over. The client has approved the storyboard and how will it be to bring a commercial to him that has changes; he might not approve of the changes. Not being on the set, he cannot appreciate that the board just could not have been produced as sketched. How often have we seen an account executive or someone from the agency sit in an editing session, storyboard clutched to his bosom, ascertaining that every scene is cut in exactly the same order, at exactly the same word—that, even, the composition of each frame is the same!

Remember that the board has been tested in animatic form. Or, it has gone through an even more thorough test with a completed commercial. In the animatic, a series of stills, in effect the storyboard, has been aired or screened to an audience and the reaction, recall and impact measured and scored. How these tests are done, or arguments pro and con the techniques or findings, are not the province of this book. (Would anyone like to hear a few choice chapters on the subject?) The score is the core of the storyboard's preemptive strength. When a test has scored well, almost all arguments for change are fruitless. The instinct the director feels about how to make the spot better and more effective takes an awful beating. Yet, the client, too, often has doubts about the total validity of the test, and there is always the chance that the director's ideas might make it more effective; thus, maybe they will take a chance. The answer is: don't give up. There is never clear-cut reason why a spot has scored well, anymore than there is a clear reason why one movie actor becomes a great star and another fine actor does not or why one stage play is a hit and another not.

If these phenomena could be computed, every movie and stage show and commercial would be successful. There is still the measurement by the seat of the pants and the director has one of the most sensitive seats in measuring and affecting the emotions and reactions of the audience. Not for certain, God knows, but that area is his bailiwick and he will be correct more times than other people. So, despite the fact that the spot has scored well, he may well be the one to put his finger on its weaknesses and suggest an alternative that will work, that will, indeed, strengthen its very strengths. There is no perfect commercial and, whether the director works from storyboard or filmed test, he should offer creative suggestions.

Before the commercial has been tested, it has already been ground down by legal requirements. This is not a game we are playing; the consumer's interests must be protected from unscrupulous advertisers. Precisely because of the powerful impact and pervasiveness of television commercials, the watchdogs must sniff out every scent of lies, misrepresentations, even omissions of truth. Let's give that to them. The networks, the federal agencies and the private organizations devoting themselves to this problem do a most creditable job. However, like all things bureaucratic, it sometimes just gets silly. If the intent of the law is to keep beer advertisers from showing people enjoying the beer, why is the major restraint that of actually having the enjoyer drink it? You can see him lift it almost to his lips, cut away to another shot, then cut back to the drinker after he has sipped and is sighing happily, wiping the froth off his lips. (Established broadcasting custom says you cannot show a person drinking beer during a TV commercial.) I doubt that many TV viewers are conscious of the non-drinking.

The nit-picking of words is worse. In order to have every statement, every piece of dialogue legally correct, everyone acting in a TV commercial seems to use a vocabulary they learned at Harvard Law School. Because, in fact, the lawyers are so involved with the choice of words, they are practically writing the spots. I have no answer to the problem, other than to call for reasonableness from the censors (they refer to "continuity") and the lawyers. I would go so far as to allow an advertiser to say his product is the very best—it is an advertisement after all and everybody (okay, not kids) knows it.

In those commercials where the legal requirements are very strict—and more and more commercials are falling into that category—the creative input of everyone concerned is frustratingly limited. This seems to be like complaining about the weather. So, the director drags his rationalization to the fore and plays it like a puzzle. How do you get around the restriction and still remain legal? The director is presented with all the taboos. Now, how can he make it a viable commercial?

Challenge or opportunity, the storyboard is enemy to the director. It is a spy reporting whether he is following instructions. The storyboard is a siren calling the director to lotus land where he does not have to think anymore. It is a mischievous elf creating confusion in the mind of a director who is on the brink of a creative thought only to lose it; the concept is shattered by the sketch in the storyboard before him. The storyboard is a vicious mistress, emasculating and paralyzing the director and his thought processes. The storyboard should be drawn under the direction of a director. The creative power of a director, together with his instinctive desire to help in the creative process, is sucked out of him by the storyboard. It is a prison, a blight that freezes the very paint of his filmic palette. To the lazy, unimaginative director, it is easy numbers to paint by. To a director of force and honor, it is a binding, suffocating chain of words that only repeat: "You must."

At best, the director can improve what is on the board somewhat. He longs and strains to overcome its strictures and build it into an efficacious and proud work of advertising art.

5

Talent

WHAT A DOPEY WORD: talent. Not that actors and actresses don't have talent, but how in lexicography's name did the word "talent" evolve? What happened to the word "performers"? It seems to infer that only those in front of the camera or on stage have talent, no one else. I was once a performer. I played guitar and sang folk songs and it was my profession—until I had to make a living. Now that I operate behind the camera, does it mean that I lost my talent? Forgive my carping, but every time a terrible actor is wished on me, I choke on the appellation. Also, words are my interest and the tools of my craft. (Although I probably will be drummed out of the Writers' Guild of America after this book is published.)

What is the relationship of a director to talent? Let us assume that the acting ability of a given actor goes from A to Z (Z being the best). If the actor has only a G ability, no director is able to get him to perform much higher, though a good director can pull him up to J. (A bad director will pull him down to B.) What I could have said much simpler is that the director needs as able an actor as he can get to realize the best performance possible. And so we cast about to hook the actor who can deliver the role as near perfection as possible. (Or does the word "casting" come from the foundry?—i.e., we create a personality in the image of . . . forget it!)

The Casting Director

The most common method of casting is to use a casting director. (Hey, there's another word to mutter about: the diminution of the impact of the word director, now that everyone has taken it—lighting director; assistant director, who is almost always the representative of the producer; director of photography; casting director—I'm grateful that the janitor has taken the title of sanitation engineer rather than garbage director. Since I direct everyone, does that make me a director director?)

As I was saying, the casting director is called in. He may work directly for the producing company or the advertising agency or he may run a private business. Much depends on his ability and dedication to the particular job. He will know what agents handle the correct type of talent for the productions at hand; he will know the individual actors and their abilities pretty thoroughly. He has his own file of pictures, home telephone numbers and so on. The casting director, in turn, calls the talent agents or the talent directly and sets up a casting session.

The Casting Session

If the agents and casting director are doing a conscientious job, the actors called in will not be the same old faces you get every time. There is no question that these same faces are good professionals who can be counted on to turn in creditable performances. They are safe to use. But what you lose by this is the occasional opportunity to find the out-of-the-ordinary but perfect face for the part. And if that actor cannot act quite as well as the old pros, the trouble is worth it. The casting director, too, should bring in people other than the ones the agency has described as correct for the character. If he does the latter, he is acting as a telephone service. A group of talent should be brought in who do not necessarily fit the description, but rather reflect the casting director's taste and choice for the role. Another group that should be entered into the sweepstakes is a collection of characters chosen from a totally different viewpoint. This can trigger new concepts for both the agency and the director; it's remarkable how often this happens.

Today, a terrible type of casting session continues to happen, but, thankfully, quite seldom: the "cattle call." Therein a mass of talent is brought into the waiting room so that the producer or director can saunter out and point to some of the meat and say, "You and you and you stay for an interview. The rest of you leave." The acting profession is thus degraded and insulted. The Screen Actors' Guild fights the cattle call. Even in those casting sessions where specific actors are called, the appointments should be staggered, giving reasonable time for each actor to be interviewed or taped with a minimum of waiting. Depending on the production's needs, the calls can be anywhere from five to fifteen minutes apart.

While my own feeling is that I want to be present at every casting session, I must admit I hate the sessions with a passion. I know that the winner will earn a decent, if not goodly, amount of money. But, I also know that each person has had to make a concerted effort to get there—correctly costumed, coiffed and cheerful. They have left children in the care of who-knows-who and driven in from the suburbs and gone to the beauty parlor and paid for parking and hoped. Then they come into the room with the big desk and the imperious group staring at them and they act their hearts out for a couple of minutes and leave. Sitting there, I know in almost all cases when the actor in front of me is all wrong and doesn't stand the chance of a one-legged man playing Tarzan and what is he even doing there! But, still they troop in, some of them my friends from having worked together before, and they look into my eyes for a sign on how they're doing and I have to play dispassionate fish. And, they go home and I know they won't hear a yea or nay unless they take the trouble to call their agents, and the agent himself might not know until the spot is shot, weeks later or even later than that. In the meanwhile, hope. In the order of which casting I hate most, it's men the least, children after that and women the most. The kids are bad enough. In the main, they're not there happily, even though they have been taken out of school for the day. It bothers me to see the unhappy child there, fidgeting at his imprisonment against his will and natural bent. I'm probably wrong but I still feel that women are more sensitive to this degradation than men; they act so much more intently about getting the part. To me, the women seem a great deal more vulnerable. (Please, could you call me a chauvinist donkey, rather than pig?)

A Director Casting

Yet, I can vote for only one person for the part and I sit there at the casting session, happy, at least, that now I have a better chance of ending up with an actor with whom I can make a better commercial. And, coldly, I give each a rating for the part. The agency has given me a list of the contestants and, next to each, I write a short description. The photos they leave are so misleading, I need something to remind myself who belonged to which name. I write something that stands out: "gravelly voice," "l.l. (looks like) Aunt Frieda," "l.l. a skinny Burt Reynolds." Then, for me, the score of one to four checks, four being perfect. A four-checker almost never comes in but, when one does, a weird thing happens: everybody in the room is in total agreement that this is the one. That's a very satisfying casting session indeed.

One director describes it:

> You sit back and you throw a question. It's like jury selection. You try to find something that would interfere with your shooting. The questions are only based on what you're doing, that you're gonna get the best job out of them. The better they can perform, the more concentration you go on to whatever subject. It's great if you can tell somebody "Now you pick it up here, you do this, you do that," and you don't have to tell them again and you do twenty takes.

What do you look for, generally?

> I think intelligence is number one. A smart person. I think in our business we have to have smart people around us.

Another director says:

> I want to get somebody who is right for the part. The agencies have a lot of prerequisites to that. I need to know that the person is somewhat versatile, can give me more than one kind of delivery. I think that's important because when you get to the set, you have your opinion and there's somebody with an agency or client opinion. We don't play scenes in commercials, really; (we) play feelings, emotion, one-liners.

Casting is as subjective and intuitive a gamble as any arbitrary decision. You get a feeling: from the way the person moves in the few steps he takes into the room, from the reasonableness of his replies to your questions, from his professionalism of slating his name before the videotape recording, by the look in his eye. Your reactions to all these factors, even before he acts out the part, is vital. Also, you must disregard his inanity of squealing rapturously about how he absolutely loves and always uses the product, or the ridiculous wax of his moustache. Look to see what kind of a person he is; in the shoot, you are going to be in a most dramatic one-on-one situation with him and his personality will suddenly become very important. Sometimes I can even tell that the spaced-out character in front of me is the type who will be late on the set or take forever in his dissatisfaction with makeup or sweat up a torrent or not be able to remember lines. God, the characters!

It is at the casting session that the director must decide whether the actor actually understands the lines he is reading. Ask some questions; actors can fool you at the first reading and then confound you at the shoot, when you find out he doesn't know the meaning of the scene. Look, too, to determine whether there is a natural energy level that will sustain the actor at least through the filming day. This weakness is difficult to spot early—it becomes evident in a hysteria and weariness at repeating the same copy.

As one director sees it:

> You don't see the magic until it's on the screen sometimes. You don't believe the thing is coming across when you're shooting and then you look at it in a screening room and it knocks you off your ass. On the other hand, some people give you a terrific reading and you look at it on screen and you say, "Oh, Jesus, it's awful." So we're learning all the time.

And another:

> Usually the agency . . . will pre-cast and I will see finalists and callbacks and we'll run through it. What I prefer to do in a casting session like that is have the producer or casting person run through it with the actor while I just watch (as) they go through the litany of what it's all about, explaining the spot. Then I begin to make suggestions and at some point I don't lay back anymore but get actively involved, explaining to the actor what I want from

the thing if I don't think it's being explained properly by the producer or casting person. You find that a lot of what happens in a commercial, both in the casting and execution, is very unconscious. I don't know where it's going to come from and when I'm going to start cooking. There's sort of a magic moment when my adrenalin clicks into a moment. That's true in casting as well. In a lot of situations, (what) the actor is asked to do is very mundane and there is really precious little you can tell him that will enhance or detract from what he is doing. I kinda watch and at some moment this click happens and then I know what I want after observing it for a while. I suppose occasionally it'll be unfair to the two or three actors who have gone by until that clicking moment happens with me. Then I think I can tell them how I think it should be done and things that might help him or her personally achieve that moment better.

We all tend to *look* intently at our actors. Some of them have such interesting looks—beautiful, funny, weird—that we forget to *listen* hard. In that way, what might be overlooked is that the voice has a rather high pitch for a man or an extremely low masculine growl for a woman. A lisp on a man who is supposed to be a jock just doesn't lie right; dentures can create a whistle or a click that just cannot be overcome. A voice—not the reading—can be rather flat. Again, I beseech the agency: involve the director more in casting. He has had to work his heart out before on just such oversights and tends to listen a lot harder than agency/client people who cast more, shall we say, empirically.

There are many good actors who are just soggy omelets when asked to improvise. Yet, it is a good technique in many kinds of casting sessions to ask the talent to act out the scene in his own words. What comes forth immediately and clearly is whether the actor has intelligence and knows what in tarnation the commercial and the character is about. He will also bring forth some interesting interpretations that you haven't thought about and perhaps the agency will detect some weaknesses in the copy. Get the talent to exaggerate the problem or minimize it. Another shtick is to dream up totally new lines that nail down the character to be played. Then you can tell much more easily whether the actor fits and understands the specific role. Let the actor make changes in the copy as he sees fit. This also helps the agency to study the correctness of the copy; it will take everyone's concentration away from whether the copy is correctly delivered and pull the attention over to the study of whether the actor is correct for the part, which is what you're all doing there in the first place. As one director put it:

> When I'm in a casting session I usually work with the actor. It tells me two things: first, do I communicate with this actor and vice versa; second, it gives me a chance to work with the script before I'm on the set. I work out a lot of my problems in a casting session. Find out what the rhythm of the copy is, what the natural breaks are. This is very important to me because I would have to spend half a day on the set finding out about that. It's always murder on the people who come in because you have to work out all the problems

with them; of course, they're not all going to get the part, but they've been the guinea pigs, which is an unfortunate part about casting. I think it's one of the most valuable things a director can do before shooting a job. You really (start) to understand your script at that stage.

Playing the script and revolving it to inspect all possibilities gives you nuances that you may very well not have thought of beforehand: an actor might grin while delivering the line—it's great!—he might look askance at the person reading to him—good! Directors tend to allow the listener in a bit of dialogue to sit there impassively. An actor can inexplicably underplay a line which should have been shrill and it works. There are surprises in casting sessions that will entertain and delight you, folks, but you have to pay close attention. According to one director:

> I explain the commercial and their particular role in the commercial. Running through the lines, I often intentionally change direction, only to see whether there is that ability in the actor to change direction.

And another:

> Again, the aesthetics of dance play a very important part and I favor body movement, body positions—the way people walk or sit, the way they can reach for a product or make a gesture. I will immediately prefer a very coordinated person to a *klutz*.

A director will be able to tell his grandson that there was a time, before that director's time, in the halcyon platinum days of television commercial production, when the casting was done only by the agency producer together with the director. Then, they brought one—I repeat, one—photo to the client to show clearly who the talent was going to be. Now and forever more it is the committee! I'm not the one to say that the new system is wrong, but wieldy it ain't. There's the representative of the client and his assistant; the creative head; the art director; the writer; the casting director; the producer (any of these categories may well be two or three persons); and the account executive. The account executive knows the personal prejudices of the head man at the client's. (There have been times when an advertising campaign and its various components have been influenced by the wife of the chairman of the board, by her telling him, "Arthur, I saw your new commercial on TV and the blonde looks like a real hussy. I'm ashamed.") *Directive:* no blondes in his commercial. Honestly, I've been given just that instruction!

Casting on Videotape

The next step is videotape:

> Now we put it on videotape. Not the first audition, although sometimes the smaller agencies don't have preliminaries. If you're a big agency and have a big casting department, you'll be seeing people all the time, weeding out the good from the bad.

From its library of videotapes, the casting department of the agency pulls out the possible performers for the commercial. They are called in and act out the part, again on videotape. Of the many that are taped, most of the committee choose several, who are usually asked to return for another session, the call-back session. From this group, a small number of contestants, often three actors, sometimes a couple more, is assembled for the final casting session. Then the director—and not until then—is called in to add his voice to the discussion of the entire committee for the final choice. That is the normal practice today in the larger agencies.

In the smaller agencies, more and more use is being made of videotape casting. However, the photograph is still important. The trouble with photos, of course, is that they may very well be a few years old or retouched or posed or lighted in such a way as to distort the genuine look of the actor.

Another value of videotape is that the actor can be seen by all in a wardrobe or part of a costume that reflects the character to be played. There are still enough non-professional decision makers about who cannot visualize how the actor will be transformed when in appropriate costume. The smart actor will find out in advance what the commercial is about before showing up for a casting session and dress himself accordingly. The photograph that he leaves, too, will show him exactly as he is; an exotic still makes it doubly hard for the deciders to see him cast in the part.

Hands

Another element too often overlooked in casting is the hands of the actors. Almost all—yes, that many—commercials have a shot of the talent's hand or hands holding the product. Of course, the safest approach is to hire a hand model to stand in for the actor. In that case, try to match the hand with the actor. (Remember, too, the almost omnipresent wedding ring; advertisers are still square about people who live together.) The fingernail polish should not be too obtrusive no matter what the latest style is, unless the spot is one that revolves about fashion. That admonition is so self-evident that you might think it is always automatically seen to by the actor and the makeup person. Not at all. Time after time I have seen my crew wait while someone raced out to pick up a mild peach nail coloring.

The graceful, perfect hand is of prime importance in a food commercial. A director who is a specialist in shooting food says:

> Hand action is very complementary to food if you're shooting, say, pudding, of having a spoon coming in down and knowing how to do it and then bringing it up and having a little hold and bringing it out of frame. Shooting a hand to me is like shooting a talent on a set who comes in, says her lines, knowing what the message is, and then making an exit. . . . When we look at a hand model, I go through a series of tests to determine if the hand model is qualified. One, I look at the hand to see if it is well scaled, as far as proportions; I look at the fingernails to make sure they have a graceful contour to them,

that there is an elegance, a quality about the hand, particularly (in relation) to food. Once I perceive the hand from the outside as well as the inside, I always determine the design of the hand, how it moves. Once I do that, I have them hold both hands out, off any surfaces, because sometimes you have hand models who are very astute and when they start doing things you ask them to do, they do it in a way that camouflages their own disabilities. So that when you have them hold their hands out, maybe they'll rest them on a table or something (to keep them steady). Through the years of experience you become very perceptive about how to determine who is a good hand model. So, after I see that the hand is visually steady, I give them a few hand actions, such as having them go through a very simple scene with a saucepan and a ladle. I'll indicate that what I want them to do is enter the scene, having them hold up the ladle, bring it back in (the saucepan) and stir around and pick it up as if they're having something cascading off it into the saucepan again, bring it back in and exit from the scene. I'll try to determine if the hand is graceful enough to move in; secondly, if they have the intellect to understand direction. That is another aspect of a hand model that most people don't realize is very, very important. As with talent, you can direct them to perform for you, but there has to be input from that talent to contribute to the performance. With a hand model, they must have a feel for what they are doing. It's not just doing it by the numbers, because then it becomes a static and stiffish kind of thing.

Mismatching

The trick of resting hands on the table to minimize trembling is only one of the ploys that talent will use to get a job. Actors have been known on occasion to rearrange the truth about their capabilities. Let me put that another way: actors generally will lie harder than a starving used-car salesman to get a job. You ask an actor: "Can you ride a bike well?" He will answer, "I was a finalist in the Boston-to-New York heat." But, you can see the cartoonist's balloon over his head saying to himself, "I must learn to ride a bike if I get this job."

One director had this experience:

> I had a spot to do with waterskiing or swim wear. The first opening shot is flying through the air from a ski jump. And you ask everybody. "Yeah, yeah, we can waterski." I wanted to get into the final selection. To have them come off the ski jump, you gotta be the best and they have had to (have done) it before. So, I insisted on being in on that final selection. Because, just by asking . . . and then one girl, I look and see she left a cane up front. She had twisted her foot doing a pilot in Los Angeles. And I said, "Is that your cane?" "Oh, yeah, yeah, but don't worry, I'll be all right for the shoot." I said, "Look, this is the most strenuous thing you can do. We're not just gonna pull you for ten minutes around the water; we're talking about shooting the whole day. You're gonna be up, down, up, down. You're gonna change suits, you're gonna do this, you're gonna come in. Sure, there's gonna be

time for breaks, but I gotta tell ya . . . ." She says, "I guess you're right." Maybe she would have fooled the agency. And then we get her out there and: "Oh, boy, I gotta rest!" And whatta ya gonna do? Finally, by questioning, just the way you would interview somebody. Just narrowed it down to a precious couple of girls. Until one—she knew exactly what she was doing. As a matter of fact, she was turning around and telling the boat operator what to do. And even the chase boat, she knew exactly where to position so that the weight . . . things that even I didn't know; she contributed greatly to the spot. So, right there was her importance.

These stories of mismatching the actor to the spot because the actor misleads the casting group are legion. Another director speaks:

> We were shooting a young boy. This was a prepared chocolate pudding and
> . . . on the day of the shoot, we realized he didn't like chocolate pudding.

It takes time during shooting to unearth these secrets. When food eating is filmed, a pail is kept nearby for the actor to spit out his mouthful as soon as the director says, "Cut." It doesn't matter if the actor even likes the stuff; after the twenty-second take, the bile starts to revolt. Imagine if you get an actor—especially a child—who doesn't like the food but must eat it and look delighted. That takes some acting—and directing. Worse, there have been plenty of instances where the actor is just plain allergic to the food and gets deathly ill on the set, saying, "I didn't think it would affect me this time."

Truth in Advertising Actors

That is a lie born of a truth unuttered. No one asked him if he was allergic to the food, so he didn't say. Another pitfall in casting is the gentlemanly approach to casting actresses for swimming scenes and not asking them to show their bodies. Wrong. A body that is sensational in a tight blouse and shorts can be a horror in a bikini. Oh, the secrets that emerge: surgical scars, outstanding moles, weird sunburn patches, flabby skin, drooping breasts, burn scars, jutting bones—on and on. If they "didn't know they had to bring a bathing suit for the casting," don't believe 'em. Strip 'em or forget 'em. Okay, so I don't hate *all* casting sessions.

The other aspect of the choice of talent is determining what the client will like. The only real answer to that is to first please yourself as the director. Almost always you will find the right person for the part and, if it *is* the right person, the client will almost always like your choice—almost always. A director says:

> In commercials, finding the right person has to do with fitting the role in the commercial but, also, (being) what the agency has in mind. First you have to listen to what those people are saying. When they say "low key," what do they really mean? Honestly, I had tremendous problems with them at one time. . . . I mean I just never got it right. The first two or three commercials

> I never got it together where everybody was happy when the thing was done. One day I just decided to go to the agency and listen—really listen—to what they were saying, and I've had success since.

What do you do when the chosen actor proves himself inept at the time of the shoot? Try crying; try convincing the agency folk to call in the second choice while the crew waits; try breaking the actor's leg so that you can collect on your insurance to pay for the day; try being lucky as was one director:

> He was in there and said, "Hey, I'm an actor paid up in SAG." Well, we discovered a star. The kid was phenomenal. The original guy admitted he couldn't do it; he didn't believe in what he was saying in this bank commercial. It went against him; that was his mental block. He was too big for it. Well, as they say in the theatre, there are no small parts, just small actors. So the talent can make your life pleasant, exciting or difficult.

Another little ol' whoop-de-doo is the actor who doesn't quite understand that he has a conflict of interest. That is, he is already in a commercial for a competitor. Even SAG decries this lack of ethics, but the naive-acting actor will pout (when discovered): "I thought the other spot had run out its time." This kind of machination is often enough discovered *after* the spot is filmed. The casting director, the talent agent and the advertising agency take an awful beating from the client when that happens and the spot has to be reshot. I think that's the only goof for which the director doesn't ultimately get blamed.

Very few stars act like the non-star who acts like a star. He's a difficult one to ferret out at the casting, this guy. There he will be as personable and cooperative as you will but give him the job and the Jekyll you cast is now Mr. Hyde, the actor. Perhaps because he knows that to replace him at that point is too traumatic for all concerned, or whatever. Now, this coffee tastes like mud and are these bagels left over from yesterday and who chose this terrible location with all the flies and he hates flies and he needs more time to make up because he has to cool off and he just won't wear that plaid jacket—it's too stiflingly hot and gray makes his face pale and . . . and. When I design the new director's accouterments, besides the flowing white scarf and puttees and gauntlets, I will insist on pointed shoes, steel tipped, and I will bring back the dropkick.

Types

I have run into precious few of the above types, but they do exist. In fact, I haven't had that problem for quite a while now; perhaps it's because we are casting such a large percentage of "real-looking" people rather than the standard beauty types. This has been a welcome change of approach. Not only is the look better and more believable, but the director's job is eased considerably—a gorgeous girl insisting that now she adores cleaning toilet bowls is a phenomenon that puts a director through somersaults, back-flips, pirouettes and

St. Vitus dance to make the scene look natural. I suppose there are two valid approaches to advertising: one is to set up a character that the viewer would like to be—a slim socko shape displaying a bra—or the other approach, an actor with whom the viewer can identify—he looks like me taking out the garbage. It is important for the director to understand where the client is trying to go. Or, is he aiming for the middle and what advice do you have to give him on that score? Also, in casting, the look of the actor might be wrong but the reading superb—or vice versa. It's best, of course, to find the ideal combination of perfect look and reading, but it behooves the director to weigh the values. It is in just such a situation—where there is no absolutely perfect actor available—that the agency and client will turn to the director to go out on a limb and make his choice. That's only fair and I wouldn't have it any other way. It often leads to a find of a most unusual choice that works like a Nuke.

A director comments:

> I think I prefer very good-looking people. And I mean good-looking as not gorgeous-looking people necessarily but interesting-looking people. That bland-looking housewife from the Midwest—many people feel it's easier to identify yourself with this kind of person. I think everybody can identify with them, but if she looks just a little bit better than what I look (like), I could identify with her better.

Another director says:

> Frequently there is a disagreement over who is better. Some agency people want only pretty people, no matter how they act. They'll make all kinds of excuses: "No, he's not as good an actor as that guy but that guy's losing his hair and he's got a mole." I say, "But the acting's far superior and that's what it's all about." "No, our book shows that pretty people with no regional accents, and especially blondes, score best." I have to get into a thing about instincts, good sense—and lose as much as I win.

Directing the Talent

A director who appeals for reasonable compromise between the look and the problems that will face the director says:

> Working with people there is a certain knack of getting something out of a talent and you have to take a lot of things into consideration when you do this. The mood that they are in, the way the lighting is, how many people are on the set and all these things affect a talent's performance.

Remember, too, that the actor has to stand in front of everyone and deliver those lines that are impossible to deliver. In the final surge of cutting the excess verbiage down to the required time, all the humanities have been eliminated. "Ands, therefores, buts, wells, you sees" are all eliminated. Certainly, there is no time for a "well." And, forget an "er" or a "hmm." The dialogue is now slogan-uttered by one and answered by another with another slogan. The director sweats in trying to get the words coming out as though they were coming from human beings; the actor dies knowing he sounds like a computer talking disembodied words. He is suffering; he is trying. Besides the camera, there is a host of eyes riveted on him, some of them his peers sneering at his travails.

The line has to be said well—and in time. The script supervisor's admonition "You're three-fourths of a second too long" doesn't help when the actor hears it each time he thinks he sounded good. The demonic stricture of time plays an important part even when there is no dialogue. Silent acting, too, requires a smoothness of rhythm and timing which is often enough at odds with the time allotted. Effective mime is seldom restricted by the stopwatch; it is often much more difficult to portray subtle emotion without words.

The actor always needs all the help he can get and I feel that one of the director's major contributions is the positiveness of the atmosphere on the set. I believe that the aura that surrounds the camera transfers itself ultimately onto the screen, though I do not mean this especially in any metaphysical sense. A happy shooting set puts a special glint in the actor's eye that you can see on the screen. There is laughter, a delight, in the look that the director put there with much of his shtick, again, one of the most important being the general "feel" around the camera.

I really buy the attitude set forth by one director:

> I like actors. I like them as people. They have very fragile egos. They have to stand an awful lot of rejection, more in one year than most people stand in a lifetime. And beside which, they are my tools. Just as a painter takes care of his pigments and his brushes and his pallette, I take care of my actors. I'm constantly reassuring (them). There are directors in this business who are notorious for treating actors as if they were the enemy. I hate to tell you how many times actors and actresses have come to me, literally in tears, because usually the director is taking out his lack of preparation or frustration on the actors. But, my attitude is that I have *one day*—you're doing a feature or something, you replace an actor, reshoot the scenes he was in. But with a commercial, you have a one-day shoot and the actors have to be right. Very often an actor will give you a hell of a good reading in an audition, then (he) comes in and just cannot do it. I will be very patient and try not to make him feel embarrassed or self-conscious. (I) try to be very congratulatory and helpful, because I know that I have to get through that day just as he does. I'm very careful that they feel loved—respected and loved.
>
> They are so nervous. You work with an actor and he's doing his lines and the client may come over to you behind the camera and say, "Hey, where's the john?" and right away the actor up there will think: "Oh, he didn't like my reading; maybe I'd better change it. They're talking about *me.*" That is the truth. So, even when an actor is doing a lousy job, it will take me a long, long time before I will push in terms of forcing. Eventually, I may just give him a line reading and say, "Listen, do it like this," but that's usually only a last resort. Most of the time I make them feel very good. Actors are responsive.

SOL GOODNOFF

LUNCH.... ONE HOUR!

Another director expresses it this way:

If it's a professional actor, it's different. But, it depends on how good his technique is and whether I know him or not. . . . . Time is spent getting them to remember their lines and do a mechanical task at the same time because generally, I like to combine something physical with something verbal. Usually, that allows me to move my camera or make some adjustment so it's not just a locked-off frame, which sometimes is better, too. But, it's gaining that confidence. I always tell them that first of all. "I've got a case over there, loaded with nothing but film which I expect to shoot on you today, even though you have only two seconds worth of lines. I know you're going to make some mistakes." If it's a pitch right to camera, I tell them not to talk to the world, just talk to me. I'm on the other side of it. I'm the only one that's seeing it. They are two feet away; they don't know exactly what I see. So, I try to be as reassuring, as self-effacing and as nice as I can and let their ego be as big as possible. I try not to be a star on the crew, just one of the guys. I try to let them see me working. When they start blowing lines and things like that, I just try to reassure them. Sometimes it's good to let them blow a couple of takes. Things like that—try to find an element of common interest, engage them in a conversation and take their minds off some of the things that are going to pressure them. Somebody will blow a line with a lot of confidence and they'll turn away, then turn back, and their entire face will be beaded with perspiration. I've seen that happen many times. Or, their hands will start to shake. And it's mortifying. You only need to know how mortifying it is to try to get in front of the camera and remember some lines. I've done that and it's really scary. Maybe it was more scary for me because I'm not an actor and I was always a very big failure at that. But, I do try to project myself into their position. I try to see all those things that would reassure me. What would I want from a director? And the rest is just theatrical tricks and training.

Beauty and the Director

There is yet another world of television commercials: the fashion spot—those products that deal mostly with the beautification of women and concentrate on portraying that beauty. In this genre, the director must pour into every angle, every shot, the essence of all his romantic notions and fantasies. The girl must radiate the quintessence of glamour, the finite perfection of femininity. The girl must awe the viewer with her stunning beauty and at the same time be so delicious that you want to be her friend. The environs should reflect this paean to love and the product a part of—and reason for—this idyll. Whether she is in jeans or diaphanous flowing organdy, the girl should be a goddess who belongs there without question. Much attention is placed, correctly, on the lighting and on the casting, but the director who brings forth the consummate personality of the player is at least as important as the art director and his minions. It has been said that a director falls in love with each leading actress he works with; in the creation of a fashion commercial, it is absolutely obligatory if he hopes to transfer that awe to the screen.

Contrary to jokes that have been made, I have found that brains most often go with beauty and that dream girls are not all that hard to find, although you do take the time to get the very, very best. Sadly, some of the beauties have only one lone thought in their little heads: their beauty. About this, one director said:

> There are some actors that no amount of talk in the world will get out of them what you want. I can take them by the hand and play a tape back and show them what they are doing wrong and then they realize what I am looking for. Others, you can't show them that monitor. (Their eyes will constantly look toward the monitor even while they are acting.)

Methods

Speaking of wayward eyes, I have a bit that I use when I'm having trouble getting an actor to look directly into the lens if the scene calls for it: I bring the actor around to the eyepiece of the camera and have him look through it while I take his place. I talk into the lens and he gets the feeling that I'm talking directly to him alone. Then, I ask him to hold up his hand right against the lens and I direct my eyes to his hand. It is immediately and forcefully clear to him that the slightest deviation of the eyes away from the lens makes it appear as though the speaker is talking to someone else. If I am shooting the camera, I ask him to talk to me or, if there is a camera operator, then to that person. It's usually best for the actor to talk to me, so I operate in those cases. This has never failed for me; the actor's eyes stay riveted on the lens and, equally important, his speech becomes a conversation rather than a declamation.

To get unrehearsed, spontaneous statements from non-actors, sometimes the camera is hidden and an interviewer discusses the product in an atmosphere that is apparently not structured. Of what use is a director in such a situation? According to one:

> We've done hidden camera work in film; we've done hidden camera work in videotape; we've done hidden camera with film, with slave* tape camera attached . . . When you work just in film, you set your shots with the three cameramen in their blinds or in their one blind and you sit in a room with a communication headset to the film men. And if you need something, you've gotta have a monitor or you really don't need a director, or you communicate strictly with the interviewer. You could direct, just talking to the man who's out there in front of the camera. You ask the questions he didn't ask. Some of those like to answer with no interference. We use the earpiece on the guy all the time. Legally, there are so many things that have to be constantly cued that even the geniuses who can interview well don't know that if they're out of sequence, they lose it. They need guidance. It's a different form of direction, but there is a specialized technique to it—to walk a man through an audience of two hundred to interview people and follow with three cameras. . . . It's a different form of directing. What they've been doing most of the time is taking these cameras and feeding them individually to separate tape recorders. . . . So, you don't edit as you go. They prefer to bring it back and edit. But, you cover. With three cameras on a tape shoot and seeing what you're doing, you can get added coverage, because you can see it; you know you can release a camera or a camera can do something. You're dealing with three film cameras, you've gotta pre-block it, pre-lay it out and then hope that all goes well.

Ethnic Talent

I like the word "ethnic." In America, each individual is of one ethnic group or another. Which is a lead into still another variation on talent:

> The acting, again, is a little different. (The) Spanish people talk a lot with their hands. They are much more demonstrative because that's the way they are. (The) American sense of humor is extremely subtle to them. I mean, there's a joke and nobody moves a muscle in their face because in Spanish it doesn't come across. If any English or European director knows about these differences, they are certainly welcome to do it, too. But, they have to know

*A film camera with a video camera attached to it so that the video picture can be seen on a monitor while the film camera is shooting it.

it. It's the same when I do English productions. I think I am perfectly quali-
fied to do English spots, which I have done without any problem. But again,
I'm not foreign to the character of the American people, to their ways, their
colloquialisms; I understand when they are saying something, the way they
are interpreting it. I can work in both languages without any problem. Like
the Ernst Lubitsches or the Otto Premingers or the von Stroheims—it's not a
problem for me having this horrendous accent. It doesn't affect the talent.

Non-professional Talent

Often, to get the ''real'' look, the director is called upon to stage a scene
with non-actors, people who have had no experience in front of a camera. The
aim in such situations is to have a dialogue or statement that plays as if it were
absolutely candid. The non-actor must convince the audience of his sincerity
and lack of guile; he must say exactly the right words in the seconds allotted.
This is not the easiest gambit for a non-pro to pull off when the unfamiliar
lights are pouring in on him and he is facing a terrifying camera, when a couple
of dozen people are staring at him to make sure he doesn't mess up, when he
has all his normal shyness, inarticulateness and neuroses to handle as well. The
director cannot refer to techniques the actor learned at acting school or delve
with the actor into the history and characteristics of the personality to be
played. Something more is demanded of the director. A few of them speak:

> That requires different handling, (a) different dealing with people, entirely
> different. You can't say, ''Now, do it this way.'' It just doesn't work. Those
> people will shy away. So, you have to treat everybody you deal with, every
> single human being—you have to size them up and then try to get the best out
> of them.

> I enjoy working with non-professional actors. I did several (commercials)
> . . . and we used people like school teachers or writers. It was very challeng-
> ing and I enjoyed it. Words mean different things to different people and you
> can't keep saying it the same way if they're not getting it. You've quickly got
> to find another way of saying it that they'll understand. With a non-profes-
> sional there's more of an open area there.

> First of all, you've got to let them know that you're glad they're there. It's as
> simple as that. I don't care where you're shooting. You're interested in what
> they have to say and what they have to do because they are individuals, too.

> With people who are really bright, and they're not actors, it's really rough,
> it's the roughest, because they are very conscious of their image and their
> behavior. (For example, the way) I behaved when I was twelve or thirteen
> years old in high school and my French teacher would come up and say,
> ''Monsieur, you must pronounce like this, you must do that. Do you under-
> stand me, Monsieur?'' And I'd say, ''I'll be god-damned if I'm gonna talk
> like some Schmuck. I'm not going to talk like that. That is acting. That's
> phony.'' And I said, *''J'entre dans la salle de classe,''* and I said the lesson

that way and I was a schmuck and I failed. And it wasn't until I failed it four years in a row and I went to France finally, and I said, "All right, I talk like *thees* if it helps me communicate." Now, I don't pass myself off as an intelligent person; I was just very inhibited about my performance. But, usually, very sharp people have a very strong sense of themselves and they do not want to perform. They feel that they can perform in their same stiff, precise way and you've gotta knock it out of them, you've gotta relax them, you've gotta do something to get them to loosen up. You can't give them a drink and you can't let them smoke a weed or do any of that kind of stuff. You just have to stand there and do it. And, it's a *bitch*. It's really hard.

Every director works out his own techniques of directing non-actors, depending on the situation and on his own personality. I recommend, for example, the end-slate: don't push the disconcerting slate in front of the non-actor's face just before he has to deliver his lines. Work out a system of hand signals with the crew so that, after a series of rehearsals (if you have to have rehearsals), you signal the sound and camera to roll and the person doesn't know he's being shot.

There is another technique and it happens to be almost opposed to the warmth that the directors have previously talked about. A director on a set is treated very much like a medical doctor who is making a (rare) visit to the home. He stands by the bedside and says, "I need a clean towel." Everybody races out to get him a clean towel. Nobody asks, "Why?" Nobody asks, "Is that the right thing to use?" The simplest statement is taken as a royal command. This same feudal relationship exists between the crew, the cast and the director, no matter how nice a guy the director is. Now, how in D.W. Griffith's name can a non-professional citizen have any grasp of the need for this discipline, or even of its existence? His reaction to this terrifying demand—that he act in front of the camera—might very well be, and on occasion is, an unbridled hysteria. It might take the form of a laughing jag or a total lack of concentration or an impossibility to remember or to say the right words or a stubborn refusal to stand or move or do what is vital. What does the director do? First of all, he should bring up from his very depths all the patience and good humor he can. Then he should change—to fit the comfort and abilities of the person—the lines, the action, the props—change anything that is possible to change that will help overcome the impasse. Change even what can't be changed. With calm, good humor, jokes, coffee breaks, chats, and good fellowship, maneuver the person into place and quietly start the scene. If that doesn't work—and on rare occasions nothing like that works—it's time to play doctor. In a stern, unyielding tone, order a few members of the crew to do some things: move a light or put the mike into position; use this businesslike approach even though you (like I) don't talk like this naturally. Then turn to the non-professional actor and, in the same tone, tell him exactly what to do and move the whole set into shooting immediately. This, you hope (and it's been successful for me in those few difficult occasions) will sober up the person by taking him by surprise. It also will make him aware of the power and unquestioned authority of the director's throne. Good luck!

The Actor's Background

Let me take an aside here about the image of the director as it appears to the talent. I have read that all people have a tendency to respond to authority figures as if they were parents. The attitude toward a parent usually has two sides: dependency on and, at the same time, rebelliousness at the authority. A director, I think, should always keep these two elements in mind: the actor depends on the director to make the effort look good and, at the same time, resents having his own interpretation rejected or even limited by this parent/dictator.

Despite his intelligence, his talent, his seriousness, his studies of the acting craft and his aspirations, the actor is still emulating the child saying, "Hey, look at me, I'm beautiful." And, his beauty may well be in his comic face or his discoordination or his very ugliness. Up there in front of the camera he is the cynosure, he is getting absolutely everybody's attention paid to him, he is loved.

The Very Young Talent

When that actor is indeed very young in years—a child actor—the director has only one need, although it is vital. He must love children. Love brings patience, understanding. A little masochism, maybe? How do other directors feel? In the main:

> A lot of patience. . . . Kids are rough for anybody; you just have to be really good. Quite often, I'm so much better to kid actors than I am to my own kids. I come home at night and I'm full of anxieties and screaming at my kids. I think, "Jeez! That kid today was an idiot and I never picked on *him.*"

The trouble with kids is that they act like children! What parent, indeed, can keep a child amused constantly while locked together for a full day? He's a child. His attention span, even on a game, is limited in direct proportions to his age. He is asked to maintain a reasonable amount of decorum for hours at a time. He will accept a certain amount of discipline for a certain amount of time. Try going the other way; permissiveness will get you everywhere where there is pandemonium. What is the answer? Love and laughter and thank goodness I have a childish mind, too.

What I've been referring to is just keeping the kid on the set without his pouring coffee into the electric Kliegl box. How about the actual performance?

> Children is (primarily) casting. In a commercial, you can usually get away with dragging a performance out of a bad kid. Not "bad"—there are no bad kids, I guess—but a kid that isn't suited to the film. It's mostly in the casting.

You've got to cast the best possible kid, the kind of kid you know is going to be able to do it over and over again, that's the only trick there.

By performance, however, we mean something much more than the reflection of orders given by the director. A child should act like a child, not a scaled-down version of an adult. This happens maddeningly seldom in television commercials. A child, correctly mirrored, has an exaggerated reaction to life. He pouts stronger, laughs harder, hurts deeper. So what if each emotion lasts for a shorter time than in adults? The emotion of the moment is total—play it! The director's function is to get the child in front of the camera so enthusiastic about what the scene is all about that he projects himself fully into the situation. All actors have to do this, but somehow the screen devastatingly shows the truth of whether a child is acting or feeling. This is not easy to get from the kid in the structured situation of shooting a specific scene. The child feels and knows intuitively whether the director is living the emotion with him or showing his teeth in a pretended smile. In TV commercials, almost all scenes are happy scenes and the director must fall into the spirit with the kid if the scene is to have exuberance and delight. He has to inject surprises from time to time, new elements to create enthusiasms. He has to knock himself out totally. Above all, he must remain the trusted friend, the kept-promise maker, the wondrous doer of tricks and maker of faces of all kinds and for different ages. He must love, really—and he will be able to get outstanding performances, perhaps even when there is take after wearing take. I have no other advice, except you might try literally beating the hell out of the kid.

No treatise on child actors should be advanced without a word about the children's mothers. I cannot get myself to say that word. I'm joshing; I met a nice stage mother once. There, I've said it.

Animals as Talent

I once had to shoot a scene with another type of actor. There was this incompetent magician and he was to make a dog disappear. He waved his arms over the dog and the script called for only half of the dog to vanish. Of course, we had a stuffed half-dog to match the live one. You would be amazed to know how many of the crew came over singly to me to suggest that we cut the actual dog in half.

Everything the directors have said about the difficulty of filming non-professional actors, bad professional actors and child actors are part of the advice to be given about directing animals. There is one piece of advice to be added: make certain you have the best animal trainer possible on hand.

There are even animal trainers who specialize in specific members of the SAG animal kingdom. There are cat trainers, dog trainers, pigeon trainers. If you don't or can't have a trainer at hand, well, any experienced director has story upon story. I have my own:

A cat had to wait too long for its turn in front of the camera and was given a bit too much catnip to keep her quiet. Result: one drunken cat who couldn't even stand, much less act. That taught me to follow the tradition of having a look-alike animal always at hand.

We wanted to show the size of a station wagon by putting a small baby elephant inside. The little elephant sat on the tailboard first; the station wagon's front end went flying up in the air; it frightened the elephant and the car crashed down. We settled for an old lion. Incidentally, it was at that animal farm that I looked down and saw it was a rather large leopard rubbing against my leg, purring.

I don't know how to explain this story; maybe it's just the arrogance of a director combined with blind luck. Maybe it has to do with the two dogs and six cats I live with and with extrasensory perception. I don't know. The scene called for a deer standing by a lake. A boy was to enter the frame and take a photo of the deer. Okay. We rented a deer, complete, we thought, with the deer's owner. The man led the handsome deer into place with a rope. He roped the deer's leg into the ground there; the rope was hidden by the bulrushes. As soon as he walked away, the deer struggled to release himself. He did, jumped into the lake and swam away. He was retrieved with much difficulty with a boat, and the struggle between deer and handler started; it seems that the fellow was not the owner but a new hired hand. Twice more the deer broke away and by now several hours had passed and the deer was bleeding from the rope burns and controllable only when rope halter and foot hobbles were used. Finally, I moved in, calling for everyone to do exactly as I said. I walked to within ten feet of the deer and told the handler to remove all ropes slowly. While he was reluctantly doing this, I spoke to the deer, explaining why his reasonable cooperation would make him and everyone happy. He looked at me intently, disregarding the handler's movements. All ropes off, I told the handler calmly to walk away. He looked at me as though I was crazy, which I was by then, but walked away. The deer still stood. I made my usual hand signal, circling the forefinger, which meant "roll camera." I never stopped talking to the deer and he never stopped listening to me. I walked backwards out of frame and told the boy to walk in. The deer looked at the boy, looked around, seemed to ponder whether he should jump into the water again, looked back at the boy and stood there. Cut. The handler came in, put the lead on the deer and they both walked out quietly.

Celebrities

Let us leap to the opposite end of the spectrum, the talent for whom you should send a limousine, for whom flowers and favorite snacks should be waiting in the spotless dressing room: the Star, the Name, the Celebrity. I have been called upon to direct ''names'' in almost every imaginable field, including the President of the United States, and I have only one piece of advice on how to handle these fearsome situations: do your job. If you concentrate on that familiar activity, all the necessary attitudes and politicking and problems will fall into place. You are a director. Direct. As always, establish a friendly, comfortable relationship with the actor; tell him precisely what you expect of him; run a controlled, professional set and do your job. There is only one additional function you have with a celebrity: to keep everybody else—crew, agency/client and talent—from fussing and falling all over the name, from being disgustingly obsequious and concerned and futzing about every detail that is your business alone. Direct.

Let's hear it from the directors:

> I did a thing with a celebrity—a literary celebrity who has done things on the other side of the camera, but (being) thrust in front of the camera because he wrote a great book does not make him an actor. And he knew (it); he said he was afraid of being exposed and of being destroyed. But he agreed because his publisher said, "Okay, you're gonna appear on camera." He had the most difficult time remembering anything. Just a total blank. You got the copy? "Yeah, memorized the whole thing." The Panavision camera rolls in on the floor of the garden with people on (it), a big thing. And the guy says, "Hi! I'm——— I'm——— How do you want me to say it?" Then we got to his name and it ended there. And everybody died because we had exactly fifteen minutes of time. I turned around, took him over, sat down and chatted with him.

> You just have to find tricks to gain their confidence. I did it with this athlete just by pure chance. It was Arthur Ashe, marvelous person, who wanted to do his best. He was very stiff. And it just so happened he found out that I had done a commerical with Bruce Jenner. And he knew Jenner was not an actor and had never done anything before. He had talked to Jenner about it because they did the same routine on ABC, or something. Jenner said it had been a very positive experience for him. And, when he found out halfway through the day I had done this, immediately he loosened up and I had his confidence. It was just by pure chance. I tried everything: the arm on the shoulder; hanging out, trying to get him loose; trying to substitute words; trying to get his mind to think one thing while he said another; getting rid of the crew. I did everything I could. It didn't work. Then, all of a sudden, he realized I wasn't going to hurt him and I wasn't going to make a fool out of him. Once I made him realize he wasn't going to appear foolish, it was easy.

> You have to know in advance what you want from them. You have to explain it to them. Some take a lot more explaining; some take psyching-up, getting them into the right mood. . . . I did a thing with Johnny Cash. He wants to do a superb job and is very suspicious of anybody that approaches him. So, in that instance, even the ad agency said, "Er, stay back there." This one's saying, "We'll talk to him first." *I* was right up front! "How are ya doing? I'm the director." And, I gotta tell ya the relationship started from the handshake. Because he felt: okay, who are all these people? From the agency, the client, this is from this—and the guy walked up and said, "Hi, I'm your

director,'' and from that moment, ''Listen . . . if I do it this way, okay?''
and boom—we were finished in an hour and he had to go on to something
else. It was a superb spot, played all over America. It's important how you
set yourself up.

They're just like real people; they *are* real people. What makes a big star is
your vision of that person. The esteem in which you hold someone makes
them somebody different. Robert Redford, were he not Robert Redford, would
be just a good-looking guy sitting next to you on the bus. And you could ask
him what time it was, or (for) change to get a paper. But Robert Redford has
become a myth in your mind, (a myth) who actually doesn't buy papers or
ride the subway or would be offended if you asked him for the time. . . .
   Actors and stars who have become involved with commercials for whatever
reasons are usually very anxious to please. Rather than being difficult, they
tend to be far easier, I think, than the normal commercial actors. The reason
is that they're smart enough to know that a commercial is something a lot of
people are going to see. . . . (Their knowing that) millions of people will
view this (is) coupled with the usual insecurities that most famous people
have, (which are) surprising to most of us who (are) at first somewhat starry-
eyed at celebrities. . . . ''What do you think of me?'' ''How am I doing?''
''How do you like this?'' What they're really asking is, am I John Wayne or
Jack Palance. ''How am I supposed to be?'' asks Joe DiMaggio; ''How shall
I hold my face?'' asks Mohammed Ali—because they themselves have only
a very vague understanding of what it is that makes them what they are and
they depend on the directors, in fact, to recreate, every time they appear in
front of the camera, the old image of themselves as the public has come to
understand (it). So, they're both anxious for public relations and anxious,
because of their incredible insecurities, to please.
   One very famous star—whom I worked with in the beginning and who has
done lots of movies and is very well known all across America—was someone
I actually had certain doubts about directing. He was a guy who towered over
me, towered over almost all my images of the mythology of the American
star. Showing up on the set that day, I had terrible fears about whether or not
I'd be adequate enough to handle somebody who had been directed by all my
favorite directors—I hardly thought of him in a commercial nor directed by
someone like me. So I mustered my strength and got my energy level up and
tried to act as mature as could be. I walked on the set and was introduced to
this character. He immediately said, ''You're the director, huh? I'd like to
take you aside.'' He took me aside and said, ''Listen, how do you want me
to be?'' ''How do you want me to be? What kind of question is that? Be
yourself.'' He gave me various versions and I realized that he didn't know
who he was. In all his pictures, each director probably had to deal with that
problem, to recreate the star in his own image, to give him confidence to go
ahead and be that famous person. It gave me a tremendous shot in the arm
and I realized he wasn't who I thought he was, but was much more human,
more approachable; it gave me a tremendous boost of confidence. Even the
most difficult people who are irascible, who demand coffee and demand this,
are usually displaying a tremendous insecurity, a desire that the audience and

the people who are on the set that day think of them as stars and appreciate them for that. Deep down, they are afraid that a crack will show on the screen and their insecurities will show through.

Therefore: Direct. When the actor is a name, the difference is slight and unimportant in relation to your job. Do not change your personality or your style. Have fun, as usual.

My Way

In this chapter, I have unselfishly given advice on how to treat talent. However, one facet of being a great director like me is great humility. I say therefore unto you: I have propounded my own style, born of my own personality and experience. (And talent and wisdom).

Let me tell you of an experience: I was shooting in a studio that had two large stages. A director I knew well was shooting on the adjoining stage and I had asked if I could drop in. It was one of the few opportunities I had had to watch any director at work. My propounded theory of directing is that the mood on the stage will be the one to be transferred to the screen. Ergo, since almost all television commercials are happy, I spend my shooting days grinning like a happy alligator. I have fun with the crew and the talent. But here was another director—a man with a heavy Austrian accent and the demeanor and carriage to go with it. When I entered the stage, he obviously was finding it difficult to get an actress to perform correctly for the commercial he was shooting. He screamed at her—screamed hysterically—to the effect that she was no actress and why do they send him these stupid models who can't act and the actress was not only in cascading tears but totally a broken-rag corpse. He sent her back into makeup. I stood there aghast; never in a million years would I have ever treated an actress like that for a commercial. I have slapped an actress, hard, to put her in the mood for a dramatic, sad scene and created an angry, sullen mood on the set, purposely. However, not for a happy commercial. I was further and completely dumbfounded when I heard that the reason was the inability of the director to get the kind of smile he wanted. How in hell was he going to get that now, after all this, I wondered? The actress returned, controlled and sober and the scene set. "Action," he called and then, to the actress, "Smile!" She came across with the most glorious smile I could ever have asked for; the eyes laughed, the ears thrust back, the very skin glowed with happiness. How did he achieve it? Did he turn her adrenalin on to racing flow? Was fear, anger, defiance, or hatred the generator? I do not know the answer and I never will. I left the stage a sadder and wiser man. I did not have the sole answer; I just had a different approach. Each director has to do it his way.

6

The Television Commercial Director

A YOUNG MAN I KNOW was once a member of the Hell's Angels, that frightening band of wild motorcyclists. He made his gasoline money by painting stripes on automobiles. He has since doffed his leather jacket and, bushy hair, bared hirsute chest and all, is now quite a successful director of television commercials.

Let me point out another extreme: I was once in partnership with three other directors in a company we called Directors Group, Inc. One of the partners specialized in sports programs and was an avid sports enthusiast. The other three directed television commercials. One day, the sport expert made some joke about a baseball team. The rest of us laughed politely. Too politely, I felt. It dawned on me that none of us three red-blooded American boys knew a damned thing about major league baseball. We had gravitated together, unaware of this amazing quirk that each of us had; in what other profession could you find such a unique percentage of squares in America?

Where do they come from, the TV spot directors? What kind of people are they? Which become successful and what do they have on the ball that makes and keeps them directing commercials? One producer in a leading agency thinks that the genre is:

> . . . wonderful. They're bright, they're good company, they're . . . intelligent, not just about the making of commercials, but about things in general, so when you're away on a trip and you have to spend a lot of time with a director, you're eating breakfast together and you're working all day for a week at a time, the fact that he's an interesting individual and can talk about other subjects and be a good companion is important. I hate to go out with

some guy who's an atomic scientist for a week and find that I've got nothing to talk to the guy about. I'd go bananas. I find directors are interesting in that regard because they don't just want to talk film and commercials. They often add to my experience by telling me of encounters and happenings in other shoots and I hear a lot of what's going on in our business, special problems, an actor who was terrific or horrendous, a concept that didn't quite make it but if they'd done such and such, it would have made it. . . . . They're always interesting people. They're not always the same people, but over the years they're always compatible compared with other (people).

Makeup of the Director

I know another director who had studied to be a psychologist. He was all ready to enter the profession but needed some money. He walked into a studio, got a job as a messenger and never left the TV spot business. He, too, is quite successful. Of the directors interviewed, one was a graduate engineer, another a Rhodes Scholar, one a magician, an actor, a cartoonist and so on.

I think I can say with no equivocation whatsoever that all successful directors are bright, even fascinating folk. They tend to be compulsive doers, even though their demeanor sometimes belies it. That compulsion asserts itself in their chosen work in almost maniacal concentration. Listen to them:

So, if I don't work my ass off now, if I don't run and lift weights, if I don't use my mind, if I don't go to the theater . . . when the time comes, if I don't read, if I don't see films, what am I going to draw on? I have no energy, no vitality. I want to be the most potent person on the crew.

Film is my hobby, too. I collect movies (but tell the FBI they aren't pirated or I'll lose my collection). Seriously! I read old books and I have a big collection of gadgets and stuff. Home movies are my hobby and that's it; I don't watch football on television. If you read about these old guys and try to pick up from what their interviews say, you can learn a lot about lighting. The way they used to do it was the best, anyway. There haven't been too many innovations, really, since the twenties. So that's where I take it from and I just watch movies and occasionally I'll work with somebody from a movie and I'll ask them how they did that. I do try to meet as many people in the film profession as I can and I just ask all the questions. It's not that hard.

Energy, it's energy; that's the whole thing. You have to just get yourself going. For years I would just sit around, just kind of wait. And I finally realized one day, it doesn't work. You do it yourself. You get up off your ass and you do it. I try to tell people that. You know nobody is gonna do it for you. Nobody will. They never have for me. I never had a guy to study under. Nobody ever put their arm around me and said, "Look, son, do this." I never had that. My parents didn't know about film. They just encouraged me.

You can be tired and beat. Yes. But, your mind has gotta be sharp. You gotta move and it's your responsibility to get to bed early and not go boogying all night. Because I know as a director that I cannot function if I'm going to abuse myself. There are times when, of course, you have stretched it to the limit. Let's say . . . you're in Los Angeles, you take the red-eye, you get off the plane in New York, you know you didn't sleep and you gotta direct something that day, gotta pull it all together, get those trucks moving, get those elephants on the left and the camels on the right type of stuff. You still have the energy, you can still pull it off.

It's your job. You can either hide behind a beer glass or you can study it day and night. And, that's what you gotta do. I learned a long time ago if you want to be good at something, you do it. You want to be a good hurdler, you just run hurdles all the time and work on your speed and form. I want to be a good director.

And, if you can't create that kind of interest and being a strong director, you shouldn't be a director—might as well be a producer. Be somebody else on the set so you can sit around and schmooze and take it easy. Probably even get the same money, even more. But, I'd say good directors thrive on it. It keeps them young; it keeps them interesting as people. They like to be in the limelight and they want to be in charge; they like the recognition.

Considering the exotic characters of these directors, it may not necessarily follow that a *mens sana* will come from a *corpore sano* but I can tell you that every director knows he has to keep himself in at least adequate physical shape. For myself, I have found that I can never sit down on my "director's chair," even when I'm waiting for the set to be readied. I stand all the livelong day even when the livelong day runs 20 hours. A director is called upon to move quite a bit even on the shooting stage, let alone do the climbing and acrobatics often necessary on location. How do other directors feel:

I get up early, anyway; I gotta run early in the morning. . . . If you want to look good, that's it. If they've asked for it, you deliver it. . . . Besides, I remember when I was working. I've always worked, since I was nine. Every job I've ever had, except this job, the time dragged. I used to sit at the clock in school and hold my breath. I could hold my breath for three minutes: it was just from practicing for four years.

I don't run but I do a lot of physical activity: carpentry work; gardening. (I) take a lot of sun and swimming. But, the most important thing is to come from good stock—good peasant Russian stock.

Yeah, as I say, it's my metabolism. . . . Somebody said to me on the set, "man, you're really going; you're really going." But, I wouldn't know what to do if I wasn't going. I think I would go nuts if I were in a position where I do the same thing over and over every day. I can't handle it. I think, with a feature, I'd really get bored with it in terms of my day-to-day work. . . . I really like this life; I feel I'm in control of it.

I love (directing). I wouldn't be doing it otherwise. Directors are a certain breed of cat. Funny thing is that every kid that gets out of the schools, that comes in looking for a job with a producer, wants to be a director; yet, they don't know the first thing about what a director is. All they know is that Spielberg did this, Frankenheimer did this and Orson Welles did *Citizen Kane* and the reason he shot it at low angle is this. They come in and they have no possible knowledge.

I was waiting for a director in his anteroom when his staff was packing up— the office was going to move. Just to start a little trouble, I said to them, "I'll bet the director doesn't do anything." Someone said, "Oh, he just gives orders." I told this to the director and asked if this was part of the enjoyment of being the director. He said:

I'm gonna tell you . . . about a director and about power. I think a lot of people look upon a director with this incredible envy when he's on set. They say, "Wow, whatever he wants, man, he's got it." The most difficult thing I've had to learn in twenty-five years is this: I would walk on the set in the morning and say, "coffee"—coffee; "cigarettes"—cigarettes; "ice cream"— ice cream; "gimme a chair"—chair; everybody's looking around: "What can I do for him next?" Tell the actor: "laugh"—he laughs; "cry"—he cries; "sit down"—he sits down. Pretty soon you get this incredible feeling of power. You control the actors; you can make them laugh; you can make them cry. You want him to fart; tell him to fart—he'll really squeeze his guts out. Just about anything you want, you've got. The lights go out, you go outside . . . you lose control. And pretty soon, it's a humbling experience: doorman won't open doors—you're no more nor less than anybody else.

I mentioned that the best line I ever heard describing "what a director does" was: "He answers questions." Every director grins when he hears that:

Yeah, you do a lot of that. It's funny because sometimes you catch yourself just saying, "Yeah, yeah, yeah." And you don't even know what they ask you. Then you say, "Oh, wait, I shouldn't do that." It's scary.

I like to tell stories about the director, Josef von Sternberg, because, despite his very real and impressive talent, he made himself the caricature of what the original Hollywood directors should look and act like. On the subject of the director's majesty on set; Sternberg one day asked me to call over the new assistant prop man. "Huey," he said to the little fellow, "when I want to sit down, I will sit down. There had better be a chair there." Poor Huey had to hold on to the director's chair and watch von Sternberg's behind for a clue all day long.

Why did this lord bit come about? One director says:

It has to be that way on the set because if there are two bosses, or three bosses, it's mayhem. People have to look for their orders on that set. You create the impetus, you create the schedules, you create the mood and, if you crack, they crack—unquestionably, every single time.

Says another:

My favorite cartoon is the one . . . about the trained seal being interviewed.
What the trained seal is saying is, "What I'd really like to do is be a director." I have that upstairs; that's my credo.

Starting Out

How do you get to be the leader, the artist-in-charge, the king of the crew?
In almost every craft, there is a sequence of apprenticeships and promotions to
reach the goal of master. There is no specific series of steps to take to become
a director. Almost any avenue is correct; but you must have that almost unde-
finable mania that produces leaders in any field. A traditional route is to start
at the bottom; in this case, a gofer and sweeper. A valuable background is to
have worked on a documentary crew, filling in where needed and learning the
varied crafts: gaffer, prop man, assistant director, script clerk. Shoot as many
stills as you can:

That's how I got into the movie business. I was a still photographer. Before
that I was an engineer and made taxi meters. But, when I got into still photography as a profession, I found it very unrewarding, or the rewards very
limited. It had nothing to do with money, just to do with how people treat you
and what your efforts become. Still picture. That's great. Turn the pages, it's
gone forever. Everything we turn out as directors . . . is remembered. You
make a good commercial, it's remembered for a year or two.

In terms of young people wanting to get into this business, I say get experience out of town. That is what I tell them when I interview them. I know that
those opportunities are still there but there are so many kids that want to get
into this business that it is unbelievable. They don't want to write the great
American novel anymore, they want to make the great American film.

I started out doing a lot of tabletop closeup type of things and usually we get
commercials that involve talent as well. We've done a lot of talent things but
we're mainly known as closeup food and micro-type photography.

I became a television director because I knew Bert Stern and, at the time, I
was making a career choice in my life. I didn't know anybody in the film
world who really wanted me in flim. I ran to Bert who, at that point in his
life, though principally a fashion photographer, was beginning a commerical
routine and was very enthusiastic about it. I was looking for someone who
would help me and we seemed to have—well, it was a perfect coincidence for
me. I went into commercial photography basically because I had a shot to go
with Bert and because he was the only person who offered me any job even
vaguely related to the film area. . . . I had had some experience with stills
but nothing beyond an amateur quality. So basically I was not a very exciting
guy and I was interested in working with someone who was inspirational and
who I could learn something from. He happened to be in commercials at that
time.

I came to New York and I beat the sidewalks in New York. I printed up five hundred resumes and got out the yellow book and went to every company and left my resume. I planned to go back to Pittsburgh on a Friday night and was packing in the hotel because nothing had happened and the telephone rang and my sister called me from Pittsburgh and told me . . . a man had called and said he wanted to talk to me on Monday morning and he called from New York so I waited over the weekend and Monday . . . I was shooting.

My intent had always been to be a director and I fell very heavily into camera because I thought that the camera was the most important tool. I started in this business at CBS as a cameraman and doing a lot of shows. I was always very upset because I thought I could direct them better than the directors who were doing it. I was just a cameraman and I gradually learned more by watching the people who did the directing, especially what they were doing wrong. In those days, everything was done live. I know a lot of things were done wrong. Finally, one man gave me a chance . . . to direct a commercial. . . . I really don't know why; I was a good cameraman and I really was and I think he figured that not too much could go wrong. Mostly, because I was taking good interest and because I had an eye for composition.

Well, the way I started working professionally in this business was to become an apprentice to a script supervisor. I joined the union and I started working as a script supervisor immediately. I worked for four years very successfully. But, there was an apprenticeship program for directors and I had three directors sponsor me and I was able to go with them on all their shoots, work actively as an apprentice director. I went to all the pre-production meetings, to everything that was really getting me one step above just scripting or just producing. At that time, I was already out free-lancing as a producer. When the time came and the first Spanish commercials broke through, they asked me if I wanted to take a chance on directing one. Then there was another and another—and I decided to open my own business. That's why I automatically got into commercials; commercials came to me.

My first film was a narcotics film that I did in one day on an idea I had thought up. I called up a guy and rounded up about four grand to make a whole film of this man telling a bunch of kids about his life. The film went crazy and it became the number one film because of how I dealt with the human element.

Well, I've always been a fan of musical comedies. When I was in college, my summer jobs as director of theatricals at big summer camps—I love doing musicals, either originals or revivals of Broadway musicals of the day. I think it's a kind of synthesis of the best in American theatre. In a good musical, you have a good book; you have much more exciting sets than in a straight drama; you have more exciting costumes. It's all a form of opera, really. We use all the crafts, all the technique. There are fewer and fewer musical comedies being done today—the kind of extravaganzas we did for Camels or for Muriel Cigars—that kind of thing. Like the Broadway musical, they've almost gotten out of hand in terms of cost. But, I also think I have a particular talent for it. I love music. I have a sense of rhythm of when things are right, when things work. It's more flamboyant, more fun doing a musical commercial.

I went to Syracuse University and studied fine arts. I was a painter. I was a bus boy (on) the athletic staff and did shows on Monday evenings. I was a staff cartoonist for six years on the *Saturday Evening Post, Colliers* and other magazines. So, my background is basically a visual one and also comedic. When I was cartooning, I was doing some telops, they were called. They were between-station-breaks advertising, such as the *Sid Cesar Show* or the *George Gobel Show* and I would draw some telops for NBC. And, I was paid a few bucks to do these little cartoons. One day a friend of mine and myself, we got a Bolex camera and we did stop-motion photography with still photographs. We made a ten-second ID and we sold it to the network for about a hundred bucks. This was for the *Sid Cuesar Show.* They liked that little piece of film, sixteen millimeter. And they said, "Can you do more of that for us?" and we did some more. . . . We were doing that for three or four years: animation, graphic design, and we needed some live footage to go with the animation for one of our clients. . . . At that time, my partner and myself had designed some very large soft lights and we started to shoot some inserts to go with the animation.

Directors of television commercials, then, come from everywhere and anywhere. They are directors because of their talent, their intuitive understanding of how to communicate varied emotions to the TV viewer, their dedication to the job at hand, their unquestioned leadership abilities and so on. An increasing proportion of directors have come directly from the advertising agencies. They were producers, art directors, writers and others from the creative side of the agency. There, they learned to appreciate what the client wants, what is expected from the director and how the agency works. They have worked with directors and been on shoots. When the occasion arose, they directed an insert or a small spot or even an important one for the agency. They have also directed the narration recordings and, often, the casting sessions. Most importantly, they have made contacts within the agency; sometimes their first business comes from the buddies they have made at the agency and client. The reel they have to show may not all have been directed by them but the spots can be pointed to as "their" work. Two directors who started in an agency:

I started in an agency, although I didn't understand how agencies worked. I did watch a lot of television and I knew commercials. I knew what I thought commercials needed. I knew how to tell a story using commercials. My heroes when I was a kid were Eugene Smith and Eisenstadt, all these guys who did photojournalism, and I find the format very similar to commercials. . . . I wanted to be a photojournalist, originally. . . . The interesting, arresting opening visual and the telling of the story and then leaving them with a shot they never forget. . . . Finding an interesting character and getting inside them and revealing something. That kind of thing.

I think the agency is primarily the way to do it. To learn the agency so that you know their needs, you know what commercials are all about and then learning so much about production, then trying to direct your own work. Do your little projects on your own, in eight millimeter or stills. Then, try to farm out the work so that you can take a stronger hand in it. Find a cameraman you like and the cameraman will teach you a lot if he's any good. Or, coming in as a cameraman and working with a strong agency person and then eventually becoming a director-cameraman, which is quite feasible. Technique and camera work are so important in commercials—arresting visuals to get your attention. So important. Editing is another way.

Knifing Your Way In

More advice to the film-lorn: There are some 3,000 schools that teach some version of TMR (television, motion pictures and radio). On the average, they turn out at least ten TMR graduates each a year, or more than 30,000 applicants for jobs. Are there more than 500 openings each year for new bodies? I doubt it. No wonder this industry is replete with dynamic, resourceful people. Only the tough—and rough—can get a foothold. I confess that when my advice is sought by a hopeful filmmaker, I do my very best to dissuade him from entering the field. I do this under the theory that if the fellow gives up trying because of one director's superior cynicism, then he doesn't have the steel and teeth and claws you need to get into and hang on in this business.

Is it at all possible for a young person to enter the field and become a director?

> Very hard. For many reasons. I think the older a profession is, the more difficult it is for people to enter that profession. When it's new, it's free and unencumbered and I think it's a great opportunity. When the movie business was young, how many people came into it—there were lawyers, there were clothing merchants, there were shysters, all of them—Goldwyn, Warner, Thalberg, they were just merchants. But, today it's run by a very tightly closed so-called movie professional. Television commercials are controlled by lawyers and the FCC, there are so many rules and regulations, so it's very difficult for somebody to come in there and be used by the agencies, because they want the security (of knowing) that they're getting someone who understands the problems commercials have today. Twenty or twenty-five years ago, you didn't have these problems.

> Look, I was never one to put down knowledge. When I was going to college, there were very few courses. USC was the only one that had any kind of extended film curriculum. I went to CCNY because that's the only place my father could afford to send me and that was because it was free. I took courses in every department. I didn't even have a major when I graduated, which was rare but—I said because I wanted to be a film director I started a film society at City College and we studied films and we wrote learned articles. . . . In the film business we have a slogan that we use very conveniently. It's supposed to be some old Chinese proverb that one picture is worth a thousand words. But, the film people don't finish the second part of that: one doing is

" ACTION ! "

worth a thousand pictures. I think that's really where you get your experience; that's where you can use your academics and your theoretical experience. Certainly, some of the younger directors who are coming along and doing very interesting work have done student films. Certainly, I wouldn't pooh-pooh the academics. I think the more you know about music and art and communication, the better you're gonna be.

Well, any schooling can never do any harm. You will learn a solid fundamental background of what tape is all about. You will learn what the basics of directing are about; what the basics of shooting are about. . . . . If I am shooting a scene and I am supporting something with nylon thread or something, hanging a radio in space and I see the light hitting the wire, I know how to get rid of that light and there are tricks I can do usually with video just by "digging" the picture. I can make it go away. (If) I don't know this—I can sit on the set for three hours trying to take the light off those tiny little pieces of wire. These are things that no kind of book learning will tell you. You just got to do it.

I didn't come from a film background but an academic background; I was a psychology major who got a summer job as a messenger and then stayed in it. I find that my psychology background from graduate school is as helpful to me as any film school would have been. It's helped me deal with the people and the craft I'm concerned with. Because we are dealing with a highly intense sixty or thirty seconds. As a matter of fact, if somebody said to me, "I want to become a director," I would say, "Go to school, study poetry, literature, psychology, some graphics." That's more important. Studying poetry is more important than how to run an Arriflex. I maintain that you can teach anybody the mechanics of filmmaking in thirty days but you can't teach them to tell a story. I think if my children wanted to do what I do, I would have them just get a good general education, particularly poetry if you're going to do commercials.

We hire people occasionally and we hired like two people over the summer. We were busy and they were young kids and we didn't have to pay them very much money to be very honest with you. They could run around and do a lot of things with very little money and yet these people must have really learned an awful lot. This is the kind of industry that you can't learn from the book because you can't read about doing a show and doing a commercial. (Author's note: until now!) You really have to learn by doing. You have to put your hands on the camera and point it and take a look at what you got. You then play it back in order to learn something.

Stick to it, no matter what. . . . I made all my breaks, all my chances. It's like they say, that in this business, if you don't have a father or an uncle or a friend, you don't make it. It's a hundred percent true. But, I had none of these and here I am smack right in the middle of it. It can be done, if you really insist.

(A comic in this business once gave this advice to a newcomer. First, it was to be born to wealthy parents to keep you while you are knocking on doors. Rich relatives in general are fortuitous; you can get them together to back your first endeavour to show as a sample. If they're really all rich, you can hire the best of writers, cameramen, editors, and perhaps turn out to be a winner right off the bat. Failing relatives, the best course open is to marry someone rich . . . in California, so that if you're divorced, you get half, which should at least open an office. But don't sign a marriage contract there.)

At one point I gave classes for established film directors, teaching them how to direct using the video cameras and recorders. Certainly the use of three cameras at a time was difficult for them because of the need to contemplate even the lie of the cables while moving the cameras during the shoot. Also, immediate editing as they went along proved to be a traumatic experience for some. These film directors would be astounded to know that there are videotape directors who never shot film and are now making the transition in that direction. A director is a director is a director. . . . The transition in "the old days" was almost always from documentary film director to TV commercial director. This was looked upon as an insult to the art of film. One director recalls:

But I remember that not so long ago I was always being put on the defensive. "Why aren't you doing features; why aren't you doing documentaries?" And this is usually by some son-of-a-bitch who's an accountant. You know, you used to be a documentary filmmaker. It's very hard to make a living. You'd go out and you'd scrounge up a client and enough money and then you'd usually spend twice as much as you were getting because you wanted it to be a great film. It was a very thin life.

Amen to that. I remember as a young lad I went to a party and there was the aging father of documentary films himself, Robert Flaherty. I was awed and spoke to him at length. The major portion of the discussion was his complaint that near the end of his career he was broke and hadn't had a job nor touched a frame of film for the past two years! (He did do *Louisiana Story* soon after that; it was his last production.)

Female Directors

In one aspect, at least, the television commercial directing field is not much different from features or documentaries in that there are exceptionally few women directors. I should imagine that the recital of reasons for that is the same as in any industry when it is challenged on the minimal numbers of women executives: tradition, chauvinistic men laborers who would not accept orders from a female, pregnancy, periodic illnesses and all that nonsense. In the TV commercial area, as in most industries, a foothold has been established and the number of women directors is—slowly—growing. Two of these speak:

> I bet you that I still would get more jobs if I were not a woman. I have personally never yet found the opportunity where I felt "I lost this one because they are thinking of me as a woman." But, there has to be that feeling out there an awful lot. But I don't think the crews are affected by it. Every person in the crew—and I've worked with NABET and IA crews in Miami and New York. I've never had a problem, simply because I'm a former crew person myself and I know what it's like. I have always had very good luck with the agency people and probably even better rapport with the client. I never had conflict in these areas. . . . This is my fourth year now. In the beginning, everybody was sort of feeling out: "Is she going to stay around? Is she going to make it? Will her first few jobs be failures or disasters?" Well, nothing of the sort has happened and I have gone to Miami on the tails of major disasters from other companies. So, I think slowly the agencies are getting more confident.

> Well, at this point, I don't think they are thinking of me, period. Every job I get I'm out there hustling for. And if I'm not making myself sell, they're not going to be thinking of me. They're going to be thinking first of a lot of other people. . . . But, this year, I have done a lot more than before. Every year is better. So, I think it is a matter of time and they will accept me and the other women out there.

I think she's right, but, until those halcyon days of equality arrive, I should add into this volume of advisements a note on accouterments. Far be it from my egotism to advise a lady on how to dress if she's not an actress on my set, but let me hide behind the statement that the client and crew have some expectations: A female director should not present disconcerting cleavage during the shoot. It is assumed that there is a degree of butch in a gal who chooses to be a director, so slacks are more *de rigueur* than a skirt. Close-cropped coiffures and minimal makeup are preferable, too. (Good Lord! I'm not going to have a female friend in the trade after this book comes out.)

And the Male

For the men: carrying a zoom view-finder to choose lenses is out. Also, forming a frame with the thumbs touching and the palms outstretched is a conceit that is passe. Tweeds are always safe if they are not tailored. In general, dress in the style of the day but always more so. For example, if jeans are in, remember where the first part of the word dungarees comes from. Boots are never wrong. The image to be projected is always one of dash and strength. If you are truly a born director, you will never have to think about what you wear or how you look. That leather vest you love or the wrist-band you wear for luck will automatically brand you as someone who is something.

Actually, in those last two paragraphs I was only kidding. The genuine advice is to be yourself, dress the way it pleases you, carry yourself the way you always do, speak in the tone you naturally do, be the nice guy you always are—or the arrogant slob you've always been. You will be successful because of your true character and any postured attempt to dissemble will work to your disadvantage. If you are the director, you *are* a character.

7

The Client and Agency Folk

A COUPLE OF DAYS BEFORE the shoot, there was a lot of bustle while dressing the sets in a Hollywood studio. We were going to shoot a commercial and there were four large, complex rooms to be filled. Most of the scurrying was being done by the representatives of the agency and client, in from New York and with little better to do that day. They were examining, commenting on and asking for rearrangement of the pieces as they were brought in.

I was reeling from the bedlam. In turn, each member of the crew sidled over to me and spelled out the word: M-O-N-E-Y. But, there are many more reasons than money that make a man choose to be a director. After a short time, I gathered the agency/client group together and wearily made the same speech to them that I had made to others dozens, if not hundreds, of times:

> I'm here to make the best possible commercial and to please all of you in the process. I trust you will all have helpful suggestions and I promise to listen seriously and respond. However, there can be only one director on the set if the actors and crew are to perform their best. All ideas and objections should be channeled through one representative, in this case preferably the agency producer. Then the crew and cast will not become confused and neither will I. Henceforth, no one else but I will address the cast and crew directly and, please, all suggestions should be presented to the agency producer, who will relay them to me. I will listen.

This little speech is not given in anger. I am seldom angered by people because I am not irritated by stupidity, ineptness or such failings that others may have. They can't help it. Rather, my wrath is turned against myself for hiring such

100

people or allowing myself to be associated with them. I am not always forgiving, I do become furious at sloth or diffidence or negativism on the job.

There was no call for anger on that California stage because everyone was trying to make the production better according to his own measurements and dictates. Except for the inordinate amount of time the folk from the advertising agency spend trying to impress everybody else with their wisdom and talent, I know them all, without exception, to be honestly concerned that the best possible job is done. In that sense, each man is on my side; we're in the same platoon.

Why the Director Is Chosen

Still, no matter how you do it or say it, it takes a kind of *chutzpah* to corral them and read the riot act. After all, they are the ones who gave the director the job in the first place. Reasonably, there should be a certain amount of gratitude for their trust; the desire also exists that they will come to the director again for the next production. Let's look into some reasons why the specific director is chosen for that specific production. An advertising agency producer speaks:

> Why we choose a director now depends so much on which creative group we're working with, which account, which client we're involved with, what our budget restrictions are, the last job the director did . . . (because as in so many businesses you're only as good as your last job)—and so it's a mix. . . . So now you're trying to get somebody whose chemistry is right for this little group. You don't want a flamboyant guy because you know this account man doesn't like any loud jokes and yelling on the set and this client doesn't want any long-haired director spending any of his money, but he wants a reputable citizen who gets his hair cut every two or three weeks.

The Sample Reel

Another agency producer insists that, primarily, the director must be a good director with the ability to deliver good work. The agency places much weight on the sample reel. Since there is quite a large committee that collectively makes the choice, it cannot be expected that each member will know the talents or even the names of available good directors. The sample reel then becomes the basic measurement. There are many very good directors who have not had the opportunity to work on outstanding commercials. That's another chicken-and-egg situation. If the reel doesn't show outstanding commercials, they don't get the opportunity to do any. Another and different frustration to a director is that the agency people almost never differentiate between the commercial and the directing. If the concept of the spot catches their fancy, the director is given credit for being a good director. Unfortunately, they can only too seldom pick out the directorial values from commercials of mediocre original design. Other considerations for the sample reel are: the director's choice of his spots in relation to the particular subject matter of the forthcoming commercial; the juxtaposition of spots on the reel; the perfection of the visual and the audio and many more aspects that have little or nothing to do with the director's talent. The sample reel is a selling tool, the most important one that a director can have and it should be presented in jeweled perfection.

Making the Impression

Again, how does the agency define a good director?

> He is a man who is interested in what he is doing, who gives freely of his time and himself to prepare himself properly, who can take into account many, many factors that are involved: politics, diplomacy, tact, strength, vision, imagination—sounds like I'm recreating the Boy Scout oath—knowing when to make the wisecrack and knowing when not to make the wisecrack, and let's not forget one thing: he also has to be a good businessman.

An agency producer recounts:

> I remember a client . . . who had a very conservative ad manager. They were coming in for a pre-production meeting with one of my favorite directors, a very colorful guy. (The director) had in his office a fabric-designed sample slogan that I felt would be inappropriate for these two clients coming in from Philadelphia to have staring them in the face. The client was coming in as an accommodation to the director, who was pretty busy at that particular time. I asked him to do me a favor, since he had been assigned to this job and I had sold him very hard to the client: to take his favorite slogan off the wall and put it away for the meeting. The slogan was a perfectly harmless slogan which these two gentlemen from Philly would agree with a hundred percent, but I asked him anyway and, after some teasing, he agreed. What it said in big bold letters was, "FUCK COMMUNISM." They would have thought a guy who hangs that in his office with ladies coming in couldn't be a very respectable person. That typifies how the chemistry, no matter how good he is as a director, has got to be acceptable. Certain clients are suspect of certain lifestyles or looks as wrong and (as influencing) the selling of their product.

Another speaks:

> You pick a director who is able to give you what you consider to be enough pre-production time so you can plan the thing properly. He can attend the pre-production meeting with your client and understand the job thoroughly. He is not involved in so much other activity that he gives you a lick and a promise and then on the day of the shoot says, "Where's that board? Oh, it's that job". Believe me, there are directors like that. You want a guy who is compatible, someone you can work with, someone who isn't so high and mighty that you can't communicate with him. There are things I say about some directors that aren't always flattering, although the vast majority I've worked with in over thirty years of making commercials have been terrific people. In

a couple of instances, I've run into guys who feel that as a director they will turn the pre-production chores and the business end of it over to others and they will just be the director on stage or location. So, when you want to talk to these directors prior to going on the shoot or even prior to assigning them the job, you find you have to talk through other people. And they get the information second, sometimes third, hand. I don't think that's the way to operate. So, having had experiences with those people over the years, I haven't gone back to them. I'm not mad at them; they are perfectly good directors but their *modus operandi* is not one that is good for me. I won't name names but I think other people probably find the same things to be true. But, maybe their creative director or their client is insisting they continue to work with these guys because they continue to be busy and they continue to do good work. . . . (One director) I found to be very good. He would take your storyboards—he wouldn't change them drastically. . . . He used to draw little storyboards of his own with the exact camera angles and the relative size, the closeups, etcetera. He did his homework. You came out and reviewed it with him in the morning and you said, "Terrific." These were all the improvements you wanted to make over your own storyboard. And, if you wanted to discuss or debate any of them with him, he was certainly open and willing. He was a thorough pro so, job after job, many people would go back to him.

Pigeonholing

The director's personality and his dedication to the job, then, are criteria for the general choice of the director by the agency. Another vital aspect is type-casting. If a spot seems to call for someone who is the "fashion" type, then the choice will narrow down to the "still-photographer director," one who had made his mark in that area. In viewing the sample reels, they will look for the "texture, the look, the style" of the high-fashion photographers. Each frame must be worthy of an ad in *Vogue*. If this look is not on the reel, forget it. About such choices:

> If you know you're doing an action commercial, you (may) feel that a director-cameraman can capture that action for you, or maybe it's got a jingle as an audio track or announcer voice-over that will sometimes influence you. Because then he's up in a helicopter with you and you're doing the thing or he's skiing down a mountainside with a special rig . . . and have a skier following him and be shooting from a helmet. . . .

> If a job is one of a highly technical nature and involves complicated rigs, props, devices that have to be an integral part of the commercial, you go with a director who has that kind of background and experience. You don't go with a fellow who has been doing commercials and is a specialist in pet food and who says he can handle cats better than anybody and his experience is heavily into cat food commercials, then maybe he's not going to be so good at filling a head with steam and making it evaporate at a certain rate for a different client. On the other hand, if you go in for comedy, some directors have estab-

lished themselves by their track record, by their reels, their experience to be very proficient at handling comedy—and it's a tough category. Certain other directors who would like to do comedy just haven't had the opportunity and so you're afraid to gamble on them because a lot of money is riding on it. So you go with somebody (who) did a lot of comedy out on the coast and he's a terrific guy and he's easier to sell.

Any television commercial director who is not an out-and-out specialist and who has a number of directing years clicking his stopwatch will probably find his history closely related to mine. Every few years, I have transferred in reputation into another "field." For a few years, I was a strong "fashion" director. Then, my reputation for quite a while was as a "sheet-metal" (automobile) director. I went through comedy and slice-of-life expertises and today, I think, my label is "people" director because my reel shows good acting by professional and non-professional talent alike. Have I lost my previous abilities? No, but a people director is what I am sold as today. That is what my reel shows and that is what I get the bids for.

I am sad that I do not get the opportunity to work on those other commercials I enjoyed so much. But, I am not angry. It is not the fault of the agency folk. Type-casting is the implacable way of life in the advertising agency world.

The Politics of Choosing a Director

The group choosing a director for a particular shoot are seeking as firm a footing of security as possible. The sample reel is a vital part of the ground but using the acknowledged "superstar" director almost absolves them totally if things go wrong. "Well, I got the best director possible." Yet, this scene described by an agency producer probably plays several times each day on Madison Avenue:

It depends very much on the group you're working with in the agency. Let's take the art director group. There are certain art directors who feel more secure if a very expensive director is going to get their job. They think it has more chance of success if the current winner of the most "Clios" this year directs it, regardless of who he is. They may not even know the man. But, they feel more confident that it will be terrific and win them an award if Mr. X would do it. X is terrific. Maybe they're even right about that. But, he's also very expensive, very busy and so it may not be practical to bid for X, let alone use him. He is one of the several top-flight directors who get a lot of money. So, you may have to convince the art director that X is possibly not right for the commercial, that he may not want to do this kind of thing, or that he's away for three weeks and won't be able to do it in the time required, or he's not within the client's budget. On the other side, you have an account man and he knows his budget for the year. He's got exactly nineteen thousand dollars left from which we must make the commercial and pay the talent. "X is not going to do it for nineteen thousand, let alone pay the talent and agency commission. Call some other competent person who doesn't have X's rate of thirty five hundred a day, or whatever his rate is. There are good directors who will work for a thousand a day, so we could get this budgeted for sixteen thousand.'' The writer in the middle says, ''Gee, when I was at my last agency, you know who did a terrific job for us? I haven't given him a job since I've been at this agency. Can you call so-and-so?'' ''Wait. So-and-so, he's not right for this thing. Have you seen his latest reel?'' ''Yeah, I look at reels on Thursday mornings.'' ''He's still not right for this thing. Because, I tell you, he's not going to get along with that art director, especially since he wants X.''

And so on. The scene will play itself out one way or another. The script will be revised, there will be adjustments and financing and compromises and some director will eventually be chosen, albeit tentatively. That director will sense a strong suspicion of his talents throughout the job despite his proven abilities and will be bombarded with discussions of personalities and politics from the producer who is trying to hold everything together. The director who had bid on the job and lost will wonder why he was not chosen and another scar will form on his poor multi-lashed libido.

I'm not sure which director I'd rather be: the one who didn't get the job or the one who did. The one directing will soon realize that every decision he makes is being doubted and questioned. He is instructed to play scenes in a manner that he thinks is wrong but he is not invited into the original discussion in which the decision was reached. As one director complained:

> Sometimes they make you feel good; sometimes you're miserable, kind of ignored . . . there is such arrogance on the part of some people that you are made to feel that you're there because maybe you've been sweeping the floor and you happened to be caught in the room at that time. . . . I think they'd get their money's worth a lot more if they really used you, used your creative experiences, your taste.

When such agency ''political'' aberrations take place, the directors—the one who gets the job as well as the ones who don't—grow an extra lump on their paranoia.

Let me hasten to state that only in some cases are the agency folk on top of the director in this negative manner. In almost all shoots they are on the director—all over him—and in an occasional spot, the director is even given a lot of leeway. One director salivates:

> Some have commercials with just an idea and some of them come up and say, ''Look, we have got this great idea and we want to put all these things together and how can we do it to make it come alive?'' These things you love to get. Someone is relying on you as a director to make an idea turn out to be a finished thing. . . . But, very seldom do you start something from scratch.

Very seldom. The implacable storyboard which the director is handed shrinks the parameters of his creative input. Yet, this book is not a polemic to change the system. It is a request, an urging, to use the director's talents to a much greater degree. It will cost no more and the client will get more for his money. Call the director in at an earlier stage. Involve him more; he will offer more. The director will be ecstatic. Perhaps someone who doesn't know the history of the client and product will not be shackled to taboos that inhibit the full range of needed new ideas. If he's an experienced pro, he won't rail at having his ideas rejected; he's happy just being given the opportunity to give his imagination some air for a change.

I can appreciate the problems of scheduling such a situation: how can you call in the director before you have awarded the job? You can't pay him if you don't use him. The agency producer should not concern himself about this problem. Present the story honestly and look upon this step as a prelude to the bidding: in almost all cases, the director comes up with creative ideas at that point in order to base his bid on what he actually intends to shoot.

Getting into the Spot

During the production of the commercial, the agency wants and expects the director's total interest and dedication to the job. They will get it from the director because that concentration is the stuff that directors are made of. His shoot becomes his entire life. He breathes and thinks and goes to sleep with the product (Sani-Flush and Preparation H included). But, if his romance with the production is to arrive at a successful conclusion, give the guy some time for foreplay, will you?

As one agency producer said, "The product may not be beautiful to the director, but he must see it through the eyes of the client." He can be of more use than that. He has not become myopic and enslaved by taboos that have outworn themselves or gone out of style. He can inject new ideas into moribund platitudes. He comes to the client with the ideas and attitudes that are in use today, or will be in the very near future, because he has been working on different commercials for different clients and agencies. He is a breath of fresh air.

I have always felt that the director and the agency should definitely come from two different "worlds" to argue the method of representing the storyboard in the production. The ensuing dialogue then sparks new, refreshing approaches. Naturally, I speak of conversation, not confrontation. A number of agency executives are quite wary of the director's input; they should know that the director is on their side even when he is pressing for his point of view. This is how one director-cameraman thinks:

> If you keep them in the picture, they are very, very flexible, too. It's when you spring things on people, or you have to go through ninety opinions, then it's rough. But, if it's coming from one or two people and they know they are working with you, that they are participating, it's okay. And I do let people look through the camera. If you offer it to people, they're not piggy about it. It's a little unsanitary, but that's another thing about being a director-camera-

C'MON, C'MON.. IT'S MY TURN. SOL GOODNOFF

man. If you're gracious about it and handle it the right way, it's not a problem. They're pretty flexible. They want the best job; they don't want to come back like a jerk. They want a promotion, they want more money, they want what I want in life, they want to be successful at their jobs.

I can tell you that when one agency producer was asked whether cameramen should allow the agency people to look through the camera, her reply was, "They have no alternative."

The Agency Producer

The advertising agency producer—I am here to praise him, not to bury him. I do not speak of the producer who is all politics and no decency—and there are some of those. I weep for the producer who works for the agency where his executive role has been usurped by the art director or others, and there are plenty of these poor souls. I speak of the majority of advertising agency producers who are creative, judicious, fair, dedicated, efficient and considerate of the views and personalities of both the advertising agency and production house personnel.

The relationship between a good director and a genuine agency producer is easily likened to the bond between Damon and Pythias. How often have I met a producer with whom I had worked on several productions and we just grinned like idiots at one another. A friendship had grown between us that can grow in no milieu other than that between two buddy infantrymen who have spent a war together. Only we have weathered several wars, side by side. We have traveled together, lived together, eaten every meal together, smoked, drunk and played together. More important, we have been beset by unsolvable problems and we have solved them together. Most of all, we have *created* together. We have sat and worked over storyboards and come up with ideas and cheered each other's creative notions and politicked together to sell the ideas and, in most cases, we have won. We have shared awards and lots of laughter and hysteria. We have argued; Lord knows we have argued plenty, sometimes in genuine anger, but we have always turned one face to the world together. Each production inflicted its own special birth pangs, but it was *our* baby—ours.

What manner of people are these, the producers, who are the directors' immediate superiors on production? Primarily, they are creative persons. They were artists, writers, photographers, actors, musicians, filmmakers. From different fields, they brought a sense of taste, an appreciation of the aesthetic, an understanding of the temperament and vulnerabilities and conceits of the artists with whom they have to deal. Even those producers who do not come from any specific field, but who came up from the office ranks, have learned and acquired the patience and flexibility it takes to shepherd a production through the problems and personalities of agency, client, talent and production people. They are politicians, organizers, hand-holders, bookkeepers, hatchet men, can carriers and, above all, an integral part of the creative team.

Earlier or later, the producer becomes involved in the conception of the campaign, chooses the production company, the director, the cameraman and the editor. He sets up the casting and monitors the casting session, supervises the gathering of the production house bids, meets with the personnel of the production house several times before organizing the pre-production meeting with agency and client, oversees the wardrobe, the location choice, the equipment to be used, the crew, the sets, the props, the choice of makeup person. He monitors the actual shooting and follows the subsequent footage through screenings, editing, changes, reshoots, recordings, music, mix, answer prints and deliveries of final elements to the proper places. All this is done while he is filling out the many forms, meeting with the pertinent agency people, keeping the client informed and happy through all stages and, at the same time, finishing off previous shootings, making changes in old spots and planning the productions that will come after. Most important, in every step of the way, he is called upon to offer creative suggestions and make decisions that only a person sure of his creative abilities dare make. Be assured that, among these activities, there are many more that involve executive office problems and politics, etcetera ad infinitum.

With all these duties and responsibilities, you would think that the producer would have the power to make final decisions during the varied steps. The clout allowed the producer differs from agency to agency. One producer complains that no matter how little decision-making power he is allowed, in every case, he assumes the responsibility for mistakes, whether they involve budget or editing or hurt agency feelings or an unhappy client. The producer is inevitably the whipping boy.

As in every field of human endeavor, there are some bad boys. Just plain bad. One director reflects: "We deal with a range of types of producers. Some are very perceptive; others you almost have to hand-hold and take them through every phase of it."

Another doesn't trust the usual norm of the pecking order:

> I think that you just have to be very considerate of everyone. But, you must really find the one or two people from the agency who are going to give you the most salient information and then you have to count on these people to give you most of the input. But you must be considerate of everyone because it's a business.

The Agency Group

Let us list the agency folk who are involved with the meetings and the shoot and with whom the director will find himself in contact; their titles pretty well describe their functions: There is the Creative Head, the big honcho; the Creative Director, who functions for the head on this particular production; the Senior Copywriter and, of course, the Copywriter; the Art Director; the Producer; the Account Executive; and, depending on the agency or the situation, the Casting Director and the Stylist. Each of these persons may well have an assistant or two along or even perhaps a superior from the agency. Along with them, there usually will be representatives from the client: the Client himself; the Advertising Manager, the Brand Man and others, including, of course, their varied assistants or superiors. (Give up?) I can't resist being snide: A study of human creativity at Yale brought forth:

> *Those who worked in groups came off poorly compared with those who applied individual effort. The quality of the work was determined, not by the size of the group of minds, but by the size of the minds in the group. . . . The moment you begin to manage an artist he ceases being one. When one person directs another you have a committee of two.*

Returning to the intent of this contemplation, let us look to other directors to determine to whose voice the director attends to produce the best commercial that will satisfy everyone. Representing the orthodox:

> I always find that it's desirable to have whoever is involved there at the shoot but my immediate contact and my immediate response is the producer. I review with him the storyboard, review my shot list. Everything is clarified and if he has any input as far as the way he thinks he sees it or the way the agency has presented it to the client, then I get this input. But, by that time I already have that because we have been through a pre-production meeting. Then, I always like to review just before we shoot just what my approach is. As far as the lighting, as far as the setting, as far as the color—that's all done beforehand. On the set we are ready to shoot and everything has been prepared the day before. Many times I light beforehand so that my time on a shoot day is utilized in shooting and directing the commercial. . . . Our shoot day is a very productive day.

Another director speaks from experience:

> There's been a big change in the agencies and I'm not sure it's for the better.
> There was a time when agency producers were basically filmmakers also.
> They knew the craft. So they valued what you suggested, they valued your
> experience. But, there's been a big change in the agencies; art directors have
> gotten more and more power. Some of them feel they've invented the me-
> dium. And, you really have to have a very high threshhold of tolerance not to
> go off, not to blow your cork, get angry. Soon as you do, you become "un-
> cooperative". . . . You have to think of this as a business and know that you
> gotta please these guys or you're gonna work less and less and less. . . .
> Although some directors have made a big success out of being highly temper-
> amental, to the extent that their clients are afraid of them.

And others:

> There are instances where you have an art director who uses the opportunity
> as a training session. Unfortunately, it affects the commercial and if something
> is wrong, the cameraman, or the director, gets the blame, even though the
> input was followed to the T, against the wishes of the director. I did a job
> where I interpreted from the art director as to how it should be done . . .
> and, lo and behold, it came out wrong.

> No generalization can really apply. But, in some cases, there's one person
> whose opinion prevails. In some cases, it's the writer on the job. That's the
> person you end up performing for. In some cases, it's a committee: a pro-
> ducer, an art director and a writer, and even sometimes their client too, not
> all of whom are agreed by any means. So, you determine early on, hopefully
> by mid-morning, who the important voices are. And you gear everything, like
> a hundred and eighty degrees: there's the actor and there's that group and
> everything you do is geared for everyone in that radius.

> So, in addition to everything else, you have to be quite a politician. Very
> often, particularly with the more "creative" agencies, you may be the center
> of a storm in which an art director, a writer, a creative director and an account
> executive have been having a lot of trouble even before you got to them.
> Whom do you please? You end up pleasing each one, shooting a version for
> each one. This guy wants it more believable, that guy wants it more comedic,
> another wants it less comedic. It's three o'clock and you haven't got out of
> the first scene yet. So, you're on the spot. I don't think *anybody* is that inde-
> pendent. Everybody has got somebody he has to please. I think we're made
> very aware of it in the agency business. And, it's very difficult, particularly
> when you have comparatively inexperienced people calling the shots.

The Agency Personality

The "creative" agency referred to is the hardest type to work for. I have
found that each advertising agency takes on a most specific personality of its
own, one that is definable and predictable. I don't know how this comes about;

is it the personality of the man on top or of the founder of the shop? One agency is notoriously tight-fisted, another buttoned up, treating all their clients like Procter and Gamble with all that emphasis on paperwork. An agency may reflect a terror of the client, refusing to buck his dicta in any way. "He says" is the ultimate measurement of all that is correct or artistic. Well, it's better than hearing "They said." Those two words are the most mealymouthed manner of winning an argument. It infuriates me when I hear that from an agency man; I don't know whether to believe it at all or whether the "they" are the agency creative people or the agency man's pussy cats. Yet, I agree with the director who said:

> On the other hand, I do know that I'm working for a lot of nervous people. The advertising business is a very nervous-making business. They are constantly looking at the sales charts. Their being always under the gun makes these people very, very nervous.

The agency group comes to a shoot loaded with fear that the resulting commercial will not reflect the pitch that they made to the client, that it will get changed in the production. Worse, there is an underlying panic that their design will not work in the finished product and that the weakness of the original plan will become obvious for the first time. Here the father image of the director must assert itself. The director cannot fan the flames of this fear by any show of indecisiveness or doubt. One director takes this attitude:

> I think one of the things that I have a particular talent for is that I think they know they're gonna get a good job and I think I instill a feeling of confidence in these people. It's almost like when my kids used to have nightmares: they'd get up in the middle of the night and those were very real fears to them and I'd take them around and say, "Don't worry and go back to sleep, and Daddy's gonna be here in the morning, and when you wake up, the sun's gonna be shining and everything is gonna be all right." It's amazing how people want to hear that.

The dilemma facing the director is: to which fear do you address yourself? On the one hand, there are times when the agency folk are afraid they do not have a sufficiently creative or successful concept. The role of the director, then, is that of the immutable artist: he can be trusted to make everything come out right, he will remold the spot into the glory that the agency hoped for. On the other hand (and the hand which is by far the norm), the agency is afraid that the producing will end up in a commercial that is not exactly like the one they had promised the client—they reject every suggestion for change, no matter how valuable the suggestion. The answer to that dilemma seems to lie in the integrity of the director's approach to the job. He has been hired to direct the production and he must follow his own intuition and impulses to create the most artistic and effective commercial possible. He is bound by certain restrictions and taboos just as the director of any motion picture: the limitations of the allotted budget, actual laws and his audience's abilities to understand or even accept his communication. In directing the television commercial for an advertising agency, these restrictions loom ominously before him as in no other film form.

> It is literally four to five months, sometimes more, on the part of the agency between what they want to advertise, how they are going to talk about it, making proposals, presenting it to the client, refining it, putting it down to storyboard. Hundreds of man hours. Then you're gonna shoot. After you shoot it, they're gonna spend maybe another three or four weeks finishing it and hundreds of thousands of dollars airing it. In actual execution, the transition period is eight hours; twelve, fifteen takes and it's over with. If you think about it, it's incredible, the months ahead of time and the dollars after wards. It's often out of balance. They'll hold at fifteen thousand dollars; they won't spend sixteen thousand. They'll find somebody to do it for fifteen. There's a disproportion.

> As long as we're alerted to what those restrictions are, we work within those confines. Sometimes, like with (a certain) Fried Chicken, you have to know how to bite it, where to bite it—and all these things are very important because not only should we do it specifically according to the proper approach but we have to do it in a way that there is appetite appeal to it.

The Pretested Commercial

It amuses me to compare a television commercial director to a quarterback. I played semi-pro ball and I feel that, even if the ball carrier can break through the defense line of the storyboard, his creativity is stopped dead by the secondary of the "pretested" commercial.

Before the money is spent on a full-blown commercial production and airing, the client very often has a low-budget spot produced and tests it in one of many ways, either on or off the air. Now, if the results of the test are positive, and client and agency are happy that the commercial is effective, how can the director convince them that, in producing the high-budget version, certain changes will enhance the effectiveness of the presentation? No way. Thay want the commercial exactly as it was tested; the slightest variation or deviation might spoil the magic of its success. Well! We have previously discussed the limiting effect of a storyboard to generating new ideas; with this, *each* drawing of *every* frame is cast in concrete! If the mole on the left shoulder of the actress showed in one scene, then show that mole. You don't change or even adjust the angles; you don't shoot closer or farther away. The test might have been done only with still pictures; the director's instincts and knowledge of pictures in motion are rejected. His ability to plumb the audience's emotions is negated; the slide rule replaces the "gut." The agency has pre-cut the spot in their minds. The director is now an organizer, not an artist. (Well, at least he is still allowed to call "action" and "cut.")

I try not to make a judgment about pretesting. It is a case of trying to argue with success. The giants among the advertisers have found this system to work well for them. I suppose that in general they must be right. However, I am certain that the system of testing is far from a totally accurate science as yet. I point specifically to the area of short-term recognition and memorability versus long-term appreciation of the product. Almost all research I have seen concerns itself with the former; my prime function as a creative director is to achieve the latter. I try to involve the emotions, to make the product desirable and important. This lasting impression, it seems to me, is ultimately more efficient advertising than the immediate test of whether the viewer recalls the commerical he saw last night. There you have it, Gradus versus the advertising monoliths, and of course I know better.

Pre-production

Short of the pretesting of commercials is the problem for the director of the preconceiving of the specifics of the production by the client and agency. The director enters the fray after the script and storyboard are done and is challenged to "make it better without changing it." But, this is the way of TV commercial life. The best time for injecting his viewpoints and new ideas is not at the shoot, but rather at the pre-production meeting. There is, at least, no time pressure of an expensive crew standing around while the discussions go on; the preconcepts are not as frozen yet—well, not quite. Most recently, I was given a storyboard that depicted a conversation between two ladies waiting outside a restaurant for a taxi. The entire dialogue took place while they stood there. At the pre-production meet, I suggested that, in order to achieve a modicum of kinetics, the latter part of the conversation should take place while they were settling themselves into the taxi. I sold that one and, even though the shoot was made somewhat more difficult, it worked quite well.

A director describes a pre-production meet:

> Usually, it's the agency producer who conducts the meeting. He has an agenda, and nowadays those production meetings are sometimes very elaborate. You're given a book—you think it's a meeting of the UN—and the book has everything written out in it and people turn solemnly from page to page like they're in a religious ceremony. The simplest things are stated over and over again. But, there is an agenda and (the producer) usually makes that agenda and conducts the meeting.

And from an agency producer:

> i think a director's main function at the pre-production meeting is to listen very carefully to all the points being expressed by the agency creative team and the client. As the agency creative team is describing this tremendous opening for this commercial—this fantastic, noisy, exciting beginning—and the client is saying, "I don't like loud, raucous commercials. Can you tone it

down a little?'', the director must say, "Hey, I can't have a noisy opening and have it quiet at the same time. So, let's talk about this a little more." By the time he leaves, he must have clear in his mind what it is he's gonna do. A consensus has to be reached. And the producer, who has to act a little bit like a referee must at some point, without too much time being wasted, say, "Wait a minute, the director is right. We can't have a noisy opening and still be quiet." So, the producer turns to the creative group: "Listen, our client feels it should be quiet. Either you're going to have to agree with the client or, Mr. Client, you're going to have to come around to this point of view. But before we're through, we want to hammer out all these questions."

This pas de deux between agency producer and director is not improvisational theatre. The pre-production meeting takes place usually a week before the actual shoot, more or less. However, before the actual gathering, the producer has met with the director and has filled him in on the problems that are going to come up and the areas in which the director should enter fully prepared and with his thoughts organized. In a producer's words:

> In cases like that, the director can be very helpful and so I'm telling you that you have to warn them . . . here are some things I wish that you would bring up; I wish that you would cover this one more time. I wish that you would add your weight to this particular problem area.

An agency producer proffers an example:

> . . . and the client says, "Oh no, we have to say "up to eighty percent more effective." We have to leave that in." That makes the commercial too long (since) we won't be able to get it all in our twenty-eight seconds of track. Now, say that we are in a pre-production meeting and all these attempts to cut copy have been made and they have all been futile and you say to the director, "It's a little bit tight for copy, what do you think?" He says, "Yeah, I put the clock on it last night before coming to this meeting this morning and it is very tight. If you feel obligated to keep all this copy in there, as the producer tells me is the case, I got to warn you that it's not going to sound like very natural conversation for this slice of life; there is just too much in there. Now, for example, I have a provisional cut and I don't know the history of why this sentence is in there, but if it was to be left out, it wouldn't spoil the message for me and would help the pacing." It might be the very same cut that we suggested that never got through the client and then he says again, "Boy, these warnings in advance—I don't know, we'd better not come back and ask why everybody's talking so fast." Suddenly, the cut that couldn't be made last week is made right in the production meeting.

Another example:

> (The director) might indeed come up with a suggestion that no one had ever heard before—just from his extra experience, he's made a suggestion and everybody jumps up and down with joy and says, "Terrific! Luckily we have got this terrific director in here." Those things have happened. The main purpose of that meeting, however, is not for him to be super-creative and try

to come up with a whole new concept. His job is to execute this as it's gone through Continuity Acceptance and Research and Development and the Client and this is what we want him to do: to execute it as best as he can.

At the pre-production meeting, too, the final decision is most often made about the casting. Usually, the videotape is shown only of the last two or three choices that the agency has made, often with the client's blessing. In fact, the specific one of the lot has already been pinpointed as the star. Now the director is asked, almost perfunctorily, whether he agrees. A director describes this:

> They look to me to see whether or not the person has the abilities. They also take my opinion as to what type of person he is. But they also have their own (opinion). It's very difficult. It's like casting an aunt. Everybody relates to their aunt and you get six people. Two think she's terrific and the other four think she's not.

As does another director:

> I've never had trouble with an actor I've chosen, but I've had trouble, on occasion, with actors who have been rammed down my throat. I ask myself afterwards, "Is that because I'm resistant to someone being rammed down my throat or is it because they were not as good as someone I would have selected?" It's a stalemate to my mind. Maybe I am resistant, but often you have to settle for the best of a bad bunch in casting. I can't think of anyone I have enthusiastically recommended who has let me down.

The director asks that the agency and client folk approach the choosing of talent with a lot less rigidity. The relationship between actor and director is too important, too delicate, to chance a marginal or bad performance. If you don't believe in the taste and instincts of the director, or in his ability to understand what it is you're hoping to achieve, then don't hire him in the first place! Certainly the director must understand that you alone appreciate the client's prejudices and attitudes, that he hates certain appearances or accents. But, if the director is fighting for or against a certain choice, know that he is fighting for the best possible look and performance. Fight for his choice or, at least, harken seriously to the man's serious protestations.

> Sometimes things come up at the pre-production meeting that never came up before because this whole collection of people never met as a group before. Now, when you're pinning down every single item and the director says, "I really think the actor should be wearing a blue blazer and light gray pants," and the client says, "Wait a minute, the last two commercials we did, that's exactly what the guy wore. I don't want that. I want him in a brown suit," it's a consensus, a meeting of minds, a talking-out of problems, and it's me the producer, giving the director a chance to ask any questions.

> I've gone to pre-production meetings where the director has participated merely by being present in the room, nodding from time to time in agreement and hardly saying a word. To the other extreme, I've been to meetings that

might last an hour or an hour-and-a-half and maybe twenty-five or even forty percent of the time is spent in discussing things with the director specifically and in his explaining (that) what we have in mind may not work because of some technical limitation that somebody in the group doesn't understand. Sometimes, if an agency producer says it, it may not be accepted as readily as from this very expensive director.

It is at the pre-production meeting, too, that the director might be able to buy himself some time for experimentation. This meet is the place where the agency folk are trying to lay all their insecurities to rest in front of the client. The director can suggest here that a far-out inspiration he has had might well make the spot an outstanding one or will at the least firm up the commercial's intent. While this often enough comes up at the shoot, the agency is more likely to accept the experiment at this stage, before the shooting plan is locked up in front of the client.

The director's role at the meeting changes, of course, from meet to meet. In almost all cases, it remains a tentative one because, here, he is not the king, this is not his shooting set. He is there as an advisor and, often, is asked to put on his dog-and-pony act to "go through the spot as he sees it frame by frame."

The Director as Companion

The requirement that a director be some kind of court jester or entertainer is deplored by one of our most successful directors:

> The only problem with the intensity is that agency people sometimes get scared because you're not smiling, your tail's not wagging, you're not happy. They get a little nervous. There does have to be a certain amount of joking around. . . . Hanging out, I've just got to be careful. I never used to smile and I'd get put down for it, but now I've learned to balance.

No small amount of attention is paid by the agency to the amount of good companionship that will be offered by the director whom they will choose. Often, their group have to live with the director on location and they look to him to be major tour guide, check-picker-upper and social director. As one director admits his concern:

> (It's like) people picking a date for the weekend. Would they rather go out with me, would they rather go with some good-looking guy who shoots fast and gets done early so they can play golf. You get very paranoid when you're not working. And, I didn't work as much then as I do now. I always put the same effort in there, and you get very hung up about it. I think that you just have to be very considerate of everyone. . . . It's a business.

How much the director has to put out depends, of course, on two aspects: his own character and the character of the group with whom he's working. I have had groups from one for whom I had to do absolutely nothing (a group who wanted nothing more of an evening than an ice-cream soda) to a pack who wanted to carouse and wench and drink all night before shooting. If there is a norm here, it is that the director usually accompanies the group to dinner when on location and then, explaining that he must prepare for the next day's shoot, excuses himself. According to one director:

> Well, I usually draw a limit. Because the real bottom line is how well you work the next day. There is a limit, although I'd say I, myself, have tremendous energy and I try less sleep. Eight hours is over-sleeping for me. So, as long as I get in some basic minimum to refresh myself, I'll be able to operate and function.

And to another:

> There's nobody there to take care of them, none of that. I mean, they get work. They get their eight or twelve hours, or whatever it is, and they get their evenings. And that's it; that's what I intend to give. People seem to respond to it. You lose a certain amount of business because a lot of people just like to go out and hang out and drink. That's the way they work. It's not the way I work. After a long day, I'll do it. But the work comes first. We're just very precise about that. I think they're entitled to a lot. They pay me a lot of money. It bought this house. I don't dress well, but I could if I wanted to. I can afford to. They put my kids in a private school across the way and I don't forget it. You know, my wife looks great when she gets dressed up and it's because of that and I don't forget it. My old man made fifteen thousand a year—his best year—after being in the navy for thirty-one years. And he was risking his life all the time. And I never risk my life, really, because I never take chances. And I do a lot better than that. I don't want to forget it.

So, to that extent, the director buys his assignments. Where and how has his dignity and pride gone? The director was once the leader and be-all of TV commercial production. I suppose it is only the good old American system of competition that is to blame. There are many good directors out there to choose from and he that offers the most *in toto* to the agency reaps the harvest. In the process he has given up more than much of his dignity; he has eroded the very potential he has of creating a better product from his own store of talent. He didn't have to. The director has behind him the powerful, rich and able Directors Guild of America and, if each spot director were to adhere rigidly to its rules, he would recover the prestigious status he has allowed to deteriorate.

Every director works for a production company, whether as a staff hireling or as an occasional free-lance employee. He is nor allowed to work for any company, even if he owns the company himself outright, if that company is not a signator to the DGA agreement. Each signator has agreed, in writing, to adhere to the basic rules. I set forth some of the pertinent factors:

DIRECTORS GUILD OF AMERICA, INC.

BASIC AGREEMENT

Article 7: Preamble.

The Director's professional function is unique, and requires his participation in all creative phases of the filmmaking process.

He works directly with all the elements which constitute the variegated texture of a unit of film entertainment or information.

The Director's function is to contribute to all the creative elements of a film and to participate in molding and integrating them into one cohesive dramatic whole.

No one may direct, as the term is generally known in the motion picture industry, except the Director assigned to the picture.

COMMERCIAL AGREEMENT

DIRECTORS GUILD OF AMERICA, INC.

ARTICLE II: WORKING CONDITIONS OF DIRECTORS

2. Conditions of Employment

(a) It is understood that the term "Director" or directing" includes directing all related functions and activities required for translating and transferring the premise, idea and/or concept to the audio-visual images. These directorial functions shall include, but are not limited to:

(i) Surveying and approving all locations and their use as they pertain to the directorial concept and need.
(ii) Directorial planning and breakdown of the shooting script.
(iii) Plotting the camera angle and composition within the frame.
(iv) Participation in determining the requirements of the set, costumes, makeup, props, etc. for their proper directorial perspective and mechanical functioning.
(v) Participation in the final casting of all performers.
(vi) Rehearsing actors, extras and any of the visual and audio devices necessary for the completion of the production.
(vii) Directing the acting of all actors, extras.
(viii) Directing the dialogue as well as the prerecording and post-recording of dialogue.

(ix) Directorial supervision of the duties of the entire crew during the rehearsal and shooting periods.

(x) Making such script changes as necessary, within his jurisdiction, for the proper audio-visual presentation of the production.

(xi) The right to the first cut.

The Director's total function is to contribute creatively to all these above elements and to guide, mold and integrate them into one cohesive dramatic and aesthetic whole.

(b) It is the understanding and agreement of the parties hereto that the rights and functions and responsibilities of Directors will be preserved and protected against erosion. To that end, the parties agree that the provisions as specified herein shall be so construed as to foreclose and prevent practices which invade the rights, functions and responsibilities of Directors and threaten the stability and security of the industry.

(c) No one but a Director member of the bargaining unit shall direct all or any part of a production such as, but not limited to: prerecording; final casting; approval of location; sets; costumes; etc.; as well as principal photography, first cut, post-recording.

(d) In order to preserve the work which had been traditionally performed by Directors in the bargaining unit, it is agreed that unless required to do so by his client, no signatory to this agreement will demand or require the inclusion in the finished motion picture production of any component part or parts hereof not created under the direction of a member of the bargaining unit unless said component or components constitute what is customarily known in the industry as "stock material," defined for the purpose hereof as material created for general usage and not for utilization to the particular finished production to be directed by the bargaining unit member.

Every company for which the DGA director works has signed the agreement to live up to these working conditions and the preamble defining the scope of the director's authority. Yet, I would seriously doubt that more than one director in a thousand instances gets to direct the post-production recording. In almost all cases, too, the director is at best a spectator and kibitzer during the first cut—in most productions, he is not even around to watch it being done. The specific terms of the agreement are being broken to one extent or another in every one of the areas listed.

Why have we descended into this tasteless humiliation? I do not defend the rules; certainly, the production of TV commercials calls for specific work programs of its own. I speak of the callous disregard by the members signed to obey the rules of their own proud organization. As a group, or even individually, we have averted our eyes and, unwilling to lose jobs because we will be considered "troublemakers," we have allowed our noble profession to tarnish. I blame the Guild, too. There has been a certain diffidence, or laziness, in tailoring the specific rules and agreements to the realities of the TV commercial field. Of course, the keepers of the DGA business will say that they have not acted because the members have not been complaining. I am complaining.

I am complaining about the treatment of non-superstar directors during the production of TV commercials. I am complaining about non-Guild people directing parts of commercials. I am complaining about the minimum amount of participation that the director has in pre-and post-production. I am complaining about the abrogation of the director's duties during the very shooting. I deplore the Guild's allowing so many advertising agencies to produce spots or parts of spots without being signators to the Basic Agreement. I object to producers or art directors or writers in the agencies directing their own commercials without a Guild director. The Guild Commercial Agreement also reads:

> Article II, Sec. 8: Dual Employment
>
> Notwithstanding the fact that he may be a director and a member of the Guild, no employee or principal of an advertising agency may serve as a Director of any motion picture for which his agency represents the sponsor, unless such agency is a signatory to an agreement with the Guild.

It is not for me as a biased individual to say what the specifics of a new agreement for the production of TV commercials should be. These should be hammered out by a substantial representation of agency, management and the Guild. I insist, however, that the Agreement as it now stands does not reflect the sensibilities of present-day commercial production and the relationships between director and advertising agency. We are therefore treating our own laws with casualness and disdain. I appeal to the advertising agencies, to the Directors Guild of America and to its members to set matters aright and restore the deserved dignity of the television commercial director.

Everybody Is a Director

The point is that, unlike a surgeon or a prosecuting attorney or a computer technician, all of whom must have specific knowledges, anyone can be a director. Not a good director, necessarily, but a director. I could take any stupid oaf off the street, surround him with a good writer, good acting talent, a good editor, script girl, assistant director, cameraman and, if that group is articulate and this schlemiel is willing to take advice, he can turn out a professional job just by calling out "action" on cue. The hilarious—and sad—part is that, after the first few hours, he certainly will be telling the actors how to read their lines. Everybody is a director.

As I have pointed out, one of the real problems for a director on the set is the agency person who questions, say, the reading of a line. It is not the questioning, it is the manner in which he announces his dislike and it is his lack of understanding of what directing is all about that presents the problem. Let me offer an obvious example: An actor delivers a line with total lackluster. He is asked, in many ways, several times, to add energy to the delivery. His very personality is in the way; he normally does not speak with any real zest. The director, realizing this, asks him to shout out the line as loudly as he can, feeling that if this is done a few times, it might spark the actor's approach or, perhaps, the very shouting by this person will be the exact amount of energy needed to sound like he is making the statement with a reasonable amount of energy. At this point, the agency person jumps up. He has heard the direction and objects vehemently; he doesn't want the line shouted. Now, the actor hears this and confusion reigns. No matter how, or if, the agency man has the situation explained to him, the actor now is more inhibited than ever.

It is even worse when an agency person calls out a direction to the actor directly (or sneakily, makes a loud suggestion to the director so that the actor hears it). Every TV commercial director has had to handle this often. They say:

> Well, that's something I try to stop and I don't make myself too popular if I find it's happening. Then what results is that the actor gets "wall-eyed." He's got one eye on me to see whether I'm smiling at the end of a take and one eye on the client. Both parts of his brain are involved with "Wonder what he'll think or wonder what *he'll* think?" So, I will tell the agency producer, the art director or the writer that if they have any suggestion or criticism to come to me and I will communicate it so we can have one simple and distinct line of command. That's not easy to enforce, because the agency guys are sitting around most of the day with nothing to do. They get bored and want to direct. So, you really have to establish your position. I've gotten very nasty at times and it hasn't won me clients, but I will say, "We establish these rules: *Do not talk to the cast.*"

> I'd have to be a fool to say that hasn't produced some better readings than I've been given, because certain times they have been better. Sometimes that happens and I don't feel threatened by it. But when it becomes intrusive, I put an end to it because I think without any discipline on the set you don't get anything done. . . . Five different directors and art directors can be given the same copy and do it differently and still have five successful commercials, in different ways. I don't think the egotism of a director has to preclude any other idea or any other person from helping. Directors who maintain that imperial feeling about their work. . . . I don't think the business is that way anymore. That kind of director doesn't exist anymore.

> And, I gotta tell ya, you should see when you get a real professional on the set, he starts hearing direction from other sources, he's gonna let everybody know about it. Because he cannot tolerate that. . . . He'll just stop the pro-

duction. . . . But, when the art director says, "When you put it down, put the box a little to the left,"—that you're not worried about. It is screwing up the whole acting business and the whole relationship with a director and how the director knows how to get them to say a line a certain way. That's a very difficult job.

The worst thing about videotape is that it can be seen on screen immediately and then everybody has an opinion on how and why a line should be read. . . . Then you get a bunch of undisciplined people standing behind you and some agencies are notorious for this. Everyone in that half dozen people, in their mind, they know how that line should be said. It makes life very difficult for the director because he, too, knows how that line should be read. . . . A lot of time you work with people on the set and they are not like small people in the agency ladder. They are creative people, account people who are heads of the accounts. Sometimes their client is there also and he, too, knows how the line should be said.

They've got some great opinions. You just have to know what to listen to. A lot of people reject them all or take them all. You've got to know what to take and what not to. I've learned a long time ago not to close my mind to any suggestions.

It throws (the actor) an awful lot. I try to do it one way at a time. I don't like the actor to know that there are five people there who think he is delivering the line wrong. I try not to let him know that. I try to keep him apart from the discussions and I will do it the one way I think is best and keep doing it until I feel that I have got the take that is best. . . . Then I will go back and have our discussion and I'll go back and approach the actor again and say, "Okay, you have done that and there is another way of doing that that might be equally as good."

Shoot it two ways.

Or three or many more ways. The demon of indecision plagues every shoot. A television commercial is the result of the workings of many minds, often racing in many directions at once. They know that the decisions do not have to be made until the editing, and each wants his own viewpoint to be represented at the edit should he be able to sell his own version. The decision to "shoot it two ways" may well have started back at the pre-production meeting and possibly before. Sometimes, the director himself is compelled to make that compromise at the outset. A representative of a production house describes this scene:

Sometimes a director will say, "This is how I am going to do this"—and there's a pause and everybody looks around in stunned silence and the advertiser—the client—says to the agency account executive: "That's not what you told me what was going to happen," and another discussion ensues. This is where, many times, a producer for an agency and the representative of the production company sit back and watch the director do a song and dance— something out of left field, something they never heard of or conceived of—

they squirm a lot in their seats and they wonder how the hell they can rectify this. This advertiser has been told by the account people that he was going to get X, Y and Z but suddenly he looks up and says, "I'm getting A, B and C. I want X, Y and Z; why am I not getting it?" If the director has any smarts at all, he'll realize: "I've got to give him X, Y and Z. I'll start with that. If I have enough time on the day and I want to do A, B and C, maybe I'll do it and in the cutting room we can show how A, B and C will be better than X, Y and Z, but, gee, I've got to give him X, Y and Z".

A director tries to be understanding of the agency's insecurity that reflects itself in "do it two ways":

> The persons in the agency can be on that account maybe for fifteen years and maybe more and very often their jobs are on the line. You're as good as your last job and I sort of have a compassion for the fact they're in that kind of position. They've got to be responsible and I know that when I'm finished shooting; they've got to put it under their arm and sell it to their client. And, I'm not there anymore. Then they'd better say as much as they've got to say, to do what they think they've got to do, to survive.

Shoot it once for the writer, one other way for the client, one even for the message that has come down from the legal department of the agency with one word removed. Can a director retain his self-respect, can he live with himself? One director:

> Yes, as long as I am always doing what I honestly feel is the best I can do under a given set of circumstances (so that I can) live with myself. You have got to remember that you must have a more infinite amount of patience than you do in other kinds of jobs, because I understand, before I get to see a storyboard, that this thing has been torn apart and probably rewritten three or four times and it is presented to the client three or four times. Every shot has been discussed with its advantages and its disadvantages. Now I get the storyboard and now I am producing it on the set, and I say that there is a great opening thing here where I can start with a closeup and move around here and come to a wide shot. You talk to the producer and tell him that you have a great opening shot here where you can start on a closeup and he says, "No, you are not." I ask why. The producer says, "Because the client has already been told that we are starting with an open wide shot." I then try to tell him that this is infinitely better, look how terrific this is. "I'll show you." You take the time and make the move. He says, "Yes, I agree with you but there is no way because it has been sold to the client and we start with an opening wide shot."

The above is the beginning of a story of "shoot it two ways" if I ever heard one. The creative suggestions of the director, however, are often appreciated sufficiently enough by the agency producer and he will run interference for the director to get the idea approved by the client. This takes a great deal of strength of character on the part of the agency producer, but that strength is there in many cases. If he can't win the war entirely, he will sell it to where the director is allowed to film his version as "another way." Some times—many times—the struggle during the commercial has been going on too long and the suggestion would be too difficult to sell. Then the producer points out the battles already won to the director and prevails on him not to be a hog.

"Fight it out at the editing"—if the director is going to be at the editing. There is a certain number of directors who are busy shooting all the time. These men seldom allow themselves enough time for editing; the financial cost to them is too great. Since they are the superstars, their presence at the edit would be greatly appreciated in almost all cases, but this is part of the price the agencies seem willing to pay for their directorial services. According to one director:

> Generally, that's it. I would like to continue with it but usually the agency spends three more months editing and revising. They've splintered the business a lot. They've separated the production companies from the editing companies. In some ways it's good but in a lot of ways it's unhealthy. I've shot jobs which I didn't recognize on the air three months later, although I did the first cut. I don't know why they made the changes they did. Sometimes you'll see things that have been improved. It's often bad. Sometimes you walk away from a job and somebody else has a different vision of the material. God bless 'em; it doesn't happen too often.

And from another:

> There are certain types of agency producers who want to be directors, so this is an opportunity for them to get involved in the finishing. Some are qualified and some aren't. Some are very perceptive and complement the shooting.

The directors of television commercials owe their living and, indeed, their careers to the folk at the advertising agencies. Generally these folk are unquestionably perceptive and understanding and intent on getting the best possible spots produced. The directors, however, have one basic complaint: that their real talents are being used less and less. It is true that, as the industry burgeoned, the director played a vital role of supreme responsibility. Certainly, there were instances where the director went too far afield in his interpretations, creating a burden and an embarrassment to the agencies. To protect themselves, the advertising agencies usurped more and more of the director's real functions and the pendulum swung around to give the agency more and more directorial functions.

A recent trade magazine printed a standard production still and the caption read (again the names are withheld to protect the wrongdoers):

> In one 30-second spot (pictured here), producer ——— directs the comedy team in planting a garden on Park Avenue. Director ——— filmed the vignettes on location.

This degradation mirrors the fact of the sad situation today. We trust that the pendulum will find its place back to the point where all participants and productions profit most.

Almost all of us have chosen our professions out of sheer love of the activity and we certainly understand that many people appreciate the delight we find in our work. One director said:

Everybody in the agency wants to be a director of commercials. Everybody. I guess they're around it so much, they seem frustrated. I feel you'd like to feel that people would recognize you for your expertise in what you do. And, in our case, fine—the company does a million dollars—I guess we're recognized. When someone gives me a hundred-thousand-dollar job to do, then I feel you certainly can hold your head up.

8

Varied Types of Production

WE HAD BEEN SHOOTING a cattle roundup in Texas and arrived at the last point where the herd was to be loaded into a train. The camera was behind the thousands of steers, ready for a long shot of cattle, train station and train, which was just coming 'round the bend. "Roll camera." The train came nearer and the engineer decided to toot his whistle. The scream spooked the cattle and they turned around in a wild stampede toward us. There was no place to go other than to scramble on top of the camera station wagon to get away from the millions of pounds of meat racing into the camera. By a sheer miracle, they split just before hitting it, although they came within inches of the lens. This carried them around the station wagon and we were saved. The camera had been left running—through no other foresight than panic—and, as such stories almost always end, the footage was terrific.

Almost every experienced director has such anecdotes (does that word connote "humorous"?) of danger to tell. Get a group of directors together and start them on the subject; they sound like stunt men recalling near-tragic mishaps or, sadly, tragic ones. I have enough of my own.

We were in an open-top Land Rover in the Ngorogoro Crater in Tanzania. I was shooting over the head of the lady in the car toward a couple of elephants chomping away at some foliage. This necessitated the use of a wide-angle lens and the elephants were too small in the frame. I told the driver to get closer to the elephants. Closer than that—and a little closer . . . This was more than the tremendous wild bull elephant could stand. He had had his back toward us, but suddenly he whirled and, with unbelievable swiftness, charged the car. The driver raced up the road, the elephant right after us. We went up a hill and, as we started down the other side, there was a herd of elephants crossing the road in front of us. To either side was impenetrable bush. There was no going anywhere. All heads turned as one to the rear and not a heart beat, let alone a breath taken, until we were convinced that the following behemoth was not coming over the hill, too. When we got back to the lodge, I went over to the "souvenir" counter and said to the Tanzanian, "I understand that when a hunter has killed an elephant, he is entitled to wear the tail-hair bracelet. Since I was charged by an elephant, does that permit me to wear one?" "Oh, yes, sir," he said earnestly, "That will be two dollars and fifty cents."

One shot in the Youngstown steel mill was the stream of molten slag running white-hot into its bubbling pool. The camera was alongside this inferno when the pool exploded, sending up a rain of fiery meteors around the camera and crew. Perhaps we ran that swiftly or just wished ourselves gone, I don't remember. Certainly, we were all lucky; no one was burned, other than their clothing. Again, the camera had been left running and the shot was sensational but, of course, the scene could not be used since it indicated that there was some danger in working in a steel mill.

My own stories could go on ad nauseam (and, I'm certain, sometimes do); other directors have as many similar experiences. One director suffered a severe concussion when a camera hit him on the head. Another director-cameraman held his camera over the side of a ship to shoot a second ship when the two collided with his head between them. The camera was smashed but the extra width of the camera saved his head from suffering the same fate. The stories, funny and tragic, are legion about planes and helicopters.

If accidents tend more to be caused that just happen, the causes in our case are from our inexperience with the changing milieus in which we are constantly thrust. On Tuesday, we might get an assignment to film a boat shooting the rapids. By Friday we may very well be out there on the boat, never having been near such a situation before and with no time to learn sufficiently or prepare the special muscles required. One director tells of having gone overboard and being saved only because someone in the raft was able to catch him by the hair of his head after he had "gone down twice." If that had been me, I would have drowned; I've been bald since I was 20.

The same type of stories tell of skiing and hang-gliding and snorkeling. One tells of mountain climbing for the first time and getting caught with camera gear under an overhanging ledge. He had to rappel down a sheer incline under shouted instructions about pitons and ropes.

How do you describe the personality of a man who would choose this kind of life—and loss of life—to direct television commercials? Is he suicidal, fatalistic, masochistic or macho—or just plain stupid? I myself have one leg an inch-and-a-half shorter than the other due to a bone graft (the result of a shattered leg), a body covered with the scars of extensive skin grafts, discolored patches derived from scrapes that wouldn't heal in tropical climates—and an abiding gratitude that one cannot remember what past pains were really like.

Yet, if tomorrow morning a production comes up that will have me hanging from a helicopter over a pool of sharks, I would be happy to take it. There is only one real description of such a personality: *stupid!*

The Danger of Directing Children

To many a director, there is another type of production he is called upon to undertake that he considers a much more dangerous, death-defying stint: directing children. The whole concept of professional acting goes out the studio door: there is no hitting marks, no keeping the eyes off the camera lens, no pronouncement of lines with any conviction, no doing anything that will make the director's lot more rational or peaceful. For myself, I find a certain fiendish fun in getting a child to act; what I find totally irritating is the nervousness of the agency/client folk, who cannot abide the time it takes to summon the patience, tact, diversions, diplomacy and just plain childishness that is required to bring out the best in a child. They want the scene to play and say exactly right—immediately. I have all the patience in the world needed to establish the necessary rapport and communication with a youngster; but it takes a pulling together of all of my gestalt to continue working with the group on my back and psyche until the kid and I get the scene right. It takes time to get the child to understand what you want; it takes time to get him to want to get what you want; it takes some improvisation to get him to understand what he is talking about; it takes fun-making, ease-making, friend-making, confidence-making. It may involve cajoling or disciplining or pretended anger or let's-not-give-a-damn. It takes knowing when the child's short concentration span is failing and what to do about it. The director may have to channel the youthful abundance of energy or he may have to boost a flagging, fatigued child who is tired of the repetition and bored with this entire unnatural scene. Besides the ability to be impervious to the strained nerves of the audience behind the camera, the director who would be successful with children must have—absolutely *must* have—an unquestioning love of children. If he has it, the kid knows it, the kid's mother knows it, the audience knows it. If he doesn't, and he runs into any problem (as he must in shooting children), he'll blow the job—and his mind.

On the other hand, if the director has foreseen the problems and anticipated the amount of time and the 200-to-1 ratio of film it may take, the atmosphere of the shoot can be less traumatic. Then, when the child is really taking direction, when he has joined the effort with enthusiasm, when the filmed laughter is real and bubbly, when the projected joy is genuine and not teeth-deep, the director completes a shoot with an immeasurable sense of delight and self-congratulation.

Wild Animals

I suppose that every director at one time or another is called upon to direct animals. The very first person the knowing director gets on his crew is an

Whether the location is on a mountain precipice or in the frightening bowels of the earth, the director inspires confidence and security in the actor.

animal trainer, whether it's for an alley cat's kitten or an untrained gorilla. He needs all the help he can get. I have made my own share of mistakes and, I hope, learned by them.

Again, anticipating problems is vital. Animals can give you one scene in seconds and then take hours to get the next scene right. Heat up the set with lights and they might get sleepy—or angry. If the stage is too hot or too cold for that particular animal, you may very well have a temperamental star who can give lessons in tantrums.

A director tells me of the time he was filming an important movie star who was to open the trunk of a car and a flock of pigeons was to fly out. During the take, she opened the door but the pigeons decided to stay put. They tried many a trick, including slamming two blocks of 2 by 4 wood at the precise moment. The pigeons refused to leave the car. They spent the entire day and never, ever, got the shot.

Stories are told of rabbits arriving on set with a skin condition and in need of extensive makeup. Whereupon they decided to mate like rabbits during the scene. A great fish story I have heard is about the hundreds of a special type of bass that had to be transported from Colorado, where they live normally, to a California lake. The many fish that were not used for the scene were left there and, much later, an article appeared in the local California news by ichthyologists who were mystified about this unusual migration of fish.

I believe this story because one day I was readying a shot in the small Greynolds Park in Miami. In and around the little lake were hundreds of ducks of varied species. They had learned to beg food from the picnickers and were clambering all over us, messing up the particular shot I was arranging. When I fussed about them to the prop man, he said, "Them's Filmways ducks." I myself had been a director at Filmways for a number of years and it seems that another director I knew had brought in a couple of dozen ducks for a scene and, one by one, they had all escaped. They were left there and ecology was once again scrambled by that intelligent animal, man.

Need I point out that when the plot calls for *both* animal, and child, the director's problems are geometrically multiplied? Fill up the truck with raw film stock or videotape and roll—just keep rolling. Even if the scene that is taking place in front of the camera between animal and child has no relation to what you're looking for, keep rolling. The very best scenes are captured that way and maybe the client will allow some stretching of the storyboard's dicta to fit the great scene in.

I know that descriptions of shoots with animals and children are always portents of terrible times and traumas. They may well be. But, to those of us attuned to such filming, these productions are really happy changes from the usual abnormalities of our work and, best of all, very often result in fun days ending with refreshing satisfactions and new little friends.

The Big Name

There is yet another assignment that can easily be hazardous to the health of a director: the celebrity. The "big name" can be either a movie or sports or television star; he can be a political figure or the client himself. Now the director really has a jittery, hysterical contingent behind his camera and a demanding, usually uncertain, nervous character in front. Here, the director must call on all his resources to display simultaneous strength, respect, patience, sincerity and humor. He has to quell the inevitable tensions of agency and crew. His direction must be absolutely definite and unfaltering, never for a second letting his reins go slack. Too often the trauma begins long before the shooting starts because the celebrity is late—I have waited 12 hours for a star to show up— and even before the first frame is exposed the director is told that he must be done "in a few minutes," which is all that is left.

Here again the only attitude that a director can take is to remember the dictum: When the finished film is projected, only what is on the screen is the measure of his achievement; no one will remember the problems of the production.

The core of a television director's talent is the ability to adapt to the ever-changing situations and personalities in commercials. Each celebrity is different; each star requires different handling. There are no set rules; some need jollity, some need serious toughness. All require total pre-preparation and definite, unyielding direction.

The chairman of the board or president of the client's company presents his own special needs. He usually has, or pretends to have, very little time to give to the effort. But, the director needs time to get him comfortable with his surroundings; if he is in his own office, he is thrown by the morass of cameras, lights, cables and people. The executive should be given at least an introduction to the equipment, to the camera, to the TelePrompTer, to the concentration-shattering clapsticks. The director should have at least a modicum of time to chat leisurely and establish a rapport and understanding with him. Above all, the intermediary persons who would try to translate the director's instructions should be firmly put out of the way: there is nothing so distracting to such an "actor" than the quivering interpolations of his assistants or agency folk. The director will find interpretations or mannerisms that need change or manipulation. The script itself, which the executive has approved beforehand, may need adapting to the personality and abilities of the speaker. It is in such a situation that the group behind the camera will most often get in the way of the director and his proper functioning. Director, quietly and surely, be firm; be tough!

Interviews

On the other end of the scale, there is the assignment of the hidden camera. An interviewer goes out to talk to someone who doesn't know the camera is recording his answers and reactions. Why, then, is there a need for a director? Isn't a cameraman sufficient? One director answered it this way:

> The cameraman is not necessarily concerned with the line of questioning and how best to get the answers out of people. . . . Somebody has to be in charge. I've had interviewers up there and I've had to go out of the truck and say, "Look, you ask them this way—they won't give us a twenty-five-minute answer," and the guy says, "Hey, you're right." Now, if he knew that originally, maybe he wouldn't have been an interviewer, he'd have been a director. Those are the things that make directors—how do you get from point A to point B in words or actions within a certain space of time? "Well, don't step with your right foot over your left foot; how about stepping with your left foot over your right foot and then you can turn around." So he says, "Terrific." That's why you're a director. . . . And that's why a cameraman is not a director. And that's why a soundman is a soundman and not a cameraman. Because they are specialists in their particular jobs.

As a director, I have been called upon often to do the interviewing myself, not necessarily with hidden cameras. You look for sincerity, naturalness, enthusiasm, words that will be approved by both client and legal and, most difficult of all, conciseness of expression that will lead to a minimum of editing. I consider the interview a failure on my part if the completed spot ends up in a whole series of cuts to make the various points within the time allotted. Certainly, the television viewer must then instinctively realize that a trick is

The director interviews, keeping his body aside so that the camera misses him and films the "people in the street."

being played on him; the words that would convince were never really said but put together from various speeches for the convenience of the advertiser.

The basic technique of the interviewer, of course, is to ask the right question the right way. For example, if you ask, "Did you like the movie?" the answer is an inevitable, and unusable, "Yes." But, if you ask, "What did you like about the movie?", the interviewee is forced to answer in specifics and you end up with a usable quote about the acting, the photography, the music or other advertisable aspects. That is a very basic example; in other situations, you ask the person to describe the softness rather than just getting him to say that it is soft. You lead him in enthusiasm with your own high spirits. That is not immoral; he is saying what he thinks but this time with perhaps a greater intensity than is his usual wont.

The Pitchman

Sincerity is the key projection required from the pitchman. Whether his presentation is high or low key, whether it involves humor or sincerity or nonsense, the audience must believe what he is saying. He must impress the viewer that he knows what he is talking about; he must sound like he believes in what he is saying. The difference is a delicate nuance that the knowledgeable director can see in his smile, in his eyes, in the verity of his accents. The product he is displaying should usually, logically and naturally be within his reach; he should not have to contort his position or his fingers to present it. For my own taste, it is not vital that he be totally comfortable all the time. I like a situation where he is reasonably compelled to move and talk over his shoulder to us for a couple of moments, for example. While it is dangerous and wrong to distract the audience from what he is saying, I feel we play the pitchman too straight, too safe. There is a point where such safety becomes just plain boring and the viewer loses interest. A pitchman who comes across as a human being will, in most situations, be much more effective.

On the other hand, the environs in which he is placed should definitely not distract the viewer's attention. The set should only reinforce the character that he is portraying or the situation. The scenic designer should not be allowed to indulge his own private fancies to the point where the audience is looking at the set instead of the player. While this admonition seems basic, it is often overlooked, so that the client and agency folk are impressed when they come onto the stage. In such a case, their money is being spent but they're not getting their money's worth. It is the duty of the director to control such excesses or mistakes.

This contemplation brings us to the two viewpoints involving the "income level" of the rooms we build on stage or the location homes we choose: Does the audience identify best with a depiction of their own homes—or do they prefer identifying with the beautiful homes they wish they had? The compromise that seems to have been made is to put "usual-looking" people into a little less lavish settings. I would myself prefer to see the sets brought down quite a bit, but, thankfully, that is not my decision. One director said, "I think it's become a tradition that in kitchen spots you always have an island. Nobody works against the wall in TV commercials, whereas at home we know that's where we all work."

Food Spots

There are directors who specialize in food commercials—one of the "table-top" spots which require their own special talents. Yet, just about every director finds himself at one time or another with a food shot to make, whether it's one scene to be used as a cut in a commercial or a series of food shots for an entire commercial to which they happen to get assigned. I repeat that directors object to being labeled as one kind of director—each man thinks he can direct every assignment that comes his way. It's the same with food.

Perhaps the most important aspects of a food commercial are appetite appeal and composition. When the different items of food come to the table to be photographed, they seem to take on a life of their own, calling for certain positioning and lighting and movement. The design and composition is done while looking through the lens, and varied forms suggest themselves: the need for a fork here, a corner of a napkin there, a bowl of low-hanging flowers in this corner and so on. The food product establishes its own personality and the framing and placement of peripheral accouterments grow out of the product's requirements. One of the most important elements is the look of the hand that will enter to manipulate the food, as has been previously discussed.

Animating the food so it doesn't just lie there is another important aspect of food filming. The rising steam, the hand, the bubbling liquid. As one director put it:

> So no two things are the same; there's always a different motion going on, whether it be a camera movement or a hand action movement or a dolly-in or dolly-out, visually there is always something going on. The most important thing about all this is that even though things are going on, the person is not aware that all these things are happening, other than the fact that there is a revelation going on.

Slice-of-Life

The function of the director in "slice-of-life" productions is to mold chunks of slogans, improbable situations, cardboard characterizations, phrases left over from previous campaigns, convoluted dialogue and imperative hortatory speeches into a logical conversation that would reasonably take place. Again, I refuse to argue with success. The advertisers have found that the resultant commercials move goods; the writers correctly follow instructions and the director must do all he can to humanize the situation. In most slice-of-life spots, the director's request for changes is given serious attention; everyone is sympathetic to his effort. Yet, certain phrases must be delivered, certain reactions are compulsory. The slice-of-life commercial presents the classic situation where a director can make a spot somewhat better than the original design; he can never produce what he feels is a true playlet. A typical reaction from one director:

> First of all, it is what we call a normal slice of life but it's so unbelievable and so phony and so much really like a commercial. Maybe it sells a lot, I honestly really don't know, but I can't believe that there aren't a thousand ways to write that thing better (so) that (it could be) far more believable. It is a typical kind of commercial that is supposed to be a slice of life; it just isn't. It is completely unbelievable and I have no way of proving this other than this is what I think.

To make the impossible job even more ludicrous, slice-of-life spots often use non-professional persons. A director says:

> The remainder of that work is usually all synch sound and it's with people who aren't even actors; they're just real folks. There's nothing harder than

getting a performance out of a real person. I don't give a damn what anybody says. It's a bitch. Because advertising people expect the same quality work from somebody leaning against a lamppost in Philadelphia (as) they do from a movie star giving a pitch for some cause. I mean, it's the same thing. You've either got to get it or come back on your shield.

The director must come back with a spot that is acted with seriousness, the pitch having been given with, at least, conviction. There should be a good relationship between the "conversationalists" and they should be in a setting that is acceptable as a reasonable locale. Before going into the shoot, the director should urge the agency to cut down the amount of words in the dialogue as much as possible to leave room for the little silences that make a slice of life play more naturally, as it does in life: time for reflection before talking, for reactions, for an "umm" and an "ahh," for a facial reaction and so forth. When the participants spit unceasing and incessant words at each other without respite, the scene does not represent a slice of real life.

To keep a sense of reality and the curse off the slogans that must be delivered as though they were ordinary conversation, I personally like to keep the actors moving and doing natural chores while they are speaking. The client generally prefers to have the golden words spoken in closeup and directly toward the camera, but the director's assignment is to make the scene play like a slice of life. I work under the theory that the viewer will accept the statements more readily if he can identify with the real life scene.

Comedy

An apocryphal story is of the teacher who asked his budding film director students to state their first direction in the following scene. A man walks into his garden and steps on a rake. The handle comes up and hits him full in the face. What is the first thing he does? The wrong answers are: "Yell, ouch;" "Curse;" "Hold his nose." The first thing an average man does do in such a case is look around to see whether anybody saw it happen, *then* he yells, "Ouch!"

Television commercials, indeed all selling, depend heavily on modern man's concern with what his peers think of him. It is important that he not be considered the clown who would step on a rake and find himself in such an embarrassing situation. Comedy in commercials usually involves true-to-life situations; no one wants to be that schlemiel who is laughed at because he doesn't use the product. He doesn't want to be the one with the bad breath whom everyone turns from or the guy with the yellow teeth or the dandruff or unkempt hair or the guy using a gas-eating automobile. The television commercial director who is given a "comedy" spot to direct should be very aware of what the comedy is trying to achieve—beyond just being humorous and entertaining—and play the scene or the character accordingly. The director has much to offer here because it is very easy for all involved to get so caught up in the fun that they go in the wrong direction. Usually, too, the correct direction is funnier because the point of the gag becomes more potent and, perhaps memorably poignant.

In some fashion, the basics of comedy should be kept in mind when laying out a scene. For example, one rule is that you show the audience that something is going to happen (the banana peel on the sidewalk and someone walking toward it); show it happen (he slips and falls); then show that it happened (the person's reation to his fall). The major difficulty in doing good comedy in TV spots is the limited time allotted; there is almost never enough seconds to play all three of those scenes in sufficient length. But, keeping the concept in mind helps you compose and plan the scene with fuller results. There is no substitute for the director's instinctive appreciation of comedy and his ability to present it. He will have an innate appreciation of the weaknesses and foibles of everyman that the viewer, recognizing the inadequacies in himself, will find funny. It is a relief to see that others have the same problems that we do. The director should, in most cases, keep the scene playing as it happens in real life to real people, exaggerated though it may be. In comedy commercials, we are allowed to expand on the emotions portrayed: the laugh can be more boisterous; the tears can flow; the fall and disintegration of the environs can boldly be given greater dimension. The best comedy is, however, rooted in reality; the most effective message is one with which the viewer can best relate.

In one spot, we had cast a lady for comedy: she had a boisterous voice, a comedic grand manner and, to reinforce it, we dressed her in a hat that was somewhat outlandish. The girl to whom she was talking was to be embarrassed by the old lady's loudness in public. Originally, the passers-by in the street were to turn to look at the lady, doubling the girl's embarrassment. But, budget took precedence: those who turned their heads would have to be paid as principals instead of extras, with all the residuals involved. The word came down: no one is to turn and look at the lady. This was fine for the budget, but how was the television viewer to understand for certain why the girl was embarrassed? My arguments finally won me one head-turner and it played real well. The walking woman appeared in the background between my two ladies, turned a startled face toward the noisy talk of our comedienne, smiled the slightest reaction to the "character" and went on. Our audience then appreciated, I'm certain, to a much greater degree, the embarrassment of our girl.

The Musical Commercial

Another involvement with "showbiz" is the musical commercial. The high cost behooves the director to prepare before shooting to the most meticulous detail. If he stumbles in his forward movement, the budget will be eaten up swiftly, allowing him less and less room for on-the-spot changes and additions. The logistics, design, choreography and the very angles must be planned and plotted in infinite detail beforehand. He should preferably have a good choreographer and be in perfect harmony and agreement with him. The playback has to be totally marked and ready. The entire crew must be primed and knowledgeable in every specific of what is going to happen. And what may happen.

As in comedy, the danger is that everyone will become fascinated with the glamour and fun of the music and dance and play the shoot for the entertainment. The director must hold on to the elusive fact that the reason for the spot is to sell the product. The agency in these cases is so concerned with the time and money spent that even they very often are willing to sacrifice the sales emphasis for the entertainment; the director must come through for them.

There is a reverse danger, too. In the hysteria to push the costly project along, the director will tend to pre-plan the editing and shoot only what he deems necessary. I am not especially an advocate of overshooting for multiple angles and giving the editor a very wide range of possibilities for editing. However, in a musical, the movements and dance lend themselves well to creative editing and sufficient coverage is definitely required. Closeups and cutaways of the entire piece will offer the editor the opportunity to enhance the excitement of the spot—or, mess it up. (In times past, the rule was always to shoot entire figures to show a dance; I do believe it is possible that, because they are interested in the effect of the dance rather than the dance itself, TV commericals have brought about the change. Dance in the movies and TV now uses many closeups of feet, facial reactions and the like.)

We have read, and always will read, in the trade newspapers and magazines wise tomes about the death of spectacular showbiz TV commercials. Then we will read of their rebirth. We should always assume that one technique of advertising will come to the fore, become copied until the form is a glut on the market and then another technique will come up to take its place. One intent of the commercial is to attract attention to itself; the musical extravaganza will always be with us in TV commercial land.

"Hi-Fashion"

The word "hi-fashion" conjures up a look of high-key photography and willowy women. This approach is often applied to cosmetics, hair products and a special handling of clothing. Other than concern for the special male machismo, there is no reason why this technique should not apply to men's cosmetics and the like. Most of these television commercials are shot by former, and present, still photographers who specialize in that look in photography. The "bright-white," high-keyed approach lends an ethereal, sterile and clean aura; it reinforces the special sophistication that the model exudes.

The models chosen are usually in the 20 plus-year-old group and are almost invariably beautiful in the classic manner. They are thin (I have seen several chew and swallow bits of paper napkins to assuage their hunger) and, whether they are promoting gossamer or jeans, carry themselves in haughty demeanor.

The director must keep in mind that this bearing is almost always a trade front; the model is as insecure and as vulnerable as any actress. There are few fashion models who have the ability to act sufficiently to undertake a role requiring an actress. It becomes even more important that there be a strong and able director on a fashion set. It also helps if the director has had experience with such models; they are of a very special—and wonderful—breed and require knowledgeable care and feeding.

Obviously, the choice of these models is a result of many long-standing studies. The woman in the audience wants to look as beautiful—and as young—as the girl on screen. I wonder whether continual research doesn't indicate changes in this pattern of preference. There seem to be too few commercials that use a mature woman as a model; certainly the "other" aspect of the audience identifying with the person on screen can come into play: relating to someone who is like you rather than someone whom you would like to be. There is a thin line here, too, after which the ladies must find their feminism degraded. Looking good cosmetically and in fashion is acceptable to almost all people but a display of neurotic compulsion to attract the opposite sex must be objectionable to many. While the advertiser indeed plays hard on this aspect, it behooves the director to play the story so that it will have a positive effect on as large an audience as possible. The client will want to go gung-ho on the sex bit; the director must keep him from going too far, in the client's best interest.

Many fashion spots use only a bare limbo background and that, obviously, is the safest and cleanest way to go. When a set is used: a bedroom, bathroom or other, the design should be of the most exquisite taste. In most cases, the whole concept of income level is voided; the sets are luxurious, even breathtaking. They exude taste and aristocratic sophistication. In ever so many commercials, for example, the marble bathrooms are orgies of hedonistic design. The choice of appropriate props in a fashion spot is also of vital importance. Whether it be a hairbrush or a hand mirror or the jeweled collar for an animal, the care in locating or designing it should be entrusted only to a person of the most meticulous taste. Of course, many props are gathered and the divine one chosen.

The same approach applies to the wardrobe. The very best stylist must be sought out. The relationship between wardrobe and setting and sales message should be fully discussed. Wherever possible, more than one piece of the same wardrobe should be on hand for the shoot; perspiration, makeup, spilled drinks or tears can hold up the filming for hours while the replacement is being chased after. Also, if possible, don't allow the actor to wear the scene's wardrobe during lunch. The wardrobe person should be especially careful that the clothing looks good for every shot; there must be no unwarranted wrinkles or anything askew. While the director is surrounded by individuals—script supervisor, stylist, wardrobe mistress, cameraman and such—who should be watching for any such aberrations, he must always remember that his is the final responsibility and his eyes must be everywhere all the time.

The other pivotal people are the makeup and hair persons. Models are usually very acute and knowledgeable about their own makeup and coiffure. However, the professionals are usually better equipped to design the makeup for the specific needs of the camera and the story-line of the commerical. Special care must be taken with the display of product used on the model: the eye shadow or the lipstick or the permanent. For them, too, there is the problem of the heat of the photographic lights, which create a temperature that is far above the normal situations. Hair will wilt, cosmetics will soften, the perspiration of the model will increase greatly and makeup will run. This requires infinite care in a fashion commercial; the "wrecking crew," makeup and hair people, must be constantly on duty. More, they must be demanding and intrusive where they feel it is necessary; what is being sold is their talent. The director must respect their finickiness and devotion to their art; in fact, he should always anticipate the need for their services.

The director is there to maintain the perfection of the fashion commercial, to make the model look good, whether it is her makeup or hairdo or the way she walks, the very aura that she creates. After that most demanding aspect of the production, he is there to make an effective whole television commercial of it all.

Choosing the Location

To go from the genuinely sublime to the ridiculous, there is the choice of environs. Here, a director must unfortunately use a bit of showmanship himself. As a director, he can tell what parts of a location will look good on camera. Therefore, he can see in a location sufficient gems of backgrounds even in a run-down locale. Shoot from this angle—there is that magnificent tree in the background; shoot from this viewpoint—there is that fascinating house; the crud all about will be absolutely hidden by the automobile which will be in the shot—and on and on. Don't choose that location! The agency/client folk can never see the trees for the forest. They will think you've lost your mind, selecting a location that is generally unappetizing. Whether it is on location or in the studio, the entire set must give the proper impression, even though only parts will be used. Often, this causes an unfortunate waste of money in building and in props that will never be shown on the screen or on a long trip to another location. But, this is show-biz and the director has enough of a job convincing those behind him that he knows what they are seeking.

My personal preference is to shoot on location where possible. It normally takes a lot of money to simulate a location in the studio with any eclat. Then, it is only simulation. The correct location has an ambience, a richness of detail and texture that can seldom be duplicated. Certainly any level of luxury can be found in some location—whether it be home or office or elsewhere. Surely there are additional problems to shooting on location: sound recording; undependable power sources; transportation to and from the location with cast, crew and props; communication; lunches; availability of shops to pick up emergency pieces of wardrobe, props, film and such; and the watchful, nervous eyes of the owners of the location.

It usually is worth the trouble, providing that the director uses the location. It's awfully silly to go to an interesting locale and then shoot into a bleak corner of one room. The director should use the scope that the location allows, even though it means some extra time lighting up the hallway and stairwell for the background.

The major problem arises when sync-sound is required. Set aside time for waiting out a siren or a garbage truck or kids coming home from school. Directional microphones are constantly being improved to avoid some of the lesser noisome sounds. The director can compose his shots, too, so that the microphones can come in as close as possible. I must repeat that the trouble is worth it all; the very worst that can happen is that, if the sound is unusable, a post-dubbing will be required. This is still usually less expensive than building a set which will prove less valuable than the location.

One director was instructed to shoot on a set rather than on location:

> We built an entire supermarket over all my objections. They spent absolutely thousands and thousands of dollars to duplicate the supermarket and it took four days for three prop men to set up all the stuff that had to be set up on the shelves. It was absolutely the biggest waste of a client's money that I had ever seen in my life. There are twenty supermarkets around here that you could get for one-fifth the cost. Not only would it look off the bat like a supermarket, but you have complete control and you can do anything you want to and all the products in the world are there. I don't know why people still do that. We did it and it cost a bundle of money like you would not believe.

It certainly makes life more interesting. One day I went out of an office in New York City to a location in New Jersey with the whole caravan carrying personnel and equipment. Fifteen minutes out of the City, it started to snow, hard. In another half hour we were in a severe blizzard and had to pull over to a diner to wait it out.

The assistant director went to a phone to report our plight to the office and to the location that was expecting us. He signaled to me from the phone to come over, a puzzled look on his face. When I picked up the telephone, I must have looked as chagrined as he: "What snow? It's sunny and beautiful here in the city!"

We once were filming a slalom racer on the ski slopes of Stowe, Vermont. The shot I had set up called for the camera on a sled sliding down alongside the markers at the speed of the skier. Three professional skiers controlled the camera sled's descent, skiing along above it and holding it back with ropes. In

SOMEONE CALL THE SPECIAL-EFFECTS MAN?

the middle of the run, the sled somehow got away from them all. The sled, camera and cameraman went hurtling down by itself into the crowds below. I don't know why no one got hurt on that one. Well, the shot could not have been duplicated on a stage, anyway—not without some "movie magic," otherwise known in the trade as Special Effects.

Special Effects

Now, every production uses some sort of special effect, whether it is the slow motion of a girl running through the forest or a marching potato or just a dissolve from scene to scene. There are directors who specialize in solving problems with special effects and their techniques are as varied as the problems: high-speed and slow-motion and stop-motion photography, strobe effects, macro or micro photography, live rigging, live and optical matte work, film and videotape mixtures, chroma-key and image mattes, rear- and front-screen projections, the Shuftan process, rotoscoping, marionettes, puppetry, hand models, space visuals, breakaways, unusual camera lenses and lighting effects, in-camera opticals, projections, prosthetics, flying rigs, makeup, rain/fog/snow/fire, explosions, electronic control systems, turntables, glass painting, miniature and mock-ups, mirrors and others.

One director who specializes in "object and figure animation," which is done by stop-motion, argues that this art is far from fully exploited in television commercials. Another director complains that the agencies still do not appreciate the value of interesting special ''FX'' in moving goods. He insists that the unusualness of the shot or spot dramatizes both the commercial and the product. A cadre of real cats singing the commercial jingle for cat food has greater impact than a jingle over the product shot alone. A demonstration of the product's values using the effect, say, of a flexible watchband twisting and untwisting itself, tells its own story with force as well as credibility. Most important, there is memorability. According to one director:

> I think for something to be memorable, it has to be able to be picked out of the crowd. In other words, you have all of these damn commercials running on the air, you know, hundreds of them, and a good percentage of them are good and I think it has to be not only memorable but super-memorable to be picked out of the crowd, you know, like the ten-foot washing machines.

A fringe benefit of a commercial that is successful because of a special effect is the publicity it gets beyond the specific viewing. People talk to each other about it and, sometimes, they even remember the product it is advertising.

The function of the director on a special effects shoot is to find the solution for the problem. How do you get a man to walk up the wall, across the ceiling and down the other wall? Solution: Attach all furniture and props securely to the set, turn the set and camera while keeping all the action on ground level. And, find a pretty agile actor. There, that's simple. Or, fly people in and out of scenes with ''invisible'' wires or jump cut objects into and out of the frame, and so on.

Don't forget that the very first films that Thomas Edison made experimented with all kinds of special effects, including replacing live figures with dummies to be mauled about and then replaced again with live people. Articles were magically manipulated and sets were blown apart. The Keystone Kops had automobiles that split apart and kept riding or became squeezed between trolley cars and came out skinny; these were also special effects.

We tend to think of special effects in large terms: space wars, exploding mountains, burning buildings. The challenge—and delight—to the FX specialist is the wide range of subjects that call for his expertise.

> You never know what the next project is going to be and you have to research every single project. There was a situation where I had to do a commercial with butterflies and the butterfly had to fly in, fly around the bottle of perfume, land on the bottle, fly from one product to the other and do all such crazy things. You have to quickly become a butterfly specialist. What you do is get every book you can get on butterflies, you study them and you go to the museum and you get as much information as you can from them. You do a lot of research and all of a sudden you become a butterfly specialist and you know what kind of a butterfly to use and what to do with it. It goes along that way, you know; today it's butterflies, tomorrow it's hot dog rolls.

Mickey O'Malley   SOL GOODNOFF

WHEN WE ZOOM-IN FOR THIS SINUS BIT,... I'LL QUE YOU TO TURN SIDEWAYS.

Some of my biggest jobs have been physically the littlest jobs. Like some little dumb pill doing something crazy was more difficult than moving forty elephants through the street. Because, in moving forty elephants, you know, you've got all sorts of help and everything else and it just happens. When you're working with this little pill, there's no one around to do anything but yourself. You don't let anybody else do it because only you know what you want to do.

The special effects director finds himself much more involved in the entire production than in any other shoot. First of all, there is the research, and then the filming itself, which takes a lot more pre-planning—and the shooting is much more involved, too, than a basic production. This special attention carries into the editing; some scenes may have been shot in reverse, or in parts of the frame or intended as superimpositions and so on ad infinitum, and only the director knows what should go where. There may be further experimentation in the editing itself, which, in the case of special effects, can be exceptionally complicated.

In special effects jobs, I never shoot until everything has been approved. Looked at and approved. So, there are no surprises on the stage. We have our meetings; we have second meetings, third meetings; we start to build; I bring the clients in during different stages of the game so they can keep abreast of what's happening. This way, by the time we shoot, everybody has the same image because they've practically seen the commercial before we've run one foot of film or one bit of tape. Because everybody's image is tinted by their past experience.

How does a young man get into the special effects field? To start with, he has to be very lucky. (A relative in the business helps.) Very often it's being in the right place at the right time. I think, to do the kind of thing that I do, he has to learn as much as he can about as many things as he can. I studied magic and became a professional magician. . . . I build models; I'm a designer and every time anything comes up I go very heavily into it. I have all sorts of power tools and equipment and I build cabinets and make miniatures. The thing is, you have to just keep learning; you have to keep doing things.

That director's resume includes: Artist and Painter (work shown at the Metropolitan Museum of Art); Professional Magician; Photographer; Engineer (Inventor of the master antennae system, forerunner to cable TV); Musician and Band Leader; Private Pilot; Commander of PT Boat. Played baseball for Dodgers Farm Team.

Ethnic Markets

Directing commercials aimed at specific ethnic markets presents some very special problems. If the director is not one of that ethnic group, he must be especially careful. Too often he may fall into the trap of regarding the group in the stereotype conceived by his own different ethnic culture. In the majority of cases, this concept is not the personality that is accepted by the people in the market for which the commercial is targeted. He must understand, or at least appreciate, the kind of character and presentation that his special viewer can relate to. Casting, for example, becomes sensitive and vital. What kind of person should represent a specific section: housewives, street people, grocers or taxi drivers. Naturally, there are fewer professional actors to choose from and it becomes too easy to compromise, to choose the talent that is not absolutely correct because the non-professional is harder to handle. The acting, too, must reflect the norms of the culture. Hispanics, for example, talk a lot with their hands and their facial expressions, and their dialogue delivery is much more demonstrative and exaggerated. Their projection of humor is definitely less subtle. If a joke is delivered deadpan, it just won't play in a Spanish situation.

The very translating of the English copy into Spanish presents a problem of time. The Spanish language uses some 25 percent more words to express an idea than English. As in all language transposition, the idiomatic expressions must be adapted. For example: In English, we might say, ''Now, that's music to my ears.'' To the Hispanic audience, that means nothing. It would have to be translated into something like: ''That's what I like to hear.''

The very pronunciations of the written word play an important part. One director who specializes in Spanish commercials points out:

> Spanish is a mother language to a whole bunch of nations, but they all have different ways of utilizing that language—different intonations, different uses of the same words. We use a neutral language and avoid regionalisms. We enforce a correct accent and don't go into accents. The minute you do, you're

alienating one group and offending another and just reaching one. The pronunciation must be acceptable to the national ethnic market, so we have to compensate—adapt it into a neutral Spanish.

We have always been conscious of a similar problem of accents in the English language. We do not allow an actor who is in a commercial for the national market to use the Bostonian's "paek the caeh" when we want the entire audience to understand "park the car."

The complaint of the director of ethnic-targeted commercials is that, because of the comparatively smaller audience, the budgets tend to be tighter:

> Is that ever a problem? Of course it is. Having to deal with that reality, a director is limited in such a way by the budget that (his) creative contribution is fighting the budget all the time. Sometimes you have to shoot with very little time to prepare anything. They give you the job at the last minute—two days before. That happens to all of you guys, too, but it happens worse to us. They hold those budgets for the Spanish commercials up to the very end, end, *end* of the fiscal year. Then they let it go three days before they have to be on the air. Then we go paranoid here for three days doing seventeen commercials without any preparation, without a decent crew, because by that time the rest of the city is shooting too. So, I get what's left. The people that I like are all busy on other jobs.

(An aside: I had a law professor once who had a thick Russian accent. He complained, "Why is it that if somebody speaks with an Italian accent or a Russian accent or a German accent, everybody laughs? But, if somebody talks with a French accent, it's called Continental!)

Once I shot in Brussels and we imported models from France, Italy, Germany and Spain. The automobile advertiser took a full-page magazine ad with photos depicting the shooting of the commercial. In the center, there was my earnest face and the caption read: "The director had to speak in four languages." It's true that I can get along in all four but I was hurt. I did, after all, use English too, which I speak—after a fashion.

9

Local Directors

ONE DIRECTOR OF TV COMMERCIALS said:

> I'm known as the "King of Schlock." I've done as many as twenty-two spots
> in a single day's shoot. . . . Just lined them up in the waiting room and
> knocked them off one after the other.

While this is not a fair description of the Local Director, it does reflect the
low budget on which the director of local advertising commercials must work.
It is almost another world from the comparatively posh production of national
spots, calling for speed and a mountain of ingenuity, withal a very special
compendium of knowledge and talent, as we shall see. The production, too,
offers a certain satisfaction to the director, one which does not include a very
good financial return. In fact, the local director is almost universally underpaid,
understaffed and overworked. With the dollars allowed for spots for the town's
furniture store or grocery or restaurant, he must give much more of himself to
extract a production that at least looks professional. He is wont to come up
with new ideas and approaches because he just can't afford formula solutions.
If ever there was an unsung hero, the local director is one.

A local station executive told me, "One thing we can't afford is a serious
director. If he tries too hard to be arty, to give the client too much, we're dead;
we just can't afford it." Just 'knock it out' is the byword for these productions
and it hurts the very core of the serious director. Occasionally, so very rarely,
the one opportunity does come through to produce a tasteful and interesting
spot and the excitement in the studio is at a pitch. More often, the richer

commercials are contracted out to the New York or Hollywood or Chicago director for his proven abilities—and hearts break in the smaller town. The image of the big city director is important to the sponsor; it spells "quality" to him. Yet, the regional director knows, as every good director knows, that he has the ability to produce a first-class spot. He knows that he has been training his crew to be ready for the big one. He knows that he can, for a lot less cost, turn out as effective a product as anyone else. Seldom is he given the opportunity to prove it. So, he continues to knock out the cheapies—as well as they can be done.

TV commercial production for local, low-budget time buying is an important aspect of the industry. The spots are used in UHF stations, on the varied forms of cable and in local theatres. Local retail advertisers can budget their advertising dollars effectively and wisely. The spots have to be produced ridiculously inexpensively; the greatest price is paid by the director's creative impulses.

In the dark, low-volumed nether world of television's 2 to 5 A.M., the local commercials bay furiously at the moon. They sell aluminum siding and used automobiles and desert homesites and apple corers. They strain mightily and vociferously to shake the soporific and sleepy viewer to attention. They do not hint nor intimate nor strew gentle and subtle advisements. They sell—and hard. Pounding these forms into shape is the director. I do not mean to say that these are the only type of commercials that the local director does; he does have the opportunity to work on commercials that call for more creative juices. But, with his budgets the way they are, his eye must be on the clock rather than on the hope of an award.

I have said that the director will find, in any situation, the opportunity to be creative. Again, the very composition of a shot, the look in the speaker's eye, the placement of props make decided differences. The viewer may look at the screen and see the speaker only. At first glance, this may give the impression that the direction was vacuous, but the director may have had to work very hard to minimize many distractions, such as eye-catching props or misdirected lighting or confusing background movements or disturbing gestures by the speaker. The director has brought the viewer's attention to the speaker and what he has to say.

There are other areas of creative thought that a local director may enter (which a director of national spots finds closed to him because of the advertising agency hierarchy), one being the very design of the commercial. For example, one director tells me about a spot he was doing for a local furniture store. The merchant wanted to reach the Hispanic market, although he himself was not Hispanic. The director insisted that the merchant himself deliver the pitch in Spanish, even though he sounded more Greek than Spanish. His accent was so bad, the Hispanic audience found the commercial exceptionally funny and the spot proved most successful.

Another story is that of a merchant whose message was that he could beat any price. The director's suggestion was that he say that there were four reasons why his store was the best place to shop: 1) He could beat any price; 2) He could beat any price; and then continue for the four times.

A director speaks about doing a restaurent commerical:

> How many ways can you shoot a restaurant for thirty seconds, actually twenty-five because they want a five-, maybe a seven-second tag on the end with their store? They're the hardest. . . . You usually open up on an atmosphere idea, then you want to show the service; you want to show the food and then you want to show the building and, of course, they want to show an hour of each. But, they're all the same because basically a restaurant has tables and basically they have the same food. The only difference (is), if you have a Chinese restaurant or if you have an Italian restaurant, it's either going to be green or red.

Another speaks of a store:

> They'll want to show the whole store. The whole secret is to make the spot look very simple. The simpler the picture, the less complicated, the better it is. The cleaner (it is), the more expensive it looks.

One director describes his shoot as "quick and dirty" because of the limited budget. A typical day for him is five locations and then back into the studio to shoot.

A "slide spot" is an even less-expensive medium. You take a 35mm still camera and shoot up the outside, the inside, the products, the bathrooms, everything. Then edit, lay in a piece of stock music and get the local D.J. to announce it for $25. If you must shoot motion pictures or tape, you expose no more, no less, than you need. Here's the way other directors do it:

> Well, the way we would do it, we would probably shoot slide commercials for them, maybe charge them two hundred bucks. Sixty dollars is the rate, so you figure forty a pop to put them on the air. Realistically, twenty dollars. And that's it.

> Sometimes the agency will really spend big bucks and give me a superslide— it might be crooked—you know, a logo or just a name and a phone number. Or else, I've been known to take their business card, cut it up and, when they don't have phone numbers, take the IBM typewriter, type up the phone number on a piece of paper and photograph that. It works. Makes everybody happy. BBD & O would kick me in the behind but. . . .

The budgets are low enough, but in addition, the advertiser often pays for the production and airing with barter. I wonder how many directors take their pay in "40 meals for two" in the local restaurant or "60 free admissions to the skating rink"?

The director of local retail spots has earned his money. Often, the announcer on camera is the retailer himself and he is the worst kind of finicky star performer. He, after all, is the man paying the bills and wants to play the scene as he sees it. The conscientious director really has a tough job on his hands. I heard of one instance where the advertiser wanted his whole family on camera—and, his dog as well! He got it.

In the words of one director:

> Of course, he's not a professional actor. Even though the budget isn't there, you want a spot to look as expensive as possible. It's tough to make him do things where you know it will make him look good but his head says it's not going to work because "I look stupid moving my hands" or "I look stupid smiling." It's tough.

The aim is to get this non-actor to present his message in a confident manner so that the viewer is not distracted from the words and intent. A pair of eyes that are popping out from the screen due to stagefright is not conducive to an effective sales message. The director's objective is to relax the "actor," to help him focus his attention on what he is saying rather than on his distracting environs. Every director uses his own technique:

> I kid around with them. I tell them, "Okay, we're going to record, stand by everybody, slate." Slate goes up, everything goes—and the guy is frozen there. And then I'll go over the talkback system into the studio, a little off mike so it doesn't sound as though I'm talking to him. I'll ask the audio man, "Is his fly open? Or, is it my imagination?" The actor will start laughing. Then I'll call action when he looks up. It works—you get his mind off what he is doing. Even though lights are on, if they think it's a kidding-around situation, they're going to perform.

> You gotta take it with a grain of salt. No budget, okay? So first, you're gonna need a set. Okay? So you don't wanna spend money? Go look in the garbage in the back. All right. So what I found is a stock wall we used before, two years ago. Nice wall. So, that's the background. We need a desk—we got a piece of plywood back there—get some nails; let's put it together. We got a piece of velvet we got layin' on the floor. So there's your new set . . . a piece of carpet. The carpet down, two chairs, an old trellis in the background, two plants that were dying in the lobby. There's your set. Okay? There's no big problem, no trick in doing it. Let's get some crap together; it's going to look great on TV.

Imagine the tremendous learning-by-doing process for the young local director. Every ounce of knowledge and ingenuity is called upon to overcome problems so that he will be able to discuss and direct with authority in the future with professional crews. I am told of situations where the director does his own camera and lighting, runs in the back to start the videotape recorder and is a total one-man show. Afterwards, he edits the spot himself, including laying in the music and mixing. All this must sound absolutely incomprehensible to the director accustomed to his "professional" system, but it does exist. In fact, when the minimal compensation earned by the director is taken into consideration, the whole affair is mind-boggling. A single person is required to produce commercials in this manner on 2-inch tape, 1 1-inch, ¾, ½, 16mm or 8mm film!

At times, there is no advertising agency involved and the director finds himself writing the spots as well. There are "time buying" organizations that will
function as agencies for the client and help in the writing, but the director's
function is always enlarged in such cases because of the limited input by the
time buyers. In such cases, too, there is often a limited knowledge about what
the camera can do or, worse, they are copying a visual effect they have seen
on some expensive national spot which cannot be duplicated with the paltry
budget. A director's story:

> I did one spot where a guy had his whole family. Now, he brought about four
> hundred people in the family to the stage. It was a chroma-key of land in the
> Poconos. And, we did it, but you couldn't see the chroma-key in the back-
> ground; you didn't see anything—you just saw the family!

The budgets include the use of the permanent staff, usually of the TV station. In many cases, this represents one audio man and two men who act as
cameramen, video engineers, tape recordists or anything else required for the
particular shoot. In the main, they are trainees who will not remain long with
the outfit; they soon move on to better paying situations or to the big towns.

The values of working in a local situation are reflected in one director's
description of the use of special effects during video editing:

> Got any fun ideas you want to do? Want to do a soft-edge circle wipe or what
> we call a Marx Brothers wipe, which is a vertical wipe which goes horizon-
> tally across the screen's soft edge? We'll do that instead of dissolve on the
> spot this time. You can have fun; you can experiment. You can fool around
> with this junk, then you go to Grey Advertising and say "I've got an effect
> for you."

And this from another director:

> This time around, we'll charge them two hundred bucks. I'll get a kid, pay
> him a few bucks for the day, say, "Here's my Nikon, I want this shot, this
> shot and this shot; get a roll of film. Come back, I'll process it in my dark-
> room." That's idiot work for me, I now do color. That's it. I'll get an an-
> nouncer in, I'll give him fifty bucks; for fifty bucks, I'll tell him, I want
> twenty spots read. If he's a little bit off, it's okay; it's more than they're
> getting in print. Broadcast is much better for the retailer. And that's it. I'll do
> about twenty spots in about three hours.

In most cases around the country, the videotape commercials produced for
local use are done in the TV station's facilities. The director may very well
also be the station's news director or cameraman. The spot usually has to be
shot when the camera is not being used for programs. The editing, too, is done
on down time. The important aspect is that the equipment, and usually time, is
available to the director to use and experiment and learn. The location shooting
will seldom comprise more than one van or station wagon loaded with equipment and personnel, including the talent. In most cases, the available light is

used with a couple of assisting lamps. On occasion, a location set is lighted but seldom with more lights than can be transported in the one vehicle. Needless to say, any member of the crew may be driving and a driver's license is a vital adjunct to any video education.

A director experienced in local production contemplated how he would set up a "commercial department" in Ohio:

> I would look for all young kids . . . the guy out of a technical college and say, "Hey, look. I'm going to hire you. I'm not going to pay you any kind of rates on the thing; you need the exposure and I need the work, so let's all get together and we'll do it!" They would get a union card out of it which is the hardest thing in the world to get and we would get a young staff like here. I have a young girl, she's a college kid, graduating. She'll be a production assistant here. It's experience. They step into the front door. I would look for a staff like that for this stuff. It's not complicated to do. I try to stay away from zooms: the less you do, the easier and faster it's going to get done. I look for a medium shot for these spots, usually. Unless, if I'm in a good mood, I might truck the camera; I do my own camera.

Before you big city directors start giggling up your sleeves, let me affirm that in many cases, the director is not working at "the local level" because he has not been able to break into the big time. Often I have found a firm, deep-set philosophy and strength that keeps the director where he is.

In practitioners of every art form, there is the personal struggle between the motivation to achievment/fame and the search for inner happiness. Does the former bring the latter? Sometimes. Often, however, it is at the price of not achieving the latter. And, what's more important? Of course, that's up to the individual. Let's hear it from the local viewpoint:

> I got it licked out here, in a place like this. I live twenty minutes from here, in the country. I happen to be a boater and my boat is also twenty minutes from here. Many times (after) we wrap a shoot, everybody goes out on the boat. It's a different way of life. So, why should I go into town to kill myself? To take the bus or train into the city, work to seven or eight o'clock and take the bus or train home. To live in the city, what for? A couple of bucks more, I'm sure, but, no. I walk out of the door here, I forget the place. If I have nothing to do any day, I just don't come in. I take flying lessons; I go flying. I'm enjoying my life.

A more pragmatic view:

> Three years down the line, when I'm thirty-five, I might seriously consider getting involved with the subway or the freeway, depending on which direction I head. I've been at this for seven years now, and it's been tremendous.

10

The Crew

A DIRECTOR IS A SYMBIONT, sharing a symbiosis with his entire crew: "a partnership of dissimilar organisms . . . an association which is mutually advantageous." One talent builds upon the other; each craft and art making the other better and being made better.

The crew is the orchestra the director is conducting, the baseball team he is pitching for. It is a group of people whose function is to remove all concerns of the mechanical, functional and specific of motion picture production from him, leaving him the energy and concentration required for his own job. One out-of-tune musician, one slovenly outfielder, can distract and ruin the entire group's performance. In the words of directors:

> If anybody can do something that will make me look better, I'm all for it.

> I've always tried to pick my crews in the same way I would invite people to my home. I want people who are not only good at their work but I want gentle people I can have sit down at my table with me. It's always been a criteria of ours. We just put a crew together for a big car job—we just came off it yesterday—and the crew felt good about being with the rest of the crew and everybody told my producer: "You cast this crew like you cast a film."

The result of such an approach to a crew paid off for another director recently. On a location shoot, both he and the prop man were running a high fever. It turned out to be the flu. Despite remonstrances from the agency and client, the perspiring director insisted on completing the day's filming which was scheduled to continue on to ten o'clock in the evening. The prop man held in there, too, and the crew really concentrated on the shoot, every man helping the other—in spite of union regulations—and moving the production along as swiftly as possible. The wrap-up came two hours earlier than the expected completion.

One important technique to get the best possible cooperation from a crew is to hire the same people all the time. They will be grateful for the income and will be better attuned to your way of working. As one director sees it:

It's very cordial. It's very much like a family. I feel that when I get the guys on a crew that I want—an A, B or C crew (after C, you're in trouble)—I feel very confident they will bust their asses for me. I don't have anybody on the crews anymore who will go off in the corner and hide. I try to involve them in the shoot in any way that I can, even if it's just to wisecrack with the second gaffer at free times during the shoot, just so he knows that I know he's there. Or make the prop man a playful scapegoat for something that fell over. Try and make a joke out of that. I don't worry anymore about their not being with me. I do get nervous when I have to go to a distant city or a location with a pickup crew and I don't know the guys and what they'll respond to. But, to me, the cameraman and the A.D. are just as important to have on my side as the actors. You tend to work with the same people over and over, some of which is a danger, I suppose.

An obvious drawback to the use of the same crew members every time is that the director doesn't get to know the ability of others in the field. TV commercials come up fast and require shooting pretty soon after the decision to produce is made. Only then can the director find out who is available for the particular day of the shoot and too often his first choice of men is not. He should have a wide range of knowledge about the men who are available for that particular day. He can't know enough if he hasn't worked with them before. From one director:

Over the years, I've built up sort of a group of men and women throughout the country that I can count on. I have a group of people in Chicago that I like to work with when I'm in the Midwest, a group of California, people in Hawaii that I know I can go to. I've got a bunch of people who are mountaineers and river guides in Wyoming and Montana. I know when I have a job in the Northwest, these people are going to be able to grip and rig and save my life perhaps as well as anybody on earth. In New York, I work primarily IA. Outside of New York, I work IA or NABET. We have two companies and we never mix on the same job, but I want the best possible people for the job. And usually, because we have worked for so many years, we have first, second, third and fourth choices we can go to if various people aren't available.

The personalities of the individual crew members assume a vital role when the director is filming a feature film and the crew must work together for weeks or months on end. But, the very fact that the TV commercial shoot will normally take only one day precludes the possibility that the crew will eventually learn to work well with each other and the director. The rapport must assert

SOL GOODNOFF

itself immediately and harmony must be established the moment the crew arrives on set. A sloppy crew is nothing less than a disaster for a director on a spot shoot. On the other hand, a professional crew will smell out a stumbling director within the first hour and, in disgusted disdain, give very little of themselves. As a well-seasoned director puts it:

> I'm very good at what I do and the crews back me up a hundred percent. Fortunately, you know, I have total confidence. I say fortunately, because if I had any doubt the minute I'm there with the crew sitting, waiting for me to make a decision whether a shot works or does not work—I have never been in that situation. I can always say I want this lens and this angle. If I don't like it or it gives me problems, I will change it without thinking twice—almost like guerrilla warfare. If you know your craft, you have the flexibility. If it doesn't work, move on. That's when a crew is going to say, "Uh-huh, she doesn't know what she's doing."

Crew members have indicated to me that they prefer finding the director on set when they show up in the morning; they go through sufficient exercise when they set up according to the A.D.'s instructions, and if they have to do it all over again when the director shows up with new ideas, the crew will generally slow down. Given a smooth-running operation, they tend to be more efficient and responsive even to the personal idiosyncrasies of a director: one likes to have plenty of food on the set to nibble on all day; another always breaks at 3:30 for ice cream. The latter director tells of a crew he usually works with finding themselves with another director, shooting in a cold winter in

Greenland. At 3:30, they asked the astonished director if he wanted ice cream and they wouldn't explain their inside joke.

The director, too, must consider that each man is proud—as proud as he is—of his individual job. I had an editor who had what he called his "putty nose" theory: When a man whose specialty is applying putty noses on actors goes in to see a film, he is likely to emerge saying, "What a lousy movie! Did you see those terrible putty noses?" That's all he sees.

> (There are) other things you really have to be careful of. I have never, ever, chewed anybody out in front of the crew in my life. Because, once you do that, they will never, ever, forget it. They can work for you for twenty years; they can be your best friend, but they'll never forget the day you chewed them out and made a fool of them, whether it's an actor or a crew person or your own people. Your own people are usually the ones most susceptible to criticism, because they're the ones on the payroll who've got to come back. Sometimes, you're a little nicer to the crew or the actors: it's your own people you tend to flog. I've never done that and I hope I never do. Control things like that: your arrogance and your ego. It's very important, because people are watching you and they pick up on every one of your moves. You see them walking around. You feel them stalking you with their eyes. They want to know what you are going to do, what you're going to ask of them. And, you've got to be really cool. You can't just play to the agency people and all that: you've got to play to everybody. You have to lead them all, all of them, or they won't follow you and you don't deserve to be followed.

One A.D. insisted that the director pays absolutely no attention to the crew. He argued that he had worked with many over a good many years and never had that impression. I could not convince him that he wasn't being perceptive enough and was assuming that he alone was taking note of the crew's needs— perhaps another incidence of "putty nose."

The Assistant Director

He has a right to his putty nose. The vital role of the Assistant Director is described this way by one director:

> You use him as your right hand. He's not a gofer. He's gotta be your right hand. He's really a director in a sense. He's not making final decisions, but he's carrying out your decisions. Being your right hand, he shouldn't be involved in many other things. He should be involved in what you are doing. If he's down the line and has to pick up the cue with the walkie-talkie or whatever, that's a terrific responsibility. He screws that up, it screws up the whole scene. So, he is a director, a mini-director on the set. But again, I say, you have to instill in the people you're dealing with the same kind of things I have to instill in the people I'm dealing with. Maybe at a different level. But, let 'em know who you are. You're the assistant director, not just an A.D. You're walking around and saying, "I'm the P.M." No, you're not the production

manager. I think we should instill in our up-and-coming people this same feeling, that the A. D. is important, very important.

Another director insists that the best A.D. knows editing! It is true that such an A.D. will understand better what the shots are.

The producer of the commercial for the production house has left a myriad of details unattended, waiting for the A.D. to take over. Some directors do take an interest in the specifics, even if they do not do anything about them. Many directors purposely turn away from any consideration of this plethora of problems, leaving them to the staffs involved. The A.D. comes into the production and is always given full trust by the director and his producer. In effect, the A.D. becomes the producer of the show from that point on. He is given the budget (without the profit markup and director's fees) and is expected to honor the figures as established. There is a tendency among some A.D.s to "cover their asses" by overspending, to be absolutely certain that the production is running smoothly. I once used an A.D. with whom I was working for the first time and, without my knowledge, he called in the crew at 5 A.M. to load the trucks with the equipment, in order to be certain that they would be on location by 8:30. This cost a small fortune in overtime for the one-day shoot. Had he first conferred with me, I would have told him that there would be no more than four hours of actual shooting and no overtime was necessary. We were through with the filming before lunchtime.

The relationship between director and assistant director is so important, so vital to the flow of production and to the welfare of the exposed nerve endings during production that directors are always vehement, whether positively or negatively, when discussing A.D.s:

> I don't rely on him at all for anything creative. There are very few guys who are capable of that. Some are. There's a guy that's got a bad reputation in the business, whom a lot of people find annoying, and I know what they mean. He will make suggestions frequently, but they are generally excellent. Whenever I work with him, I listen to what he has to say.

> I love a guy like ———. Do you know him? Because I know that he's with me from start to finish. He's not the most wonderful personality in the world. He's sort of edgy, he's skittish, but I know he's busting his ass for me. He will move the shoot along and, in his bumbling way, he's working hard for me. He's not always telling anecdotes like some of the others, who are telling stories from the past. He will be over my shoulder all the time and if there is a prop that needs to be gotten in a hurry that someone forgot or that we need for a new dressing, he won't look around and say, "Who's gonna go out for it?" He'll be gone and he'll be back in five minutes with the thing. I do love that kind of concern for the job. There aren't that many A.D.s I work with who are that concerned. A lot of guys go through the motions: "What would you like with your coffee?"—that sort of thing.

. . . not much. What I ask of them is to stay close to me, keep the set quiet and keep the crew moving. That's really all I can expect. Anything else is a bonus.

Well, the title Assistant Director is, I think, really a misnomer. Assistant directors should be called producer's assistants, because very rarely do they assist the directors in directing. The A.D. may assist the director in having things ready, seeing that the next set is prepared, moving you along, taking care of all the dirty work, the homework, the paper work and stuff like that. But, if you work with a guy over a period of years, he becomes very valuable to you. It takes a lot of detail off your back.

I have found that a director who is let down by his assistant finds the experience nothing short of traumatic. The director trusted the assistant, looked to be cared for by the assistant, expected concern from the assistant for the production and for him. He then feels double-crossed—more, cuckolded. He was spurned, scorned. Really. Directors are always either vituperative or rhapsodic about their assistants.

For myself, I never have run across an assistant director who did not know his job fully. The value of the assistant to the director depends totally on the A.D.'s attitude toward his job. There it is again. The word attitude. There is not an A.D. in the Directors Guild who cannot do a superb job if he puts his mind to do it. Yet, like every other director, I have worked with a few who proved themselves more costly to have along than if they had been left at home. As one director experienced it:

That A.D. was really operating by rote. You don't have to yell "quiet" before you yell "roll it" (when) there's no noise. It annoys people. Anybody who operates by rote, I don't like. It's a marvelous function . . . it's a real art to itself. If you're an A.D., you know when you've done your job right and you're not running around on the day of shooting; you've done your preparation. That's something only you know. You just sense when you're running a set well or if it's falling apart. It takes sensitivity in handling a group of people.

No matter what name you give the A.D., he does, in addition to the producer's job, the job of production manager, even if there is a P.M. back in the office.

The importance of the A.D. is stressed by one director:

We hire assistant directors prior to the job and during preparation. I hire assistant directors earlier than the time prescribed by the Guild only because of continuity. You don't want to have to bring somebody up to date the day before. Better to invest a little and have that person two or three days earlier. It helps in the function and running of the job and, the easier that that is, you are essentially buying more time.

Their over-importance can often create problems. From one angry director:

> They get in and "Jeez—I got a job!" And then they sit down and then they forget that I said, "Don't walk into my office without a piece of paper, a pad, because if I can't remember it, how are you going to remember everything I tell you to do, or that I need, or that I want to get done, or that has to be done on the set."

Conversely, from a reasonable director:

> First, I make all information available about how and what I intend to shoot. If an assistant director doesn't know what a director's shot list is or what his intentions are for the day, he can't really do his best job. He's got to know that in order to do his job as an organizer of the set, (he must) think ahead and actually assist me. Let's say you have a scene with three or four kids; I might ask him to take care of several of them.

An assistant director described his role as someone who must act "laid back" and strong at the same time. "Laid back" so that he doesn't antagonize the crew and others on the set and, of course, strong, as any leader must be. He has the official responsibility of keeping the crew's morale up, keeping them informed of what is going on or what is going to happen or why the shoot has suddenly come to a stop. He eases tempers, keeps the crew on their toes without ruffling their sensitivities and maintains an avid watch that each man is doing what he is supposed to be doing. At the same time, he is ascertaining that the acting talent is signing their contracts, that they are not disturbed because they are being mistreated or paid insufficient attention, that they are getting their hair and makeup completed. The genius A.D. does all these functions and still manages to be right at the director's side every moment.

In the production of television commercials, the A.D. also has the added concern of the agency folk. He must make certain that there is an adequate number of chairs in an adequate place on the stage or off, that coffee and Danish pastries are available and that the lunch is planned and reservations made in an appropriate restaurant. More important, he must be sensitive to the moods and angers of the clients: the A.D. should be a living barometer and communicator to the director of what reactions are occurring behind the director's back. He should help keep all the agency folk *off* the director's back until, at least, they have all in committee come to one specific request to the director, rather than the jumble of conflicting opinions that is wont to come from a group. For that, he will need to call on all his strength, diplomacy, patience and sensitivity. He may also be the lucky one who must go to the agency people and tell them that if they want certain changes from the original storyboard, there will be an additional cost to them or else the change will not be made. In many cases, he'd better get the approval for the payment in writing.

The point is to keep these details and all bothersome politicking away from the director's concern or even his notice. The director looks to the A.D. to take care of the production and to take care of him. He needs the A.D. to be an assistant but also, at the same time, a leader of men. A director caps it with:

> Yes. Not just to show up in jeans and all wiped out from the night before. This is a very important responsibility. Because people will notice; everybody notices everybody else. And when an A.D. really contributes, at the end of the day they say, "Boy, wasn't he terrific" or "This one is great." All directors evaluate every job (an A.D. does). We don't just let it go by. Somebody screws up, that's evaluated too.

11

The Director of Photography

IT MIGHT SEEM ridiculously obvious to state that the vital, basic measurement in the choice of a Director of Photography is the ability of the director to communicate with him. Getting the exact—the meticulously exact—picture from the D.P. that you have painstakingly described to him is not very common. The director viewing his rushes is constantly grimacing: "It should have been just a little faster pan." "It should have been framed more to the right . . . to the left . . . higher . . . lower. . . ." "He should have led her; she's too centered." "It's all too bright . . . too dark. . . ." Ad infinitum. Seldom is the communication wrong between two good professionals; it's just almost never precise. It takes a lot more discussion and communication between the two if they have seldom or never worked together before. Therefore, the director is prone to hire a D.P. whom he knows and, most importantly, whom he trusts.

A director describes a D.P.:

> A guy who is flexible and a guy that ultimately I am confident will see things through my eyes without me having to necessarily block every shot. I usually do block most shots, but you work with a cameraman often enough whose work you respect, and who you usually respect as a person, someway—not all ways—yet, I would like to have him as my best friend. But someone who knows what my eyes are all about so that on an elaborately choreographed shot where everything is moving—the camera and actors—he'll see a frame the way I see it and I'm not going to discuss it with him.

Another director:

> There are certain cameramen . . . I don't even have to look through the camera. I can say, "Let's set up just above the knees," or "Give me a

closeup that I can really cut." Working with people, after a while they get to know you, too. (Then) I rarely have to look through the camera; they know where I want to be. I make some minor adjustments, but for the most part they get pretty good compositions.

The director, then, will work with the D.P. he knows for many good reasons. At that, each takes careful handling and guidance. The younger director, for example, has an additional problem. Working with a D.P. of long experience, he must find that delicate point between using the knowledge of the D.P. without relinquishing the reins of decision. This always requires tact and a good deal of inner strength.

To elicit the maximum possible input from the D.P., one unhappy fact of financial life of TV commercial producing must be severely questioned: The D.P. most often appears on the set and asks that frightening question, "What are we doing?" Because the cost is seldom added to the budget, the D.P. is not hired a day before the shoot; he arrives never having seen the storyboard. Perhaps he has been told over the telephone what the gist of the job is and asked what should be done to overcome some visual problem—but seldom anything else. The price for saving that day's pay is high in shooting time lost and the loss of the D.P.'s creative ideas, which are usually quite valid and useful.

In the case of the D.P., the dictum of finding the right man for the specific job holds very true. The director can look to some D.P.s for exceptional speed, to some for a special ability to shoot high fashion, to some for dramatic lighting. This "type-casting" or "pigeonholing" is as infuriating to most D.P.s as it is to directors. Each knows he can do almost any type of photography as well as anyone else can. But, it's a fact of production life. One director explains:

> I choose different cameramen for different jobs. It's not in terms of their photographic competence. If I'm going to do four days of vacuums or scrubbing power, I might choose someone who has the patience, the lasting power. Some people get impatient and bored with four days solid shooting. I can't afford that. Their personalities are important. I look for someone whose judgment I feel comfortable with. You get to read different people differently. You know when he says "good" a certain way, whether it was really good or not.

It doesn't take long to find out what kind of an "eye" the D.P. has—his compositions; his discoveries of elements to include or exclude in the frame that the director has not noticed or concerned himself with; his understanding and appreciation of the play of lights when the switch is put on or off during a shot; his directing of the viewer's eye to the correct element in the frame and so on. He will suggest the use of diffusions or smoke or colors. He will use filters to warm or cool a scene, depending on the need. He will, in short, use every technical possibility and trick to achieve in specific what the director is asking for in general: he will keep in mind that photography is an art and his function is not merely to present a picture that is clear and sharp. Like the director, his attitude toward the production must involve a total interest and dedication. D.P.s who shoot feature films find that the TV commercial is not only a means of additional income, but a break in their normal routine. They get the opportunity to shoot an occasional day, instead of the concentrated bulk of shooting for a feature and then the long layoffs. In addition, the TV commercial gives them the exposure to different challenges day to day, plus the excitement of trying new techniques and ideas.

Given the occasional need to find a new cameraman, a director must exert as much energy and concern as though he were seeking, well, not a new wife, but at least a new mistress. A director bemoans:

> I guess the way to start is to look at reels of his work and see whose work you respect. But, that's really a bad beginning. It has to do with how you get along with people as to whether he can do the job great. I don't presume that everyone is going to be professional on the set. . . . You have to look at a reel and say, "Yeah, I like the way he does that, the way he lights, the camera moves." And even then, of course, you don't know who's responsible for that conception. I've seen reels that I loved and (then) worked with the guys and they've been disasters.

Again, as with every other man on the crew, the D.P. wants his personal work to look as good as possible, sometimes even despite the reasonable need of budget and speed. One D.P. said:

> You can say slow is careful, but slow is not always careful, slow is frequently slow. I can't bear that. I love to keep moving, as quickly as possible, without anyone feeling that we're hurrying things just for the sake of getting it in eight hours.

The director is dependent on his D.P. for the very movement of the production. The D.P., after all, usually decides on who should be the assistant cameraman and, at least, the head gaffer. How well, and how swiftly, they work together is a key factor in the speed of operation.

I have found that even with the best of crews, it is of primary concern to the director to set the pattern of pace immediately in the morning. It is never a simple task, curiously, to get all the pertinent people together, cast and crew, to block out the first scene. When the D.P. and gaffer know what is expected, they will get to work and be quite content that all is going well. However, it takes, first, the preparedness of the director when he walks onto the set; it takes getting the makeup people to let the talent out of their grasps and not ask for the "just a couple of minutes more" that can stretch out into an hour; and it takes the gentle whip of the A.D. to push (physically, often enough) the D.P., gaffer, prop, script and other personnel away from the coffee complete with the long tale of what happened in 1972 and toward the director, who would like to speak to them.

The D.P. takes over after the director's talk. He has the content and mood of the scene in hand and it's time for the director's coffee—but never the end of his watchfulness. A director should have an eye and knowledge sufficiently adequate to determine whether the composition and the lighting are going in the direction he has indicated. Every artist tends to paint a picture according to his personality and D.P.s are no exception. He may be creating a beautiful picture or mood, but it may be his own concept.

The D.P. has other concerns as well.

> He also is right there when the lighting is done on the set. He changes it when it is necessary as I do many times. If it is not right I immediately change it because I can't wait until it is all finished. I see a lighting director or cinematographer taking a wrong tack on setting the lighting that I know instinctively is wrong, I don't want to wait until it is completely finished to tell them it is wrong, because (then) you have eaten up another hour of valuable time. I'll stop it right then and there or bust.

> Well, I'm very involved in lighting; I think it's sensational. I use a lot of color gel for everything. It may be that they used to do this in nineteen-twenty all the time. Nothing new. I've been on plenty of sets with just regular lighting, but I enjoy doing a little bit more: cross-lighting with little colors in between.
> . . . I'm always asking questions and making suggestions to the gaffers.

Obviously then, each director involves himself more or less in the actual cinematography as is his wont. Many directors in TV commercial production who do use D.P.s often operate the cameras themselves, some all the time and some on necessary occasions. About the hyphenated function of director-cameraman, more later.

Let us not forget that the D.P. also has the agency and client folk riding on his finder, too. Most often, they will want to know, even for the bid, who the D.P. will be. They will often make a specific choice of those proffered; sometimes they will ask for a certain person, even someone with whom the production company or director has never worked.

One director told me a long story of the production where a D.P., not of his choice or ken, was forced on him for a shoot. At one point there was a disagreement between the director and D.P. about the lighting of a set. The D.P. went over immediately to his "friend" at the agency. The director then reported:

> And even though I'm a cameraman-director, the agency man says, "Well, I think he's right." What are you gonna do, walk off the set? Well, you state your opinion. And you make it as emphatic as possible. Then you have to go on. They are the client in essence, too. So, lo and behold, it comes out on the editing machine and, "Oh, my God, the lighting's wrong. Gee, we're sorry. Can we print it up in the lab?"

For videotape lighting, the ability to see the completed picture on the video screen even while the lighting is going on is a great source of information and satisfaction to the D.P. However, the director, makeup person, agency and client folk are there to lend their assistance and viewpoint; it is too often lighting by committee.

12

The Director-Cameraman

THE ADAGE APPLIES to the Director-Cameraman: "If you want some stupid s.o.b. to do something right, do it yourself." At the very least, there is no problem of incorrect communication. What the director wants, the cameraman will understand and get it for him *exactly*—and that's no small hurdle hurdled. When a scene is shot, a director hopes that the cameraman got the scene as the director had envisioned it. The director-cameraman knows without doubt that he's got it. He planned the visual, set it up for himself and saw himself get it. Exactly.

During the shoot, there is one less cook to spoil the broth, one less creative attitude and argument to deal with, one less personality and sensitivity to handle and assuage. For the agency, there is one less person to convince and bring back to the client's need and thinking. Also, in the preparation and pre-production meetings, they had the opportunity to speak with the D.P. since the director was also the D.P. and met with them. There is a feeling that, if the director understands the agency, there will be no D.P. to lead them inadvertently away from the planned design.

The director-cameramen proffer those arguments in favor of their dual functions. They have many more reasons why the role of D.-C. is valuable. Those directors who argue against the combination of responsibilities liken it, generally, to an overloaded electrical circuit: It's great to have all the electrical appliances available to you but what good are they if the fuse blows? The anti-D.-C.s say that the many values are negated because the D.-C. cannot do both jobs well at the same time. Let's hear it from both sides:

Speaking of one problem that arises when the director uses a cameraman, one director-cameraman said:

> The poor son-of-a-bitch (D.P.) is there and he's thinking: "Oh, God! Do I have the balls to ask for another take?" But you're the director. If you want another take, you take it, take ten, take twenty if you want. It's your money; it's *my* money. There's one director here and it's my dough. If I screw up and I want another take, I do it. I do it; I don't have to be asked.

Another D.-C. says that when he scouts locations himself, he shoots stills with the same stock he is planning to use and is far ahead in the decisions of choice of location, with regard to factors to be included in the frame and the resolving of visual problems to be faced.

Another D.-C.:

> Oh, that's easy. I mean, lighting is easy. If you know what you want, there's no trick to it. First of all, you get yourself the best gaffer you can get. I've been doing it a lot of years now. I taught myself lighting from watching movies and asking a lot of questions. You can pick up a lot about lighting, surprisingly enough, when you read about old directors of photography. There are a lot of journals and magazines.

Another D.-C. refers to directing as the choreographing of different movements—and how can you mold the pattern if you don't see precisely where everything is and where it's going?

And others say:

> Operating a camera is the same thing. It's an extension of your body, and that goes for any form of it. On occasion, when I do have to handle details that are very difficult, I'll call in an operator; I set up a second camera. That happens occasionally. Or if the dialogue is intricate or if I just get weary, I'll bring in somebody else. I mean, I'm not a *fool* and I want the best possible work. But, when I used to be just a director, I used to stand by the camera and smoke three packs of cigarettes or just tense myself up and lose five pounds in the course of a day just from nerves. And the camera is good. It gives you something to hold on to. It's like when you're a little kid, you play with your dick. It's great, and the camera is just like that to me. It's exciting; I can hide behind it; I can amuse myself with it; I can have fun by myself. I can do all those things and I love it. It does not get in my way and I don't think it has inhibited my work in any way.

> I was not only able to do both, but I was able to purify my work, and I didn't make unnecessarily complicated shots anymore to prove my technical virtuosity. I went more for story content; I simplified my technique. That allowed me to observe the action as well as the performance as well as make smooth shots. The operation of the camera becomes instinctive to you, almost the same as tying your shoelaces in the dark.

Still another argument for the D.-C. is that knowledge of what the camera can do saves time as well as giving an extra facility to the director to bring new and interesting ideas to the shoot.

But:

> It's very hard to be a director-cameraman.

> I think the first thing anybody needs as a director is the ability to sustain himself physically through the day. If you can't make it to midnight during a long shoot, don't be a director. If you're winded by two in the afternoon, forget it. You've got to be as sharp as possible at midnight as you were at eight-thirty in the morning. A director working with a cameraman has the advantage that he is relieved from time to time. He can stop and say, "Okay, do your thing," and he goes off and talks to the agency or the talent.

> When you work as a director-cameraman, you're up there constantly because you're dealing with a crew, the cutters, the lights, the dolly. You don't get any rest and it's tough. It's a hell of a lot tougher than just being a director or a cameraman basically because your time is totally occupied.

> I disagree with those director-cameraman techniques, too. Because I look through the lens and I operate the camera. I've been doing it now for a couple of years. Not exclusively. I tell you that you cannot see the boom shadow—the woman crossing in front of the light where the light hits her wrong because she's off her mark—and watch the performance and judge whether the zoom timing is good. I don't care how good you are.

The D.-C. will argue that the director entrusting the camera to someone else sees the entire scene happening. He does not isolate that portion of the action that is being photographed. A director who has peered through the eyepiece several thousand times answers:

> Yes, at this point, yes. Because I already have enough experience—enough on-the-set training—(to) know exactly what a seventy-five millimeter is doing, what a nine millimeter is doing if you're shooting sixteen millimeter. Already my eye thinks in terms of the lens.

There is a school of thought that decries any technical knowledge of the camera at all. It follows the theory that the ignorance relieves any restrictions on creativity; not knowing in advance what traditionally can *not* be done allows more freedom to come up with new and innovative ideas.

> In tape, I really think that it should not be the same person. It should be a separate lighting director for tape. It is infinitely more difficult to light well on tape than on film. Film has its automatic gray scale built in. You could throw a soft light on a film set and that's all you need. The stuff comes out looking good with a soft light because every little nuance and every little shading of gray will be picked up on a piece of film. You try that on tape and it's a disaster because everything will look flat and washed out.

> . . . after that I became a tape cameraman and from that I became a director. I never really thought as a cameraman-director. Some of them are quite good and really believe in what they do. I find it very difficult to do both at the same time. If I had someone to do the lighting, I could do the camera and directing; I do that on occasion. If a shot is very intricate or it takes me too

long to try to explain exactly what should be done, I grab the camera and I'll do it by myself. I do that quite frequently. . . . If you're shooting a tabletop or someone standing up making a pitch to the camera—that could be done. But, if you're doing something that has drama to it or you have people reacting to people, it really needs a hundred percent of the director's ability. More power to the guys who do it because I don't know how in the hell they do it.

Finally:

There are certain commercials where I think that can work. If you're doing inanimate objects, if you're doing documentary type where you don't control the people but you're recording actuality happening, I think that works. But I think that for the majority of commercials it does not work. I think that either one of those jobs is a full-time job—directing or camera. For a guy to attempt both is, I think, a very bad mistake. I don't see how you can look through the lens, worry about the framing and the line-reading at the same time, or whether the scene has developed with the inner rhythm that you want, still wondering (if) your zoom is smooth, (if) there is a little chatter—I find the two things don't mix. . . . I don't believe in it.

13

The Assistant Cameraman

PERHAPS UNIQUE IN THIS WORLD is the job whose efficiency is measured by a hairline. The tiniest tip of a hair caught in the gate of a camera and allowed to remain there unnoticed can destroy thousands and tens of thousands of dollars of production. The man whose function it is to see that this does not happen is the Assistant Cameraman.

When a director starts to work in the morning, he will soon, or immediately, get to the camera to look through and prepare his shot. Just as he assumes that the set will be standing, he assumes that the camera will be ready for him and that the assistant cameraman is there, instantly, ready to help: to focus the lens roughly on the director's subject; to zoom; to move or raise or lower the camera. The director expects the A.C. to have all the lenses at hand. Since the director will walk up to the camera many times a day, he does not want to deal with any bumbling, inefficiency, or slothfulness. The most gentle of directors is disturbed when he cannot mumble into the camera, "I want the focus on the man in the foreground," and have it happen as though he were talking into a robot machine. That miraculous A.C. is there, always, functioning quietly with all his gears perfectly meshed.

But, it's a robot with an intelligent human head. The A.C. should be aware of what's going on; what the scene is trying to do. He should be on top of the scene's content while the director is setting up and during each shot as it is being made. For the director, the good A.C. is most valuable during setting-up time. I have had good A.C.s who even consider it their responsibility—not the A.D.s or D.P.s—to make sure the dolly grip is standing close by when the director walks up to the camera. Then everyone is immediately ready to change

SOL GOODNOFF

FORGET IT AL, THERE'S NO TIME!

the camera's position or make a trial move or such. For my own taste, I prefer that this kind of operation—indeed, the whole day's shoot—take place with a smooth quiet ease—and mostly quiet. I do not like to have the A.C. gab at me while I'm dreaming up an angle or complain bitterly out loud about his equipment. If there is any specific problem about equipment, the A.C. should take it up, out of the director's hearing, with the A.D. or the D.P. It certainly is true that the squeaky wheel gets the most oil and the efficient A.C.'s work goes by absolutely unnoticed, but he should toot his horn in some other way than bring the director's attention to himself; the experienced director will, after the day's shoot, review the day and remember the A.C.'s efficiency only because there was no trouble. However, many directors—and that includes me—appreciate suggestions from the individuals on the crew; some directors find this distracting and time consuming. Most will be polite nonetheless, and the crew members must determine what kind of a director they are dealing with.

The busy A.C. has much to contend with. He watches out for flaring lights hitting the lens; he must be sure that the microphone boom and its shadow are kept out of the frame, that the camera and its many accessories are in meticulous working order and that whatever may be called for, whether it is a certain strength diopter or the grip's hi-hat, is close at hand. A terrible change of rhythm is imposed on the director when he must wait for a magazine to be reloaded; there certainly should be sufficient magazines loaded with film. There absolutely must be a sufficiency of charged batteries to last an entire day. If either of these is not about in reasonable number, the used magazines should be reloaded during those minutes when no one notices that the A.C. is in the darkroom or changing bag. The used batteries should be recharged with the same magic. They must be done and ready so that the forward movement is never stopped. This, of course, can only happen with an A.C. who appreciates his responsibility and is concerned that he never falters or attracts attention to his job.

Another personality aspect required of this painstaking worrywart is the strength of character to hold off all the nervous people rushing him to move his camera from one setup to the next by saying, "Wait until I check the gate." There is not a single reasonable professional on stage who will object to the time taken to check the camera for those little pieces of hair or grit or flecks of film.

Another assuredness of his personality must reflect itself in his communications when he suspects that there may be a problem—with his focus or with the camera or whatever. If he is weak, he may keep quiet and pray that the good Lord was with him and no one will know. If he is a confident professional, and he should be, he will tell the D.P. about the problem before the move to the next shot. The D.P. and the director are owed this information.

On those occasions when there is no script supervisor for some unusual reason, the A.C. is looked to to keep some kind of notes about the scenes. No matter what the union rules are, I am greatly disturbed by an A.C. who says to me, in the moment of that emergency, "I only mark down which takes to print." I expect the A.C. to label the cans with every possible important piece of information before sending the film to the lab. I've seen too many cans go astray, film shipped to wrong places or even film developed incorrectly because an A.C. labeled the can cryptically or with insufficient information.

Generally, the director assumes that the good A.C. is doing his job quietly. He is keeping the lenses dusted, tape-measuring the focal points of the scenes, checking the speed of the camera, the camera level and on ad infinitum. He is worrying about and fussing over and fondling his camera and its parts.

Some comments about the job:

> He sticks right on your ear. . . . It's like the best caddy for the golf pro. You don't need somebody to ask, "Hey, would you give me a number two." It should be right there. And that is as simple as it comes down to, that he is there and as alert from the time the guy starts until the end of the day.

> A good assistant cameraman, professional assistant cameraman, they're highly regarded. They don't just sit down and say "Let me have another cup of

coffee and shake this.'' They're there. And those guys make a lot of money. They're very valuable. They don't want to be anything different.

Is there something else that they have to do? If there is, let them go do it. It's as simple as that. It's that concentration.

14

The Continuity Supervisor

I REMEMBER WHEN they were called script girls. Later, script clerks, when men entered the field. Call them what you will, they can be life savers, averters of disasters; they are dedicated guardians of the right. In the words of a director:

> I try to sit down immediately with the script girl, the A.D. and whoever is in charge of the agency, usually the producer, get a unanimity of opinion on what the day is going to be like, what shot is going where, what the interpretation is and roughly what time it should take. That's usually accomplished in the first fifteen minutes of the day. Then, I feel like I can do my job. I always make that my first order of business. I rely very heavily on the script girl.

The most important function of the director at that time is to get the script person to understand the shoot. The script person has almost always shown up on the set with absolutely no knowledge of the storyboard; it's another one-day shoot, that's all. The immediate goal of the script person is to get a timing of each scene, since that is the major aspect of the job. However, the director should try to change the focus and get the script person to understand the whole job and the director's intent. Almost never do I get a script person who will say to me at one point something like, "But shouldn't you have a closeup here?" That would indicate a grasp of the day's work; it never seems to take precedence over the timing.

Almost all directors stress the need to cover the storyboard as it is presented, making certain that each frame drawn is reproduced in the shooting. Then, the director feels free—and obliged—to add his personal concepts and experimentations. Normally, the director feels imposed upon and perhaps subconsciously negative about shooting the storyboard as drawn; he prefers his own ideas. There is where the need of a good script person shows itself clearly. The director will forget—really forget—to make one of the obligatory shots.

The suggestions I look to from a script person are more than that mechanical. Once again, in the rush of the forward movement of a shoot, the director may well overlook a shot never called for or thought about but one that might potentially be quite useful. Let us say, a reaction shot of a listener during an actor's peroration. Such a shot is invaluable, of course, to the editor, who might want to shorten or change takes or otherwise amend the original take. A script person who makes such a suggestion, whether or not the director heeds it, is my kind of person. This helpful needling applies to many different shots: additional closeups, cutaways, reactions and so on.

I do not want to minimize the importance of the correct execution of the technical aspects of the job. It behooves the director to cast an occasional eye on the correctness of the slating and the printing of the correct takes, to see to it that the script person checks out the desired takes at the end of the day with the assistant cameraman and the sound mixer. The script notes should then be sent on its way to the editor and so forth.

Nor do I belittle in any way the frighteningly vital importance of correct timing in the shooting of television commercials. Where a demonstration or scene must be filmed in three seconds, no more, the script person earns every dollar in the envelope. The thumb on the stop-watch tripper must be alert, agile and certain. The mind behind that thumb had better not be hung over or apathetic. Just recently I worked with a new script person for the first time and I could not trust her all day long. It seems that, in this simple shoot, the narrator's sound track was already supplied. The script girl came in and started to read the copy out loud, timing the scenes. In consternation, I pointed out to her that the only correct timings could be taken off the completed recording. That took a little while to sink in and, with a devil-may-care laugh, she told me she hadn't slept much the night before . . .

Another director speaks:

> I don't like a script girl who, after the first take, asks me whether to print or
> not. (I prefer) somebody who will go through the board and look for where
> we might pick up half a second somewhere else—make that contribution, that
> suggestion, all with good judgment. Not just a recording person but (one) who
> is actively trying to solve problems when they exist. That's a very important
> person.

I cannot remember one incident where I was let down in the major area of continuity supervision: matching. Every person I have ever worked with has kept a furious watch over each take and angle, which is the basic function of the supervisor: is the glass raised with the correct hand, the tie worn the same way, the people in the identical positions, the talent heading in the correct direction and so on. This is not to say that they were always correct, only most

SOL GOODNOFF

I'M KINDA' WORRIED ABOUT THE TIMINGS.

of the time. A major job of the director, of course, is to pay as much attention to these details as his script person, so that a memory slip on the part of either can be discussed—I even called for a vote by the crew at one rare impasse.

Then, there's the "line," that immutable 180-degree line which, when crossed for another angle of the same scene, causes the actors to jump from one side of the screen to the other. The script person as continuity supervisor is in charge of that line. And it's not an easy job:

> That one, boy, you learn the hard way. Going over the line, around the line, under the line . . . The hardest thing for a director would be screen direction, to be able to feel that without having the script girl do it all the time. You know, in tape there is an advantage over film. You can always play it back and check it. My script girl is an associate director and she's very good, got a memory like a hawk and a pair of eyes like a hawk. Numerous times, she'll say, "Let's go back and look at it." Now, some script girls are just super. They have everything, really they do. I've watched them: little drawings and figures. They're very good.

> And the other thing is exiting and entering the set. That's in every director's primer. But you learn it. If he goes out camera right, he's gotta come in camera left. It's so easy but then you get all mixed up. I remember learning that. And then, if you've actually moved the camera to another set and he's

making his entrance and the camera's facing a different direction—there's a song in *Oliver*, "I Guess I Have to Think It out Again," which is a perfect thing for a director to do. If you get a good script girl, they know it backwards.

Everyone has his own theory on the subject of the 180-degree reverse shot, whether you then move to the left or right or whether you do it at all. The argument is a manifestation of the permissiveness of today's editing and the frustration of the continuity supervisor. In days gone by, the audience would accept the concept that time has passed from one scene to another only if there was a dissolve or fade in/fade out between scenes. In the sophistication of the viewers, this dictum became obsolete as, indeed, almost all rules are being violated or at least questioned today. Just as an accomplished painter can, after he has learned the traditions of his art, break all the rules, so a director should heed his continuity supervisor's cautions and then break out into whatever form he sees fit.

One director argues:

> You don't feel (the edit) because it's shot correctly. There is a smoothness or there is a continuity of the change of the pictures made by using the rules of screen direction. Otherwise it might be very jarring to the human eye; therefore you would lose the copy point that has to be said.

A creative director of an agency counters:

> So what? Granted that the glass will be in his right hand in one scene and then jump to his left in the next. So what? If the visual works best that way, then those rules don't matter.

Do not be concerned, dear continuity supervisor—there will always be a dire need for your assistance even if all continuity as we know it goes out the window. The directors know full well how much the agency folk lean on you for information and discussions about copy and timings and props and all the minutiae with which they are too embarrassed or decent to bother the director. We know how much effort and patience it takes to handle their problems, and we are grateful for your ability to communicate.

Not that we love every part of you. It is remarkable how many directors have the identical complaint: the script people are constantly chatting and gossiping with the crew members, most times, it seems, with the sound men. For myself, I hate that mumbling and sometimes laughter that is distracting me or making my communication with the talent and others difficult. What gripes me more—and is mentioned often by other directors—is the script person who always manages to speak to the talent in the wrong tone for the occasion or for the talent's personality. A script person can inform talent that a mistake has been made with a voice that barely, if at all, conceals a sneer or an impatience or derision or disgust or even anger. It can embarrass or confuse or distract or anger or freeze and in many ways hurt the performer, his performance, his memory, his relationship with the director and crew. I have often asked the script person to communicate with me and not the talent—and in a low voice.

I rely very heavily on the script girl/person. I always opt for a quiet, intelligent person. It sounds like motherhood, but there are people like that. I hate people like ————, that whole crowd. She's always auditioning for something. I'm not sure what it is; it certainly is not the job at hand. They make noise and noise and confusion means mistakes.

Well, a script supervisor is strictly a good technician. And, if she's good, she'll be tough. She won't let you say, "Okay, we'll make up the time on the next scene." She knows goddamn well the next scene's gonna run even longer. And, with the time restrictions we have, you really have to be careful. If you get a good script supervisor, you want to carry her with you as long as possible. My attitude toward the crew is, again, like Ingmar Bergman. He likes to feel that every job is like going on a picnic and as long as you're going on a picnic, you might as well go with friends. I think that's the way I feel about the crew.

15

Allied Crafts

LET ME TOUCH ON some other crafts that the director must deal with:

THE SOUND RECORDIST

There are too few directors who pay sufficient attention to the quality of sound recording they are getting. The visual, naturally, takes precedence, but a microphone is more than an annoyance to the cameraman and something that has to be kept out of the shot. It represents an assuredness that the viewer will ultimately understand and receive the maximum impact from your communication—and communication is, after all, the name of the game. The audience for a television commercial will not have to strain to understand what the players are saying. Your art form is called audio-visual, not the other way around. The director, complain the recordists, spends all his time trying to get the best visual effects and then hurries the sound crew along to save time. It would be better if the director spent at least a few minutes with the sound people to discuss ways to achieve the best possible sound recording.

There are a few directors who like to wear headsets while the scene is going on. I have found, however, that even among them the reason for the headsets is the help it gives them to concentrate on the scene itself and block out extraneous sounds. However, the headsets must automatically inform them of the quality of the sound.

In most other cases, the director puts all his trust and faith in the sound crew. All he asks—and it's not easy to get it—is that the mixer tell him loud and clear whether the sound is okay or not. Just that, but it's more often the case that the answer he gets is a purposefully noncommittal one. If the cameraman said he wasn't certain, wouldn't you do another take? How often does the director accept a tentative "pretty good" from the soundman and move on to the next scene?

Perhaps behind this director's thinking is the knowledge that, in an emergency, the track can be looped and a better sound dubbed in. Looping for TV commercials has long since gone out of style. What with radio mikes and almost invisibly tiny mikes and increasingly superb technical advances in sound recording, the unreal and dead quality of looped sound has been avoided.

We have not as yet overcome totally the false perspective that the lavaliere microphone gives. The mike placed so close to the mouth gives the quality of a recording rather than that of natural sound. I think that that is what disturbs the soundman and elicits grudging approvals to sound takes, he is being compelled to compromise between what he knows is good and correct sound and a sound that will not, in the production, slow down the shooting with microphone shadows, boom in the shot and such, and b) a sound that will be intelligible and clear to the television viewer when the sound is played back to him finally on his audio-poor television set. So, he minimizes and sacrifices the true sound with its ambience to make sure the words are recorded loud and clear.

I wonder, too, whether his lack of sincere interest, the concern in his effort makes the soundman too apathetic in his function. I'm sure that the professional does his work as well as it can be done, just out of a functional pride in his work. Yet, perhaps that is why he's the guy who's always yakking away with the script person. Maybe he doesn't have enough to do.

I must quote this story about a soundman, It may have nothing to do with the subject other than indicating that a soundman can be the director's friend, but I just love the story. In the director's words:

> I lament, sometimes, not having elements that do attract agency people (such as wild histrionics while directing). A guy I worked for who is now a producer, was a director for a while. He had heard playback from people that he was too quiet on the set. There was not enough apparent emotion going on, not enough excitement. Yes, he was doing the job perfectly, but there was no compelling reason to go back to shoot with him. So, he arranged one time with the sound-man, the boom man, actually, to drop the boom in the middle of a take. Midway through the shoot, the guy did. Also, prearranged, he threw a tantrum. He said, "Get off my set: you'll never work with me again. You're a clumsy so and so!" (He) chased the guy off the set. (The) agency adored him, gave him three more packages after that. It can work.

THE PROPERTY MASTER

Outside prop, inside prop or set decorator, what the director needs is an octopus with eight different-sized arms. He must have superb taste, engineering acumen, mechanical genius and an overwhelming love of his craft. He should be able to communicate and be communicated with; he should have the consummate philosophy of life that will allow him to continue his effort without exploding at the agency folk, the scenic designer, the assistant director, the director the many others who will tell him how to do his job, find fault with his work and hurry him along at the same time. He must be able to read the mind of an inarticulate director and, above all, he must anticipate the needs that will arise during shooting.

The director should choose the prop man to fit the job. For example, one man is great on trick gadgets but he very well may be the type who doesn't particularly do well when heavy furniture has to be moved around a lot. The director can measure the worth of a prop man by noting several salient points: Does he understand what the shoot is about? Has he contemplated the needs of the production before the day's shoot? Has he tested the FX he will be called upon to produce before the moment of truth? Does he have three each of the breakable or spillable props—ten if a child must handle them? Does he stay on the set and keep watch over every prop to see that each looks and performs perfectly? Is he, indeed, a perfectionist? In a nutshell, as one director put it: ''The prop man I use to handle the props must be superb; he's worth his weight in gold.''

Unfortunately, the director cannot, when he uses a prop man for the first time, look into the kit that a prop man brings with him. In that magic box is an impossible amount of the weirdest items: assorted dyes, glycerine, razor blades, glitter, tiny saws and drills and jewelers' screwdrivers and metal shears and assorted hammers and pliers and clamps. He has all the basic types of adhesive tapes and pencils and pens and monofilament lines and cleaning and polishing and dulling equipment. I remember the old gag about the man who invented a banana with a feather and whistle attached so that if anyone should stop him on the street and ask him if he had a banana with a feather and whistle attached. . . .

Look to the prop man if you need anything at all; a good one knows his town inside out and sources for whatever you might dream up. There is an additional impishness in me; I delight in the need for an impossible prop or task. I grin when I challenge the prop man with it. You know what? He grins when challenged. We love it.

THE GAFFER

The head man of the electrical/lighting crew is certainly royalty in the hierarchy of a shooting crew. He is most often chosen by the director of photography or at least hired with the D.P.'s approval. Not only does he supervise his assistant (the Best Boy) and the other electrical men but the rest of the crew seem to bend a knee to his position in command. The best of gaffers work with

PROP
DEPT

SOL GOODNOFF

**O.K.,.GOT BOTH PRODUCTS... BUT
FORGOT WHICH IS THE BAD GUY!**

a quiet dignity and swift assuredness. Under his definite order and hand signals, the lights seem to appear, get set, scrimmed, focused and gelled with a surprising minimum of bedlam and a maximum of speed.

When the gaffer is called in on a production, he will often suggest, or insist, that the lights be preset the day before. Usually, this is an economical ploy, for it saves much overtime for the whole crew, for the talent and stage costs. The decision to set lights before the day of shooting is almost always relegated to the director. There are rare occasions when he will feel that the gaffer is over emphasizing the potential problems or, in some situations, he will know that the unavailability of the talent before a certain time, or some other delaying factor, will give the electrical crew enough time to set up on the morning of the shoot, which saves a day's pay for the gaffer's crew.

Unhappily, this decision takes a lot of guts and tact on the part of the director. The D.P. and gaffer consider their expertise questioned and they don't like it. The result may very well be reflected in a lighting situation that takes an inordinate time to accomplish. Did you ever see a crew slow down on purpose? Whew!

During a good shoot, the gaffer understands thoroughly what the D.P. is about in lighting a scene and goes about his work with great personal artistry. A picture—any picture—is only lights and shadows and colors. By any definition, a gaffer is an artist, even though he is mostly carrying out the lighting design of the D.P. He also knows the D.P.'s preferences and attitudes and anticipates what he will ask for, time after time.

Like every good crew member, he, too, will not turn his back on the set when the lighting is done. He will maintain a worried watch to see that no light is dark or incorrectly moved during a shot. Each change of the action by the director may very well call for an adjustment of a light or two. I urge directors to call upon their utmost patience when this "piddling" takes place and affects the rhythm of their directing. It's all for the good.

In the comparatively smaller crews of the TV commercial shoot, the gaffer will be all over the place setting and adjusting lights himself. This often requires the agility of a monkey combined with the strength of a bull. Add those abilities to his having the sensitivity of an artist as well as executive capabilities, and you can see that a good gaffer is quite an extraordinary man.

The gaffer may very well find himself squeezed under the dashboard of a moving automobile. Or, he may find it necessary to hang a light where there is no skyhook to hang it from. One director's experience:

> We had a case where we were shooting on a location upstate, doing a food shot, and we had to get some key lights on this long table we had with the product on it, and it was very, very tough. And we knew it was tough. We looked through the lens and it just wasn't there. The electrician hardly hesitated when he realized he wasn't getting it. There was an old moose head above. He went up and threw a plank across its antlers, put a couple of little lights up there and key-lit from the moose's head. It solved the problem—it made the table look gorgeous—and we accomplished the job without any real loss of time.

There are very few location shoots these days when a generator is taken along. The gaffer must find himself sufficient power from whatever source is available—and he does. I can almost swear that I've seen a gaffer get electrical power from the proverbial udder of a cow. I can tell you honestly that I knew one gaffer who had to moisten his fingers when he placed them on the bus bars of an electrical box, claiming that he couldn't get enough of a feeling if he didn't. Also, he said he could then tell whether he was getting a shock of 110, 220, or 440 volts! Honest!

Let me complete these short notes about the gaffer with a word about the wrap. It is, of course, usual for a director to shoot the long shot of a scene and then move in for closer shots, going closer and closer with each successive move. Thus, many, and then most of the lights used in the long shot are no longer necessary. The efficient gaffer will have his crew progressively wrap up those lights that are no longer needed so that the final wrap of the scene will be minimal. He saves the director a lot of time (money) this way. But heaven protect the bumbling director who forgets a long shot or changes his mind or is a bad planner and must then return to the long shot. . . .

THE HOME ECONOMIST

Home Economist—that's a weird title for the people who prepare our foods and tables. If there is one thing they pay little attention to, it's economy. They are after only the best and the most beautiful. If cooking is an art, then the combination of cooking plus the presentation of foods requires a most special eye as well as a delicate palate. The home economists, too, are quite special people. According to one director:

> I work with selected home economists who, I think, when they purchase the foods and prepare them, have a sense of design, a sense of taste as far as proportion and color, as far as selective elements, garnishing and arranging. . . .

> It is most unfortunate that the H.E. is usually not involved in the pre-production meeting of a spot that includes some important food shots. The H.E.'s input there would be most advantageous. The director himself should brief the H.E. on the needs, the look, the amounts of food required. The H.E. will then advise him of the help that is needed—sometimes two H.E.s are required, sometimes a helper or two. Whether an H.E. will accept a prop man as an assistant or insist on a professional H.E. is up to the relationships of the unions, as well as the production company's desires. The H.E. does the shopping for the food, all of which must be top drawer. Every vegetable purchased seems to have been the model for the Burpee seed catalogue. Every piece of meat looks like it can be happily eaten raw. The H.E., too, has special sources that cull the finest of viands for the shoot.

The director of a shoot must work in tandem with the H.E., as one explains:

> On a shoot day, after the home economist has ordered everything and starts preparing it, I review my schedule and what scenes I'm shooting. Sometimes this changes because some food preparations take longer than others. . . . So, based on the involvement of the home economist, we proceed in scheduling the scenes to be as productive as possible in the shoot.

The director might scan the facilities prepared for the H.E. before the shoot day. Normally, there should be a separate kitchen with running water facilities, plenty of counter space for work and storage, a double or counter-top oven, cook top, blender, can opener, dishes and utensils, refrigerator, freezer, paper towels, cloths, sponges. Any missing item can cause a stupid delay in the shoot. The H.E. is ordinarily called in an hour or so earlier than the basic crew so as to get all in order and start the cooking. By 8:30, the foods that can be used as stand-ins for the real things are ready and can be placed for lighting.

The director is also vitally interested in the H.E.s work as it progresses. Several comments from directors:

> As she is preparing it, I'm totally involved, so if there is a question about arranging it or about the mound of peas or potatoes or whatever, I can approve the finishing touches. Once that's done, we go to the set and start shooting. We often go through many takes on a dish, then the home economist is there to freshen it up or redo an area or brush some oil on. But, there can't be too much (of a) time-lapse between the final preparation and the shooting. That's very necessary.

Once you become motivated in the first scene, you may have to cool off because something is not ready. Then you have to charge up your batteries once more to get the feel of it all over again. You have a stop-and-go type of production, where there is no relative relationship from one scene to another, so it's important to keep the continuity going constantly, shooting constantly. When there is dead time, there . . . is a lack of feel and you have to get back into the swing of it. I always work with home economists who are spontaneous, who anticipate, who have things ready when I'm through with one scene and they're already working on another scene.

Pity the poor home economist. Can you see the dilemma? The director wants to have each food at the ready to move into the scene he's shooting as soon as he wants it. Almost no food looks its best when it is kept warmed; the juiciest, most appetizing foods are those which have just been freshly cooked. The H.E. can't win.

THE MAKEUP ARTIST

There is yet another artist with whom the director co-works—another individualistic personality, another varying viewpoint, another in the team to be led and simultaneously driven, another proud artist to be steered toward the director's view.

The director has little time to spend on the particulars of makeup, certainly little time to be at all creative in the art of makeup. At best, he hopes for a result that is functional. The director's most important contribution is an articulate description of the end result he is seeking and this requires a knowledge and subsequent decision of what he wants.

In the traditional type of commercial, the makeup called for is the "natural" look. This is done so often that the director, or makeup person, may very well become lulled into using the same approach in most all circumstances. A bride, for example, should look more glamorous, a tired housewife, dull. But for a girl out on the town, you might pull all stops out, except that the makeup must complement the individual, the situation and the environment. Because it is easier to have someone else do your work, or because it may not seem to be worth the hassle while you have so many other things to oversee, the director may easily fall into the trap of allowing the agency folk to supervise the makeup. Wrong! Makeup is a vital part of the visual message, even though the spot may be about roach powder. The director has been hired to get the best possible picture up there and he'd better earn his pay. This is especially true of commercials about cosmetics. If the director is not sufficiently knowledgeable about makeup, then that is one product type he should pass. Don't throw away the impression others have of your expertise in so many other fields by standing there with a lost look while the makeup person takes your place in the jousts with agency folk!

Even in spots that call for the least attention to makeup, problems do appear. Talent may show up with too much natural suntan, or not enough, or pimples or scars or facial or body hair that had gone unnoticed or had been cleverly hidden during casting. The surprises come often enough; it is always best to arm the makeup person in advance with as much information as you have. Then the artist can show up with the kit prepared for that particular job and those known problems.

The job does have its problems, according to one makeup artist:

> Sometimes the lighting is very bad in my makeup room. Sometimes we do makeup in a hallway or in a car, in so many different places where there are no lights—or different (lights than) they have on stage. It's amazing what bad lighting can do to makeup.

Coming from a bluish light in the makeup room into a reddish-lit stage can totally change the look of the makeup. Indeed, I once walked into a good makeup room and approved the makeup of the actress (standing in her slip), but when she walked on stage, the look was ghastly. The orange-colored wardrobe she wae wearing reflected precisely the wrong color for her makeup. The color of a set, too, whether background or foreground, affects the makeup tone.

A reasonably special expertise is required in the application of makeup for videotape production. Here, fortunately, the director can see (on a perfect monitor) what the end result will be and can easily call for any corrections.

The monitor is a blessing, too, when no amount of makeup changes seem to help a bad look. Too often, the makeup person is blamed for inadequate or wrong lighting. A harsh shadow in the wrong place can be a disaster. Most good makeup people have sufficient knowledge (and fortitude) to tell the D.P. of his lighting mistake.

Then, again, there are times when it is easier to change or correct a bit of makeup than to change the lighting or some set colors. The D.P. and the makeup person (along with the director's two cents) should be able to choose this option in time.

Speaking of the director's two cents, one makeup person made this plea to directors:

> Just be kind, respectful and have lots of patience even when you have to work fast and time is very important. But again, just—no matter how it bothers you inside—try to relax. That's the only way to get me to work better.

The makeup persons, too, ask that the director drop in the morning of the shoot to say hello—often many directors pay no attention to the makeup people until they are annoyed for some reason. Say goodnight, too. One makeup person swore to me that at a recent shoot, she never found out who the director—or even the assistant director—was!

Okay, but how about the directors' major gripe? One director says that he places a chair near his and informs the A.D. to order the makeup person to sit there throughout the production time. Where do they go and why can't we find them when we need them? The proverbial joke is the "call" for Makeup. T'aint funny. That joke may never have started if the makeup person had always been there doing his job. If that were the case, the first one to realize the need for a makeup adjustment would be the makeup person.

THE EDITOR

Last, but not least, is the Editor. A director speaks:

> Well, like all things, time changes everything. At one point we had an editor on staff for over five years and I was totally involved with editing. To me, shooting is one thing and finishing is the optimum of everything. When we had editorial services in our own studio, it was the greatest pleasure and privilege to be involved in editing. I just loved it. I think, with editing, a director becomes much more perceptive. He can see things, do things by degrees and enhance a commercial enormously. I would say that the economics of production, of utilizing specialists, has resulted in everything becoming fragmented. And sometimes such specialization results in lack of motivation, of interest, of the same continuity that you perceive at the initial stages.

And from other directors:

> Editing is, for me, many years later in the business, almost a lost cause, I'm sorry to say. I will always go to the first editing session and make my recommendations in an attempt to get something resembling a first cut—which is really a kind of fiction if you're working with the agency people. I try to get my ideas through, but those battles are very quickly lost because the agency had other things in mind. They will give up a good performance for a shorter take that allows the product to be on longer at the end. I've fought that battle often enough to know that very rarely will you win, very rarely will an agency producer or creative team listen to you and say, "You're right."

> After fighting for the first editing day, or for a couple of hours, I just give up; it's as simple as that.

> The agency pushes you out. They want to play. They want (you) to get out of the office.

Almost every director feels this great loss. He is, after all, a total filmmaker. Most often, he has had long experience in editing and loves the craft. A great potential of his growth is taken away from him. How better to learn from your mistakes than when you are faced with the obligation to overcome them in editing. You don't make the same mistake often after that. But, you don't learn if the editor "saves" you and you never even hear about the particular.

It is not possible for a director to articulate every cut he has planned—certainly not every different *possible* cut—to the script person for her notes to the editor. As the editing proceeds, he will recall what the plan or possibility was. He must be at the editing sessions to offer this input. The director cares. The production was *his* baby for a while and he is quite concerned about how it is finally going to be put together—for his own peace of mind, for his own dignity. His business acumen tells him that a basic reason for his being kept away from the editing is money. My survey of directors proves to me that a system of lower pay for editing time would be quite acceptable to almost all television commercial directors.

The director, knowing that the final editing is out of his control, can go in either of two directions. The first (and unfortunate) road is to shoot only the scenes indicated—and each only long enough so that the editing must follow his original design, there being no alternative. This can very well result in a loss of the effectiveness of the commercial. The other alternative is to overshoot; this is costly and a waste but at least it offers the editor every possible combination and permutation of cuts. As directors express it:

> If I know I'm going to supervise it myself, I give myself a lot more coverage. I try to plan it so that I can give the editor (or myself, if I'm going to supervise the editing) not only everything he needs, but alternative situations, either to pick up the pace or slow (it) down, play long shots long, play 'em short, use various angles.

> Sometimes I overshoot. I overshoot now because I own the company. Nobody is saying, "Why did you go over the film budget?" And, again, there is something for everybody.

Because I hold a brief for the director's active participation in the editing process, please understand that I am not in any way denigrating that other vital artist, the editor. That the editor often enough "saves" the director is no idle statement. That the editor often enough adds a sparkle and zest to an otherwise dull commercial is absolutely true. My point and plea is that the two heads, director and editor, are needed for the best possible result. Nor do I minimize the input of agency producer, art director and all the others. They are talented, knowledgeable people; it's just that they did not visualize the minute specifics of each shot as the director did and they should contemplate what's in the director's head. They should appreciate the minutiae of the director's version and vision.

Still, the editor, and the editor alone, has, in addition to his special talent, a treasure to add to the effort. Neither the director nor producer nor any agency person can bring to the editing the unique perspective that the editor can. He alone has not been encumbered with the past, with the meetings and the dicta and the nonsenses and the difficulties of shooting and the preconceived ideas. He alone can truly measure good from bad in terms of audience acceptability and effectiveness with total disregard for politics and personalities and problems. His should be a strong voice and vote.

The classic example of editing is the closeup of a face. The director knows the emotion he was looking for—and achieved—in shooting the face. The agency folk have their own version of the particular emotion they see. The editor, virgin to these preconceptions, sees only a face. In editing, the emotion that the audience will finally see in the face is that which the sequence of cuts before the appearance of the closeup leads the audience to see. This is the editor's art and his strength. Depending on his cuts, he can make the audience either laugh uproariously or shed a tear when that same closeup appears on the screen.

In the discussion of the editor, I must say that I have been thinking only of *film* editing. When I shoot tape, I find another life for myself entirely as a director. The director is almost always there for the editing and the first edit is usually a completed edit on videotape. The editor, too, is another sort of animal under these conditions. The whole system of relationships changes and the mode of working is different. There are a few videotape editors who function much like film editors, but very few. Under traditional circumstances, the film editor is given the rushes and storyboard, he views the rushes several times, making his notes, and then, with a resolved total plan, proceeds to edit the spot. Not so, in almost all videotape editing. When the editing is ready to start, the editor will turn to the director and ask, ''What's the first scene?'' He will lay that down and then ask, ''What's the next scene?'' I have even worked with many tape editors who ask me what the code number is of the frame I wish the cut to be on.

In such videotape editing, the director is back on his own again. He is basically editing the spot. The tape editor, while he may be sufficiently creative to offer suggestions or arguments, is still making the cuts under the director's command. I have found that the very language and idiom of these commands are as yet mostly unintelligible to the agency and client. That gives me the opportunity, at least, to see the cut as I would like to present it. Only then, when the agency folk see the specific cut, can they ask for a change, either in the place or in the optical effect I dreamed up.

Directors are editing again—and it's beautiful!

Finally, some words from a director who had this story to tell about his crew and a wrap-up party:

> And we had this ball; we danced until dawn and all the wives were there. Not everybody knew everybody else because they'd been on different jobs at different times. Guys flew in from Chicago. We had a ball! It was great; the best time I've ever had in my life. I don't even dance and I danced until the sun came up. That's because we spend a hundred and fifty days a year in motel rooms. You've got to hang out with the right people. It's like a marriage of sorts.

16

The Business

LET'S GET DOWN TO the nit and grit of directing television commercials.

The Company

A director either works for a large company, or he free-lances, or he has a small company (a boutique, it is disrespectfully called). Company sizes vary. He may have on staff a full complement of assistants: a representative (salesman, that is), a producer, a production manager, a bookkeeper, a secretary, a general assistant or more who are learning gofers. That's a lot of overhead for one director to carry but there are a number of successful shops that operate this way. Some of them spread the burden between two directors. With more than two, you might want to call the shop a "large" company. The staff patterns are pretty much the same, with a company adding a stylist or a casting person or someone on staff doubling in responsibilities.

On the other end, there is the director with only one person doing all the above jobs, who calls in the appropriate free-lance help when needed. Still photographers who enter the TV commercial field often carry over their assistant photographers and those assistants are the producers for the company.

The problem that the one-assistant companies have is that the rep also must act as the company producer and that means a lot of time is lost when he should be out in the field turning the earth. Several good reps have told me that that requires making some hundred telephone calls a day, each day, besides their other functions. It requires a thorough and up-to-date knowledge of the marketplace, who's fired from what job and what agency producer is taking up at what new agency in that revolving-door world of insecurities.

The primary function of the rep is to get agency people to view the sample reel of the director and thereby bring in storyboards to bid on.

The Rep and the Bid

Given a storyboard to bid upon, the rep is often the person who does the bidding. In many cases, of course, he may be the production company's producer, too, but the more opulent companies separate these functions. In most companies of small size, too, the director himself does all the budgeting and bidding. A rep should have the ability to bid, should the producer and director be out of town on a shoot.

One director has full confidence in the bidding ability of his rep:

> My rep knows my habits. He knows the speed at which I shoot. He knows my weak points and he knows my strengths. And, when he bids a job, he understands that. Whereas somebody else might bid a job for three days, he might bid it for two days. Whereas he might look at a set and interpret it through my eyes and speak to my scenic designers or speak to me, and we arrive at how long it would take to build, the kind of set and so on. All this affects the price—and we say you're not interested in price but that's the name of the game when it really gets down to it as ninety-nine-point-nine percent of all jobs are based on the bid system.

A rep who has received a board says:

> So the next step is to come back to the home base, sit down with the director, discuss it with him to see what he sees in the commercial, what he feels the schedule will be, how long it will take to shoot this, what his production requirements are, what special equipment he will need . . .

Another rep says:

> If the director's available, obviously, let him make decisions about lots of things. I also think if there's a set designer available or on staff, it's a good idea to bring him into your thinking. Numbers are only as good as what they represent. I can do a budget many different ways on a single project. Sometimes, I have to insist on a direction. Sometimes I have to say (to the director), "This is the way it's gonna be. Here's the way I figured it out." He might say, "Gee, I. . . ." But, it's important that a director never embarrass his representative, either, because the rep, after all, is the director and the company until people that you contact actually meet the rest of the company. You're the calling card. If you make a promise, the rest of the gang better keep that promise or you're no good, because you don't do anything else as a representative but tell the truth, seem to know what you're talking about, answer questions as intelligently as possible. I say, "I don't know but I'll find out for you," if I don't know. But the director has to be behind you. No matter what he says to you in private—"You son-of-a bitch, what did you do

to me?''—he must never say it in public. He must say, ''Okay. If ——— said it, sure.''

Representatives are concerned about the director's attitude toward them. One speaks of the need for ''mutual respect.'' Another:

> He must respect the person for his or her overall maturity and judgment, for something as simple as saying, ''If I'm not there, he or she can represent me. And I don't have to worry about what she says or how she says it.'' I keep saying her and his because more and more I find young ladies are in bid sessions where I find myself.

Another rep admonished directors to be ''as much an aid and comfort as possible to the rep.'' He asked that directors give a hand in the sales effort wherever possible: ''The director should be available to go to a lunch. . . .''

A rep explains the all-encompassing nature of the job:

> It isn't right to sell a job and disappear, go out and get the next one. . . . I am still the salesman and there is nobody else. So, I have to consider myself as just the representative competing with other excellent representatives and I have to watch my p's and q's so that I can maintain the position in which I find myself. You can't just ride it; you have to be interested in every young producer who comes along, every unimportant assistant producer, because tomorrow, they're going to be the producers. They remember, and they should. So, you must maintain your integrity, your intelligence and your dependability.

Any good rep will tell you that the measure of his success is related directly to the work, the personality and the reputation of the director he is selling. While every positive aspect helps, a close contact with the agency buyer is usually of little help other than being, perhaps, the reason his being considered as one of the bidders. The director may very well be a favorite of the agency but they have other favorites, too. Then, the bid takes precedence.

Yet, the basic labor of the rep must never stop. He must get the sample reel shown and extol the qualities of the director to all who will listen—in terms that the director could never in good taste use himself. His message must be that the director is not only a superb artist but a pleasure to work with in every way and so on.

A director says:

> I've always said to reps, ''Figure out how we bought and you'll know more about how to sell. How do I choose a cameraman, assistant director, script supervisor?''

A mixed blessing is the pigeonholing of a director as one who does a certain type of commercial well. The director is assured of a continuity of such jobs, making the rep's efforts limited almost to order-taking. However, that very singularity keeps the director from getting productions of another sort, confounding the poor rep.

If somebody has shot three commercials for soup, he becomes a soup special-ist. Through his whole life, he'll never get a chance to shoot anything but soup.

A rep:

> I have been called by an agency producer to pick up a storyboard. What I look for and hope to get from him is a frame-by-frame understanding of what they want. In addition, I want spelled out clearly what the specs are: who does what; who pays for what; who supplies things. For instance, who does the casting? Does the agency supply us with the color-corrected product? If there are special props involved, let's say, that have been used in a previous commercial the agency has done, the agency would be supplying them. And such things as who supplies the wardrobe. If it's our responsibility, I like to get an idea of what the agency sees these people wearing. I want to get an idea of what should be spent on that. If there's some dialogue or if there are voice-over lines, I've got to know who's recording the lines—I have to know if it's our responsibility, if it's going to be supplied to us by the agency. I've got to know whether it will be on quarter-inch or magnetic stripe or whatever. I always would like to know who the other bidders are because it gives me an idea of who our competition is and where we are positioned as a production company and where my director is positioned in the eyes of the agency.

Eliciting a Bid

The rep would prefer to find himself bidding against the top superstars. Then he knows that his director is considered one of them. He might be among the "food" companies or among the "schlock" outfits. His presence within any specific group does not absolutely delineate the agency's attitude toward his company. They may want another type of bid or a different viewpoint. Or, the rep's very charming personality may have earned him a chance to bid on a job. This happens, but not very often. What is more prevalent is the friendship factor between the rep or the director and the agency purchaser. The social relationship is still the most potent force in selling—all selling, I suppose.

Among the many factors that decide an agency on the use of a specific director are: the sample reel; previous experience with the director; personal relationships with the director; the director's working personality. Are the agency personnel comfortable working with him? The client personnel? Is he difficult to talk to? Is he cooperative? One rep sees it this way:

> Writer, art director, producer, account people—when they leave that set and say, "Oh, I can't *wait* until I come back and work with this guy again, he's great!" Hopefully on the next day, with the dailies, that's confirmed, and you've got a customer who's certainly going to consider my director on every-thing that's important. If you louse up on the set; if your dailies are bad, if you make a lot of mistakes, if there's disorganization and disunity and havoc on that set—even if it comes out beautifully—they're gonna remember the

havoc, the disorder and they're gonna hesitate about coming back to you again. Perfection is the name of the game. And it isn't even as simple as that and that's very difficult, because it's somebody else who decides what is perfect.

A production company might not get bid because it, or the director, is not considered sufficiently business-oriented. The director may have a bad reputation of paying no attention to the budget. The company itself may be known to be in financial difficulties or not precise in itemizing expenditures in cost-plus productions. There is a real concern by the agency that a foundering production company might fold during a production, creating all kinds of troubles for them with the client. They like to work with someone who has been in business at least a reasonably long time.

Every production company is accustomed to the occasional "exercise" bid. An agency normally gets three bids for a production and that allays the concern of the client that he may be paying more for the choice of the agency person instead of the lowest possible price for the best possible production. The production house, when one of its representatives is on intimate terms with the agency producer, often gets a board to bid on with an admonition such as: "Bid me thirty-two thousand, five hundred on this spot; I want to give it to X and I need two other higher bids." The production house then goes through the exercise looking forward to the day when they will be X. Or, if the bidding has been legitimate, the friend at the agency may well call you to say: "If you want the job, come in at twenty-nine thousand, five hundred. I have two slightly higher bids."

The Clio

When an agency producer wants to "sell" a director to the client and to his own agency people, a very strong argument is, "That director won a Clio this year." Winning this prestigious television commercial award indicates that the director is contemporary, successful and able. However, the strongest value of this achievement comes from having won it *this* year—especially if the spot is one which is widely run and has attracted everyone's attention. Because of the many different types of Clios handed out each year, saying that a director has won a dozen Clios over the years is no great shucks. This year's win does it.

On the other hand, I get a lot of mileage out of the ability to say that my work is represented in the "classic" archives of the Clios. That's impressive.

Time after time, the names of the "superstar" directors appear on the latest Clio list. The envious might say, with good reason, "Sure, they always get the juiciest spots to shoot." They do. And they get the fattest budgets. And for very good reason. They're damned good. Still, in many places, there is strong refusal to use these people; the dictum that comes down from the client is that "they aren't worth the money." Well, "each to his own gout;" that leaves more potential business for those directors whose prices are in line with the client's definition of his needs.

The Bottom Line

An agency producer:

> If I recommend certain directors and discuss production backup, I'm listened to. That's not considering twenty-year friendships—whether they're right or wrong and all that jazz. Money does play a big part and I have yet to see a series of bids where they were all very close. Some places will bid forty-nine, others will bid fifty-two, and that is close enough for my standards. But the third was ninety-nine and that infuriates me a lot because you know there is no need for all that money. In that case, I called the production company and asked, "Why didn't you say you were busy? I could have called someone else. Leave me with some sort of an option." That has happened a few times and it is not strictly my own example.

Having worked for a production company before joining an advertising agency, the same producer says:

> If you assess the board you say, "Realistically, this is two days worth of styling, plus the time needed for the shoot." If you work for a "fashion" production house, you tend to collect a very good wardrobe room. Maybe the director would say, "That dress, that dress and that dress (from his own wardrobe room) will make it," and that would mean the stylist would not have to go out and shop. So, we'll be booking her for less time. But, I would still put down the three days I originally counted in the budget because the agency didn't have knowledge of it. I think that all companies are entitled to making a little bit of money. What bothers me is when there is an enormous amount of exaggeration. When I see four days for a stylist counted in the budget for a one-day shoot that involves an hour shopping to pick (things) up, that's when I call people on that.

I must include this aside on the subject of selling. A director says:

> You know what the business is like: it can be very, very corrupt. Makes you sick, but it's a fact of life. It's like politics. A lot of people in this business are very, very crooked and I try not to work with them. They know that I'm straight and they try not to work with me. We don't take wives on location at our expense and I don't give kickbacks and I don't raise the bid. I don't do that and I don't like that.

More than one volume could be written on that subject alone. Yet, the same prose, changing the name of the industry to any other, would apply. Let it lie there in its filth.

The Job Is Awarded

Let's get back into the sunshine: the selling is successful, the job is awarded to the director. A rep:

Now the dust is settled, the job is ours and the director now has to ready himself for the upcoming production. He probably has not had any talks with the agency producer at all. So, I feel that this is the time where the director and producer should get together and have a discussion between themselves with me there, because I have been the go-between, and talk over the nuances, the fine points of the job, to make certain that the two minds are now aligned and that they are going in the same direction. This is an important session. If the director and the producer haven't worked together at all, or if it has been a long time in between, a lunch is a good idea because it can be an informative session on how the job should be handled. Maybe there are some distractions at lunch but we can rekindle any friendship that may have fallen by the wayside, or give the producer an understanding of who this man is who is going to make this commercial, and it is generally a good time for each of them to get to know each other. So, it really is a pre-pre-production meeting.

This is a vital moment for the director, whatever relationship he has with the producer. Even the best of professionals, you and I included, are guilty of wishful thinking. At this point, however, the director's dreary function is often to prick the agency's balloon. Even if the production budget is $10,000, the agency has been selling the spot to the client over a long period of time, while at the same time selling itself. By now, the mental image of the production is one of a $100,000 spot and the director, as well as adding his creative input, must bring the project down to solid earth. The combination of demands is not easy; the director himself wants to fly, but there's that budget. Not that a $10,000 production cannot be as artful and/or as effective as a $100,000 spot; the ultimate success depends, of course, on the combination of the concept and the production.

The Company Producer

At this point, too, another person enters the fray: the company producer. Not the agency producer—I curse the narcissistic similarity of titles—but the person who will be the liaison between his production company and the agency from that point on. The rep bows out, basically. The company producer might be the production manager playing two roles or he might be the business partner of the director or the free-lance assistant director or, in the case of the still smaller company, the rep himself. The ideal company producer has only that function and applies himself totally to it. The director needs and depends on his producer as though the producer were his security blanket. The importance which the director applies to his producer can be heard in this hysterical description from one director:

> She's the best in the business, the *best!* She can do budget, she can entertain you, she can shoot a camera, she can load a magazine, she can cut. I trust her taste in clothes and hair as much as anyone's around. She knows the business from the bottom up. I put her against anybody: Hollywood, New York, commercials, film, anything. And, she's gonna be a big star someday. Kills me,

because I'll lose her. But, she's the *best* and when they talk to her, they get the straight stuff.

And, indeed, the company producer *is* important. An agency producer insists: "I don't ever think about a job first really in terms of the director. I think in terms of the company, which for me means production backup."

I take no little umbrage at this but it does point up the sober business side of directing commercials. And, the surging quest for security by the agency folk. They need a person to lean on for details other than those fielded by the director. They need a whipping boy because the director is usually too austere a figure to whip. They need answers to questions—fast, correct, honest answers. The company producer must play the additional roles of diplomat and, at the same time, the mailed fist of the demander of additional monies for requests originally unspecified.

An agency producer:

> I go into any company I am about to work with under the assumption that the director likes and trusts his producer. There has been one instance where I was very dissatisfied with a producer. I felt that this man did not care, was not servicing me at all and was, in fact, maltreating me and my agency. It was a very tense job with a lot of politics going on. I thought that perhaps the best bet was to call the director right away. I told him that I was sorry to bother him with this type of problem, but I wanted to know which stage we were shooting at! I wanted to know how come his stylist didn't show up for the fitting! It was really disastrous. There was no backup at all.

The Director as Businessman

The above, the director can do without. It usually works the other way: the company producer has to stay on top of the director to keep him reminded that the TV commercial field is indeed a business. A couple of producers have the same point to make about a director:

> I would like to know that the man has a sense of business because it is a business and it has to be adhered to. He shouldn't lose sight of the fact (that) he's budgeted to work an eight-hour day and he shouldn't let his so-called creativity stand in front of that. He's got to bring his job in on budget. If there are changes precipitated by him, it's still got to be on budget unless the client agrees to pick up the tab for something special.

> He, too, has had some administrative background, which is useful in a director, because so many directors are interested in a so-called creative result and as long as they are not paying the bills they don't care how they come to that exciting commercial, the one they can put on their reel, the one they can tickle the art directors' fancies with. What I look for in a director after the basic talent that is so necessary is a man who understands that this commercial field is in fact a business. And, if you lose just a little bit on each job, it will take you just a little longer to go out of business. If you make a little bit on every job, you can grow and prosper.

Naturally, the rep and the producer must know their director's approach before the bid, as well as: his pace, about which one agency producer said, "Sometimes you don't have a fast director. That is okay. I don't think fast or slow means good or bad;" his penchants (I always like to have a wild wall on the set ready for me if I want to expand or reverse a shot, even if it wasn't originally called for); his insistence on plenty and constant food on the set and so on. Yet, the director must practice plenty of self-discipline and, if that determination slips, it's great to have his producer as his forceful conscience.

From one director:

> I respect him as a producer and if he tells me we have to get finished in ten hours, we get finished in ten hours. . . . I try to let him be the boss on the set, even though I might be the owner of the company and the director. On record, I feel the producer who's in charge of the dollars has the final responsibility. I think the director can at times be too self-indulgent.

Behind the Director

On the other hand, an agency producer protests:

> I think that directors are sometimes overprotected by their teams from the trauma of directing. If the team is going to over-protect, then the team has to be strong. The team has to go on the line.

That refers to the director's group that keep him, for example, from overworking, from attending too many useless meetings, from handling too many details by himself.

> That puts me, as an agency producer, in the position of having to bumble through with the art director as to why the director doesn't have time for a fitting, or why the director doesn't have time to look at the casting tapes when they've known for a week that it's going to client and, in essence, why not have a director's input.

These are the times when the director owes the agency his time and input. One fair agency producer insists:

> I wouldn't expect so much as thirty seconds of a director's time unless he had actually been awarded the job. That is, unless he's an old friend, or perhaps he is a director who has worked for the particular account for quite a while. There are still single bid situations where you can say, "Hey, Ben, we're ready for the next package." I'm glad to see it still goes on.

Details of the Budget

The producer for the production company has the completed budget in his nerve-tightened fist now. Listed in those pages are some two hundred separate, specific estimates of individual costs. These details have usually gone to agency and client; they expect the production company to adhere, if not to the penny for each category, then to the total sum.

To put it hysterically, things can go wrong. The stories are legion; I like the example of the nine-story mockup of a product box that was to be set up in a dry river bed in Yugoslavia with hundreds of extras relating to it. The cost of building it escalated fiercely during construction; there were days and costly days waiting for the bad weather to let up. Finally, when the shoot was imminent, the river had a flash flood, destroying the construction. The whole production was started all over again in Israel.

What happens when that happens? Or, what happens when a crane is budgeted for the shot and the director insists that the commercial would be greatly enhanced if a helicopter and the flying camera is used? It depends on two factors: the contract with the agency (whether a firm bid or cost-plus or firm fee for the production company and costs) and whether the agency or client tend to allow costs to rise.

I have found that the "personality" of the agency plays a very strong part in this attitude. In any case, it never bodes well for anyone if the budget is exceeded for any reason whatsoever. Everybody looks bad and there is anger and embarrassment and a lot of questioning and demands for proof of the necessity for and of the exact amounts of the additional billing, and then the payment, at best, comes in very slowly. The most fearsome words you can hear are: "The client won't pay; the agency will have to eat the cost." Then the hatreds and retributions explode like a *Walpurgisnacht*.

So, the budgets are set out quite meticulously for the bid and every effort is made to be quite clear about what is going to be given and done by the production company for what monies.

A company producer:

> It is now a matter of course that no longer do we only give a bid; we also send along a cover letter which explains the director's viewpoints on the commercial. This is also a selling tool, no doubt, but it's what the agency wants.

Another company producer:

> No advertising agency comes to a studio, or a location, and brings their own lunch. They expect to be wined and dined and fed a lunch or a dinner, or both. You cannot rely on your budget to include that. It makes it kind of difficult. Some money has to be spent there, but as far as agency people are concerned, they brought their lunch in a brown bag when it comes to figuring the final budget from their point of view.

The budget, of course, depends vastly on the pace of the shooting. Overtime is very expensive for the most part. An extra day is always costly, too; however, too often the shooting falls into so much overtime that it would have been less expensive to work another day at straight time. The wise director considers this balance very carefully—including the complication that the agency pays the talent—before the bid is sent in or when the shooting goes late.

A director:

In this job, boy, you come to work at seven-thirty and it's a *race* until five-thirty or six. I mean, you're going a mile a minute. But it's great! Everybody's on you for answers and you try to give them and you try to do that and you can't have any beer during the day 'cause it's going to slow you down. You just can't wait until they say, "wrap," and it's over and you can just sit down and take it easy and help with the wrap—or don't use your mind. So, I like the pace; I like it a lot.

Another director:

I think the demands on a feature film are much more than on commercials. I think commercials have the cushiest job. Sometimes we'll get a fortune just to do two shots in a day, in the right light. And, you can't do that in a film. . . . No wonder their work is incredible looking. They wait until four-forty-five to push the button and if (it) ain't right, and if a cloud comes out, they come back the next day. We can do that. I like to shoot pastoral work in the best light. If you shoot it at noon, it's not gonna look as good. If you just tell them up front: "Look, do you want me to bid this for the crack of dawn and the magic hour" If the agency says yes, well, then do it. And you can't do that in any other profession. The hardest thing about shooting features, if you're a technician, is matching. You gotta shoot at noon, you gotta shoot early morning, you gotta shoot late afternoon, and then you gotta shoot on days when it rains and make it look like it's sunny. That's why commercial guys have such a tough time sliding into features. A director can't even think that way. Poor cameraman. You know, it's really a bitch. I do a lot of that. This spring was really rough with weather. We had to use a lot of lights, but God help us, it did look sunny and light. So, it's rough.

Still another unknown factor of the budget that must be rather blindly estimated is the amount of film raw stock that will be used. If the spot is one of grand scale, then one producer's dictum is valid:

I believe that a director should understand that, in most cases, film is the most inexpensive item in your production budget. I think you should use it intelligently, but don't stint on film. It's a foolish saving.

Yet, the many spots done on a sparse budget cannot reflect this comparative extravagance. The exposure of film affects costs other than the stock itself; it increases the budget of the developing and the printing and even the subsequent time of the editor and negative cutter. The budgeting of film stock must also take into account the approach of the director, the talent of the actors and, as in every aspect of budgeting, the personality of the agency and client, who may call for less or more or a maddening amount of retakes on each scene.

The "weather day" is almost always budgeted separately and, if the weather turns bad on the day of shooting, the client pays for it, usually at a lesser or no markup. I had a shoot of an outdoor patio barbecue for a soft drink spot and, after all was set up, the weather turned and it looked certain that we were in for a strong shower. A quick decision was made for a new story-line, since we had nothing to lose but the film to be exposed. We let all the preparations stand and, when the downpour hit, shot a great sequence of the talent swiftly gathering up the foods and barbecue equipment, getting drenched uproariously in the process. Then we moved into the house and filmed the setting of the tablecloths on the floor, with the fireplace, a guitar playing, the eating and drinking, and it was delightful. A shot of a boy seeing the sun come out and then we moved out to finish in exterior. It worked.

Another director's story:

> We were at our most critical shot recently on a soft drink thing with a very elaborate special effect on a picnic table outdoors and it just started to pour out of nowhere. And, we just had to do it. That was just ordinary field experience where you send a prop man to a local hardware store which is five minutes away, get some plastic drop cloths, tape them together to make a twenty-four-foot awning and continue shooting and get the thing.

I know that this sounds ridiculous but, after you have saved the client the cost of a weather day, it is very difficult to collect the money from them that it cost in time and extra equipment. It's much easier if you sit on your fanny and call it a weather day. That situation has been previously accepted and the payment is forthcoming much easier!

Those were just examples of the complications of the budget to be contemplated before the bid. It takes a mind-reading rep or company producer to foretell what the reaction of his director will be to the bid. In most cases, the director should involve himself with the bid before it goes out.

Unless you are awarded the job, the agency producer will in most cases not call you to tell you so. That really stinks. A rep:

> Two reasons come to mind immediately. One is that there is some embarrassment, and number two is that they never intended to work with you in the first place. A third answer could be, and I'm a very forgiving man, that the poor sucker is busy and doesn't have time to do it.

Sure.

Pre-pre and Pre-production Meetings

But, let us say that the rep is awarded the production:

> Well, I immediately go into a dance, whistle "California, Here I Come" or whatever and inform the personnel at my company that we've got such-and-such a job. We're going to have a pre-production meeting at the agency at a certain day, so let's sit down and discuss it ourselves so that those of us who go to the meeting know exactly what's going to happen, when and where. . . .

This is the pre-pre-production meeting that takes place at the production company. Immediately after, another pre-pre-production meet will take place between the agency producer and the director, preferably, as noted, over lunch. There, the director is oriented into the many aspects of the production: any politics, the intent and aims of the undertaking, the creative approaches, the missing elements of creative concept required from the director and so on. A team is forged between the agency producer and the director, who, from this point on, should operate together. Each item is meticulously and completely discussed so that there is perfect understanding between the two.

An agency producer:

> If the timing works out (which it seldom does), I'm usually in the midst of casting when the job is awarded. I open my mind to any suggestions that the director might have. This usually happens when he says, "Now that I'm doing the job, why don't you call in so-and-so?" I think that is invaluable. The directors I have worked with all seem to be very involved, especially in casting, if indeed they were not responsible for the casting. . . . I think that a director should feel quite bold about saying, "Okay, you guys have decided that he's the one for the part; I really don't think he's your best bet." I think that is fair, whether he wins or loses. He really should go on record because he is the one who is going to be blamed if the performance is not good enough.

Occasionally, too, the art director of the agency will want to talk with the director privately to get his licks in so that the spot is produced the way he sees it.

Now let us march in solemn pontifical ceremony into the pre-production meeting, which is almost always held in a conference room at the advertising agency. A production company rep speaks:

> I go, together with my company's producer. Possibly the director of photography will be there because there are certain things he may have to know. If we're doing the casting, our casting person should be there. The stylist should be there. If it is a commercial that requires the services of a highly skilled hairdresser, the hairdresser should be there too. If the set is going to be built, the art director who will design the set should be there. The number of people will vary according to the requirements of the particular job. It is conceivable that the director will go with a retinue of people.

As does an agency producer:

> . . . the creative team from the agency: the writer, the art director, the producer who runs the so-called production meeting in almost every case, also the account group and the client. (Also, our casting person and our stylist.) The purpose is to make sure everybody involved in the project hears at the same time exactly what is expected, so that when the job is shot and edited and you sit in the screening room, there isn't a lot of "how-comes?" In that meeting, we settle on a cast. You look at the recommended cast on tape. Usually you have a backup or two in case there's a problem with the client or someone objecting at the last minute to one of your choices—or someone not being available. . . . You review every single detail you can think of that can

be decided in advance in relation to that commercial. Wardrobe: is she wearing a skirt and blouse; is she wearing a turtleneck; is she wearing dark or light clothes; is it a summer or winter setting. . . . You can spend a half-hour talking about nothing but wardrobe; you can spend another half-hour talking about sets. Certain things have to be decided. Is the commercial in its present written form legally approved by the client's lawyers? If not, what's holding it up and why can't we get that settled? Is it approved by all three networks' continuity acceptance? Because, after it's finished, is CBS gonna come back and say, "Oh, you say it clears your sinus cavities. You're supposed to say, it *helps* clear your sinus cavities." Did you forget to record the actor saying "helps clear"? Does R & D have its stamp of approval on it? Can every claim be substantiated? Does the color-correct product exist? It has to be a very close resemblance to what's on the shelf. The pre-production meeting is usually a week before the actual shoot. So, in the week from the time the pre-production meeting is actually held some of the loose ends can be tied up, but we try to have everything ready before then.

Obviously, many of the items to be discussed and checked between agency and client are out of the director's bailiwick; it's best by far that he keep his mouth shut and stay out of those details. He will be turned to, soon enough, to discuss his understandings and input. By the time he enters the pre-production conference, he should have studied the spot sufficiently to speak with authority on any frame or fallibility of the storyboard.

An agency producer:

I've been to meetings (that) might last an hour-and-a-half and maybe twenty-five or even forty percent of the time is spent in discussing things specifically with the director and (with) his explaining that what we have in mind may not work because of some technical limitation—that somebody in the group doesn't understand.

Another:

You get a director who comes into a pre-production meeting and yawns a lot, looks like he's preoccupied with another shoot or a feature he's planning; it's a different fit. It has nothing to do with the guy's ability (but) with his bedside manner.

And another:

At this point, the director should be in charge. He knows the answers now. He's learned the requirements of the job, he knows more from his pre-pre-production meeting with the producer, he has taken the time to study the storyboards, to sit with a stopwatch and maybe draw some thumbnail sketches as to how he sees the shots. He has planned whether he's gonna do the first shot first, the middle shot first or the last shot first—how his day will be worked out. (He has) an idea in mind of what color schemes will be involved in the set, the set decorations, the minutiae that take up a director's time. He will have done his homework. He will have made every effort to find out everything that will happen during the commercial from fade up to fade out.

The director who was speaking about the resentment that agency people have to creative contributions from the director during the pre-production meetings says:

> You make a suggestion—how can they admit it might be a good one, because there are six other people in the room and if you make a suggestion, why didn't the writer or somebody else think of it first? I used to have a whole routine when I was working with major agencies. . . . I'd say, "I have an idea . . . forget it." They'd say, "What do you mean?" "No, forget it. You guys probably thought of it and rejected it." Or, I'd start out with, "Jeez, I wouldn't have your job for all the money in the world," and finally they would wheedle it out of me. You have to be very careful as to how you make suggestions. On the other hand, there are other agencies where you are looked on as part of the team. It is true (that) they have a very difficult job, coming up with a new concept, with one that will be approved, one that will get through clearance, one that's competitive and so on. You don't know all the problems; it's very easy to be critical.

From an agency producer:

> I think the best a director can do is say what he recommends. After all, he is the one who is experienced in directing and he should tell them what he wants. Everyone has a little bit of deference for the director. Even the most unruly of people will reach a point where they will sit back and listen. This man is on the set every day. I'm on the set every other month. I've got to listen to what he is saying. There are a lot of ideas that sound good, but the agency people just don't understand a film. They don't understand their options and they think they can do anything suggested. . . . I think a director should be outspoken within the parameters of his knowledge, experience and common courtesy.

With that common courtesy, do include a generous portion of tact and diplomacy. How hard does a director argue for his own viewpoint? He must be able to perceive when a point or an image is engraved in immutable stone. When and how he gives in depends on his own personality, but he should, at the least, have the wisdom to know where the agency and client stand and he should try to probe that while he is arguing. Also, it would be wisest not to ignore the muttered objection of that mousy looking guy in the corner. He may well be the "master" with the final say.

Again, the personality of the agency or its producer plays a distinct part in the approach of a director. According to one director:

> If I'm working for a volatile producer, the pre-planning will be much more specific than if I'm working with someone who is like-minded to myself, who is looser, who will accept suggestions and changes on set. So, the sketches that I do, frame by frame, will be much more elaborate. (One agency producer) will blow his top if the prop table is over here instead of here and make that the cause célèbre for the day. So I'm very specific on entrances and choreography. . . .

In this crazed world of working right up against unmovable deadlines and challenging creative personalities, the final decisions arrived at during the pre-production meetings often ain't so final after all. For myriads of reasons, the copy will be changed, even while shooting. Talent will not pay off, colors will clash, the legal, R & D or several other influences will arrive on horseback with fresh problems. It takes a goodly amount of eggshell-walking and tiptoeing to amalgamate the new dicta with the remembered final rulings that came out of the pre-production meeting.

I have a story about a pip of a change. Would you believe that I was awarded a simple spot that was to be shot on the steps of the Statue of Liberty—and we finally shot it in the jungles of Ecuador? It's true. The agency could not get the permission they promised to shoot at the statue and I was asked where we might find another famous long series of ascending steps. Among others, I recommended the pyramids in Mexico. This was approved, the budget was changed and I notified my Mexican crew of the shoot. A week before the filming, a notoriously great-bosomed actress was photographed bouncing down these same steps and the President of Mexico was infuriated at this irreligious display at a holy monument. All filming was outlawed at the pyramids from that day on. Now (with my own funds, since this was not an agency problem anymore) I had to find another location. The Mexican crew informed me that they had just been shooting at the Mayan temple of Tikal, in Guatemala, and that it would be perfect. The agency and client approved the location and we went to Guatemala City only to find out that it was okay to shoot theatrical productions there but *no* commercials.

I offer the following as a definition of the word "chutzpah": It was vacation time and there were no airline seats to be had to get us to Tikal. But, we not only got to Tikal to shoot the illegal commercial, but we were taken there and back by the Guatemalan air force!

Yet, that's not all there was to the story. In the early afternoon of the one-day shoot, while I was hanging by my fingernails (the cast was on the high steps; the crew was balancing on the highest outjutting of the stones), I was informed by the pilots that a storm was brewing and we had better leave soon. Well, there was the one more shot, and the one more shot and we took off quite late, but the storm hit and the plane was forced to land at some weird tourist outpost in the jungles, where we spent the night in thatch-roofed huts surrounded by monkeys.

17

Shoot and Edit

LET'S TAKE IT BACK to the moment when the director and his group have left the pre-production meeting, replete with the "blue book" of agency instructions in all matters concerning the commercial, changes in the storyboard, names and phone numbers of the cast and agency producer, perhaps the color-corrected product in hand and all else. This is where the director takes over the reins and leads the production. Or, at least, this is where I think he should. There are a number of successful directors who are quite busy and find it more efficient to have their company producer run the show, making themselves available for consultation. That may be more efficient and more profitable, but I cannot believe that it is more creative. Or, let me put it this way: in such cases, the company producer becomes the director for this period and the level of creativity rests on the personal talent of the producer. For my productions, I trust my own talent (over everyone's!) and prefer to track the details myself.

The Director Takes Charge

A rep agrees with my view:

> This is where (the director) begins to work and it's my opinion that where the person who is titled the producer for the production company now becomes the executive producer, this is the point where I want the director to become a producer-director. I want him to take it upon himself to look into every angle, every stage, every step—not relying on a soul, never feeling that anyone is going to do his job properly—to ask questions, to double-check, to make sure he has every piece of equipment, every prop, every piece of ward-

205

206 DIRECTING: The Television Commercial

robe. Never should a director assume that anyone else is going to do a job
well, because this is his ball game.

Directing the Designer

We will start the director on his way. Let us first face him with the need for
a set design. There are many situations where the set design has been made
prior to the pre-production meeting. This is preferable because the sketch can
then be shown to the agency and client together, and the uses and reasons can
be discussed and any changes made without a whole series of meetings afterward—with the subsequent necessity of sending the sketches to the client for
approval of changes. It also helps the director during the pre-production meeting to explain more clearly what his movements will be and what each frame
will include. But, in our hypothetical shoot, we will start the set sketch now.

Two heads come together: the director's and the scenic designer's. (The scenic designer is also called—to help our industry's confusion along—the Art
Director, not to be confused with the Agency Art Director!) The director's
function is two-fold. He will proffer his creative ideas for the design and plot
the physical form of the layout to conform with his technical needs. He will
anticipate entrances and exits of the talent, calling for a doorway here and a
door there that swings in this or that direction for easiest movement. He will
request that a counter be kept in a certain area because he doesn't have the
extra seconds needed for the actress to walk around the counter to the door. He
will know which fixtures and equipment should be workable during the shot
(''practical'') and what the income level of the occupants of the set is, as
ordained by the decisions of the pre-production meeting and the Blue Book.
He will discuss with the scenic designer such things as the amount of clutter,
the fireplace setting, the view out of the window, the time of day the shot
depicts and the personality of the room—whether the furniture be period or
Regency or contemporary or whether there should be drapes as well as curtains,
and so on ad infinitum! He then must inspire the scenic designer to note all
these details, go home and then return with a sketch that will be imaginative as
well as functional.

All this planning will be done together with the company producing person
or personnel—the producer, the production manager and/or the A.D. He will
also instruct them to search for a certain type of location, a certain look or feel
and degree of opulence of the house or institution, or a pastorale and the specifics thereof. One of them will move out to search for and find several possibilities, returning with Polaroids of each for the ultimate choice. With them,
too, he will discuss the equipment needed, the makeup and special people he
wants for the crew.

Directing the Details

These nagging little details are the substance of the director's efficiency and
talent. He has a keyboard of many notes to manipulate, any one of which can

sour the entire composition. In how much of the specifics should he involve himself? Which should he delegate to others? All this depends on his personality, his method of working, the trust he has in his assistants and many other factors. His job is to see that every detail is taken care of, totally and well, no matter who is responsible.

When the set sketch returns, he will check to see whether there are any changes he wants. I must note here that I am constantly amazed and delighted with most of the designs done by these miraculous people. Despite the plethora of restrictions and demands placed on them, they still manage to make the sets look like they had been completely free to create their own fantasies. The sketch is then sent to the agency and ofttimes changes are made, almost always slight.

Now the Polaroids depicting several locations come in.

> These will be looked at by the director and the agency producer; they select several that they feel might be right and then the director and agency producer should physically go out, look at them themselves—keeping in mind the time of day they are going to be shooting, where the shadows will be, where the sunlight will be. For an interior location, they have to know what background sounds they have to worry about. Are there men sawing trees in the next yard and will they continue to do so on the day they will be shooting and what can we do about it? Maybe they can convince the men to stop. The director will also have to think about how his D.P. will light the location; can they bounce light, can they get power? Sometimes the director rehearses in the locations. Many times, if it is an interior location, the D.P. should go along to figure out what he will need to light it. He knows at this time what the director wants to get from paper onto film. How will he give it to him?

All those details. Another director objects:

> Preparation is different with every director. Some directors, rightly or wrongly, feel they have to be in on the most minute detail. I have a staff that's been with me for a long, long time. I have a terrific producer, terrific scenic, terrific D.P. My people are extensions of me. If I were to get on every job and check those details like some other people do, I think I'd be boxed out by the time I'm on that set.

The set sketch approved, the grips are working with the carpenters and painters (forgive me: the painters are called scenic artists), and an electrician is standing by to turn the lights on or off, depending on the time of day.

(Have I betimes been too snide about union rules? I'm rather sorry, since I am very much a union man and have done a stint in my early youth as the business representative of the then Association of Documentary Cameramen. It's just that, as in all union situations, Labor has had to make doubly certain that their rights and incomes are not impinged upon by Capital, and the pendulum of power has in some situations swung too far from the bosses to the worker. Still, I do not believe that our democracy could remain fair or even possible without the existence of union strength.)

As the set is being completed, the director calls the agency producer to the stage to affirm that all is resolving as planned and promised. The director has made several trips to the stage during construction and during the deliveries of furniture and other props.

> If he is going to have a prop for the set and it arrives and he finds that it doesn't fit at all with the set, he's going to say, "My God, that's terrible. I want something else." This is part of the director's role.

In many situations, the director has outlined the first shot, usually the long one, to the D.P. and the gaffer. Toward the end of the construction, the gaffer enters with his crew to pre-light the set, setting his lamps in the general area required, whether they stand on the floor or are hung or placed on the catwalks.

Back at the agency, usually, the talent has gathered to try on and display the wardrobe. The worrying director is involved here, too. In fact, the advice of the D.P. is sought for his knowledge and feeling of color and textures.

Creativity of the Director

All these, you might say, are details. But, long before his entry on the day of shooting—and up to the last moment, including the night before—the director has contemplated more than detail, more than technique. He has had ideas, perhaps brilliant touches of his own he would like to add, but he remembers what the producer has said:

> To the client, it is a very important thing. That copywriter might have written at least twenty five specific points, and done a hundred tests—storyboard tests, writing tests—and it is not unusual to say that fifteen animatics were made in doing this commercial, only to have them tossed out. It is very hard. It is *drek*, but it has to be done as well as possible, given what it is. A lot of directors who have lovely, lovely reels don't really seem to know about advertising as much as I think they should.

A fellow director says:

> I think we have to think in terms of the broad strokes, of the selling proposition, of the ideas, of the whole charisma of the commercial. It's like over-painting or overproducing. Sometimes when you paint a picture, it can be over-painted, over-detailed. I think a lot of guys are prone to do that.

The director, then, concerns himself with the whole, although it appears he is involved only with the specific scenes. The slightest look of an actor, the most minute hold for a reaction can underline or even establish the drama of the story-line. Perhaps it will even create a story-line or a flow that was not in the final writing; the director, however, feels that the original intent of the writer was to put it there, only to have it get lost in committee meanderings. The director will not actually change the storyboard; he will have it acted out so that the total story comes through. He sees the commercial, perhaps every commercial, as a little story or at least as an interesting lecture.

A director:

> There's a slogan we used to use in making teaching films and training films in the army, which was: tell 'em what you're gonna tell 'em—tell 'em—and tell 'em what you told them. And, I think you've got that in a commercial. Very often, you have to state the problem that the coffee is lousy and this girl has bad breath or somebody has dirty fingernails, or whatever. You offer a way out, then you show the happy conclusion. That's the way, particularly in slice-of-life commercials, which are mini-movies: you state a problem, which may not be earthshaking but is a problem for these characters. You say, "Here's a possible solution; why don't you try it?" In the third act, they try it. The sun comes out; everybody's happy. So that's why I think of it as an opera in three acts.

The director reviews in his mind what spots he has seen of the same product. In many cases, he has a flock of them screened for him long before the shoot. He may feel that the characters do not generally relate to each other sufficiently or there is generally an air of unreality to the scene or dialogue. He has been at the location. Since a storyboard has drawn the scenes in explicit lines, it is not easy for a director to change the angle or even the props and furniture as planned. However, the location is almost always found after the board is drawn, so location shooting allows much more freedom for the director to plan and design various aspects of this shooting. He gets a lot more opportunities to use his "what-ifs" with the agency producer: "What if we shoot the scene this way?" What if we get a couple of extras and move the camera around?" And so on.

Given that the set has been completed the day before the shoot—and, unfortunately, too often the set is not completed until the last moment—then the director has had a chance to mull the possibilities of the shoot quietly and without the pressure of time. I tend to stand there, imagining each shot, moving around with each move of the future dolly, probing the potentials.

A director:

> In choreography, you have to compose movement for a specific amount of space. You are involved with rhythm, with timing and fluidity, continuity of movement . . . and almost everything I have said relates to film on an equal basis. I think film deals with motion, with rhythm and all these, plus one extra thing: the camera lens. You bring in a third element. As a film director, like a dancer (as I am) who uses his body to communicate, you use the camera to communicate.

Like a matador the night before the bullfight bending the knee to the Virgin Mother and calling upon Her strength, the director contemplates the next morning's shoot in his lonely room.

Although I have been on the set planning the shots and on location walking through the scenes, I never put my shot list on paper until the last possible moment. This moment, senselessly, is almost always at two or three in the morning before the shoot. It's not that I have been "blessed with insomnia" or that I am too nervous to sleep; it's just that I don't want to stem the flow of new ideas, which a written shot list tends to do. Also, on location, I have dined with some of the agency people and inevitably some of the discussion is about the shoot and then new ideas are often generated. To contemplate all the new thoughts and work them into the shooting, I find myself with the storyboard stretched out before me in the early morning hours as I start to jot down the final order of shooting, the shot list and, perhaps, some needed sketches.

I have never minded for myself what the morning call is. It makes little difference whether the clock rings at four or seven. It is as difficult or as easy for me to rise and my body or mind doesn't seem to tell the difference. I know that for others an especially early call is traumatic. So, I have my steak and eggs for breakfast—I added toast when I learned that carbohydrates are a better source of instant energy than protein.

The Shoot

A company producer:

> Okay, I'm shooting. The director should be prompt. He should be on the stage or location at the right time, prior to the client. He should be busy directing the people as to setting up the first shot, how he wants it, looking at the props. When the camera is set and the location is lit, he should be able to say, "This is not quite right; let's change it." Then he can let the agency guy take a look before he shoots. But, the director should be prompt and should arrive with the storyboard in his hand—to be used for himself as a memory device. If he's made a shooting board for himself, this would have been gone over beforehand with the agency so that when the agency's client comes in—who's not necessarily very knowledgeable about production—the client might want to know why the director is doing that scene first when it's almost last on the storyboard. There's got to be a reason, and he's got to know it.

In the morning, the agency writer and art director are rhapsodizing about the talent. Most often, they were the ones who were most influential in the choice. The director had already had his say before the final choice and, if his advice was not taken, he should have availed himself of an opportunity to voice his complaint. Nonetheless, these are the actors he is to direct and get the best possible performance from. I can say that in most cases, under-direction is wisest: almost always the talent has been chosen because they physically, and in personality, represent the stereotype of the character desired. Let them play their own selves out: most often that works best. Just make sure they come across with an understanding of what they are saying and looking vibrantly alive.

Everybody in the studio is standing around watching and listening to the director handle the actors. This is their entertainment and, for some people,

SOL GOODNOFF

I KNOW...BUT HE HAS BEAUTIFUL HANDS!

their concern for the day. They study the director's technique and ability. Is he communicating well; is he leading the actor into the correct direction; is the actor being molded into the correct character?

One director:

> If they're professional actors, I try to learn the style they learned in and try to relate to that. I've had some training in that over the years and I still audit courses from time to time. It's very useful. I've many friends who are theatre actors. Speaking and hanging out with them is very important to pick up new techniques, how to make adjustments—there are some good books on it, too.

And another:

> Well, acting school is the most important thing. You don't have to get up there and do it yourself, but you must learn what it's like to feel like an actor and be an actor and all the actor's needs.

The Director as Leader

Many, if not most, of the directors have come up from the crew. It is a good background. Leading the crew, giving orders, rushing them, controlling them for silence or for attention—these can be quite frustrating efforts. The basic personality of the director plays a vital part in his success with the crew. As I have said, there are two basic and totally disparate ways to lead: either be a friend to all men and they will follow you out of love or be mean and tough and you will be followed out of fear. Either way, the crew must have respect for you and your ability to direct.

Discussions of leadership always tend to give the impression that one must act like a leader. I don't think you can act like a leader. You just are. When I walk onto a set, I am never at all concerned about, nor do I give a single thought to, my ability to lead the crew. I know I am a leader, therefore I am.

The peripheral vision I keep working plays on every member of my crew. This includes my producer (or A.D., if he is acting as producer). Even with my back to the agency and client, I am concerned, too, about whether they are at least satisfied.

A company producer:

> Sometimes (the agency producer) is ignored completely and the copywriter and the art director are doing all the talking. Sometimes the agency's creative director is doing a lot of the talking and sometimes the agency's account guy speaks up because his client is there and he wants the client to know that he is doing a great job as an account man for the agency. At this point, it has become almost like supervision by committee. Hopefully, at this point the director should make it known to all concerned that he is in charge. It has been determined previously what is going to be done and he wants to do it that way. If he wants some variations, he can do them later.

A director:

> If I feel I'm getting hassled by clients, by the agency, I'll give them exactly what they want, and that's it. But, I've been on sets where they have problems among themselves. And, it's infectious; it permeates into the talent. In such circumstances, the best thing to do is to give them what they want and get 'em the hell outta there.

A production company producer:

> If (the director) is not too smart, he's going to follow his own line and say, "I'm going to do this my way and (you should excuse the expression) screw you guys; I'm the director, it's my show." It's not the case: it is a mutual effort.

How sad. Either approach is, of course, a surrender—either to self-indulgence or to self-debasement. In either case, whether the director insists on his own way or meekly (or in disgust) gives up his dignity as an artist, there is a misguided interpretation of the role of the director in the production of television commercials. Simply put, the director is there to get onto the screen what the agency has put onto paper, adding his own personal creative input. And, he must do it within the budget prescribed. To get as much of his own ideas into the spot, he must manipulate various people as, indeed, he will be manipulated by them. These are the ground rules; play them or get out of the game.

Power of the Budget

A note about the budgets. Long ago, I heard that the budgets for the new spots were much lower than they used to be. Recently, I have heard the same thing and I would expect to hear that same complaint far into the future.

I make no claim to having done any research into the matter: I know no statistics, if, indeed, there are reliable statistics. But, I say with assuredness that there will always be lower budgeted commercials and that the "blockbusters" will always be done as well, whether they be aired on network, cable, home players or any other way. It may be that those who complain about the lack of plushier budgets just aren't getting them—or did once, and aren't getting them any more.

The availability of a larger budget brings another blessing: the time for experimentation. So, the director who gets the plush jobs because he has proven himself as an innovator gets the opportunity to innovate even more—a luxury that the director working on a lower budget production sorely misses. He, poor fellow, must push along, knocking off scene after scene so that he can finish in the allotted hours. No overtime for him.

"It's a Wrap"

Three welcome words, yet, they bring a special type of sadness. All that planning, meeting, shopping, casting, politicking—done. The light banter of the camaraderie with the crew—over. The lovely set, sparkling under the clever lights, darkened now and not yet resigned to the oblivion menacing it. The thinking and almost mischievous creativity to be stopped this moment and forever for the project. Wrap.

For myself, I tend to stay back on the stage if at all possible and unwind. Perhaps it's because I hate to leave this old friend, or enemy, whichever it was. I don't like the occasional wrap party—no more than I like attending wakes. I suppose, too, that the production—the lousy one-day's shoot—had built up to an important part of my life and now it was gone . . . Well.

The many eyes of a director are still using every bit of peripheral vision. Are the props being readied for proper return or will they be stolen? Are the color-corrected packages going back to the agency? Will the set be left standing until the rushes are viewed? Is the date set for the screening? Are agency and client's taxis or whatever waiting for them, and do they have any last requests or complaints? Has he kissed goodbye all the females that need kissing goodbye? Have the script clerk, the soundman and the asistant cameraman matched their notes to make certain all requested prints will indeed be printed on both picture and sound? Enough. Good night.

The Dailies and Editing

On to the next morning and viewing the rushes—for the experienced director, there are few surprises; he knows what the camera will do, what he had the actors do and how the scene will play. But, there are occasional aberrations. How the heart will slip down into the stomach when a flick of an actor's eye that went unnoticed ruins the best take. Or a deeper shadow than the director expected hides a vital factor, or worse, when it is realized that a shot that was planned was never made! Everyone might be huzzahing at the general look of the rushes, but the glazed look in the eye of the director signals his distress at a specific that went wrong.

The director's toughest job at the screening is explaining to the assembly of agency and client personnel that the scene which plays terribly in toto was printed because there are a couple of moments therein which are superb and will play beautifully in the editing. But few understand and it is very embarrassing, for the director knows that the overriding concern is whether the editor "will save this director's goof."

How often the editor has "saved" a director's work by using a piece of a scene or making a certain cut that the director shot to be used in the first place. The street-wise director usually anticipates the need to avoid concern at the screening by never printing any take that is not totally perfect, even though it means shooting it over and over again—unnecessarily—until the scene plays perfectly from clapstick to "cut." If he adds or changes a scene, he will inform the agency folk right at the shoot so that there will be no agonized surprise at the screening. This bright director, too, will rhapsodize at every angle, "selling" his work as the dailies unroll. I have never mastered this powerful technique, dammit; I'm intently looking for the detail which did not work. From this moment through the editing, the director, no matter how vast his experience, is learning. He will learn from his mistakes as well as from the occasional lucky break where something that he never intended works beautifully. He'll use that trick again somewhere.

A company producer

> I want the director to tell the editor, "Here are my script notes; we've circled the number of prints of each scene," and the director should know what his preferred take is. He should tell the editor how he wants the commercial to be edited together. . . . I've always heard, but I'm not sure whether it's a rule anymore, that the director had the right of making his first cut. It used to be that way. In today's world, where there are a dozen directors who are constantly directing, they rarely, much to the agency's chagrin, have time to attend the editing sessions. They get away with it. The majority of directors don't.

A director:

> The business has changed and fragmented. We all know about the director's first cut. There are very few agencies that are gonna give you the first cut. This is not Hollywood and features anymore. A producer, who is a lady on the job we just did, said, "We have a new editor, but we want to give you the first cut." Now, it's refreshing, in a sense. She doesn't do a lot of work and she has been taking courses in television. . . . It is still taught in the textbook that the director gets the first cut. Now can you see X giving me the

first cut on what we're shooting? Or Y? All of these guys you know. I'll tell you how you get your first cut. You shoot it with some of your own footage in there with the hope that it gets in.

In the editing session, the committee atmosphere of the shoot prevails, only the director has no way near the authority he had on set. There are always more ways to splice a cat commercial and everyone in the crowded room has something to say about each cut. A lot to say. But, the spot does get cut—and that's not the end of it. The tremulous environment that has been caused by all the aired objections, concerns and arguments has created a pollution of fear: The cut is not perfect; how can we go to the client with the commercial which is not perfect, or at best a compromise?

A producer:

> Everybody hates to do it, but it's done more often than not. They will cut another version, other versions, and I personally dislike these situations very, very much. We've got together a group of talented individuals who have their thoughts aligned in a certain way. Trust your own judgment. Cut it the way you want to, If it is lousy, change it. But, don't cut another version just for the sake of having another version. All these people involved should know whether their marketing goal has been achieved or that what they want from their marketing goal has been achieved. They should not have to flip a cloin to decide, or second guess what is wanted by cutting another version.

When the first editing session is over (there will be other sessions), the director's job is indeed done. The agency and client folk will pound him on the back and tell him what a wonderful job he has done. I have never been told that I did a lousy job; probably no one else has been told that, in our world of gleaming-tooth politesse. No matter, the director knows darn well what kind of production he has delivered.

After the Edit

When they're all finally gone and I'm alone in the street, a curious mixture of turbulence and peace takes over. I am still full of the angers about edits that were made that seemed wrong to me, about the several unfairnesses visited upon me by the powers that be during the shooting, about how I would have cut it, about scenes that would have been so much better had I insisted on the time to do them my way—all the frustrations, yes, and all the self-congratulations included on special touches I added, seethe in a maelstrom of turmoil.

Yet, the commercial has been completed. Whatever they are going to do with it is totally beyond my involvement and I can only hope that "my baby" will be treated well. Now there are no more props to get, locations to find, no more shot lists, no more planning and concerns. Most curious is the realization that there is no more need to dream up any creative ideas. Or solve any problems. What shall I think about now while I'm shaving or driving, or even, I must admit, while I seem to be carrying on a polite conversation? The sudden void is a little sad, a little frightening; there is a definite feeling of resentment.

The directing of that commercial has been done.

But, that Kodak spot has to be shot next Wednesday. What kind of a family should play. . . .

A SPECIAL NOTE

I have dedicated this work
to our Ray Fragasso.
But, I must acknowledge here
the infinite
sacrifice and patience of
my wife, Terry, during its
long gestation
—without whose cooperation,
as they say, this book would
certainly not have been possible.

Appendix

THE BLUE BOOK—
(OR GRAY BOOK—OR GREEN, etc.)

This is the "booklet" handed to each person entering the pre-production meeting. The contents of this particular opus is an amalgam culled and edited from several different agency booklets. The product, company, agency and names, of course, are fictitious. However, it is a true reflection of the approach; some agencies are more verbal, especially when a new product is being presented, some less.

ADVERTISING AGENCY

PRE-PRODUCTION MEETING

CLIENT: American Soap Co.
PRODUCT: Soaps
DATE: Today
PLACE: At Agency
TITLE: Pretty Soapy
NUMBER: FRCS 9412
TYPE: Film
FINISHED IN: Videotape
TEST OR AIR: On-Air

PERSONNEL

FOR THE CLIENT:
    RICHARD BOSS   DIRECTOR OF MARKETING
    ROBERT SUPPORT   BRAND MANAGER/NEW PRODUCTS

FOR AGENCY/ACCOUNT:
    WILLIAM HOLDER   MANAGEMENT REPRESENTATIVE
    JOHN UNDERWOOD   MANAGEMENT SUPERVISOR
    SHERMAN RUNNER   ACCOUNT EXECUTIVE

FOR AGENCY/CREATIVE:
    ELLEN THINKER   CREATIVE SUPERVISOR
    BEN PAINTER   ART DIRECTOR
    RALPH WOODS   PRODUCER
    ROSE SUNSHINE   PRODUCTION COORDINATOR

AGENDA

"PRETTY SOAPY"
:30 REVISED

I   OVERALL FEELING
II   SET
III TALENT
IV   WARDROBE
V   PROPS
VI   TITLES
VII FRAME BY FRAME OBJECTIVE:
    a) Scripts (Alternate versions, if any)
    b) Music tracks

    c) Voice-over tracks

    d) Sound effects (In demo section possibly)

VIII MISCELLANEOUS:

    a) For videotape Commercials—Purchase tape stock?

    b) Consideration of Potential Difficulties When Viewing Commercial in Black-and-White.

PRODUCTION INFORMATION

I. PRODUCTION COMPANY: Ben Gradus Productions, Inc.

                         625 East 47th St.,

                         616-4302

           Represented by

                  DIRECTOR: Ben Gradus

                PRODUCER: Horton Overton

            CAMERAMAN: Billy Bitzer

              EDITORIAL: Tapes Cut

            RECORDING: The Brand New Sound

                         822 East 52nd St.,

                         654-0211

       STUDIO LOCATION: 625 East 47th St.,

        SHOOTING DATE: Tuesday, June 11

II. LEGAL REQUIREMENTS:

    a) Status of network continuity acceptance:

        ABC _____ CBS _____ NBC _____O.K._____

    b) Production affidavit required? Yes ____ No ____

    c) R&D clearance obtained?

    d) Legal clearance obtained?

    e) Music cleared?

III. AGENCY REQUIREMENTS:

    A) Shooting Board: Attached

    B) Color-corrected product availability: Have been prepared.

PRODUCTION SCHEDULE

	DATES/WORKING DAYS
1. Estimate Approval	5/19
2. Agency/Client/Production Co. Pre-production Meeting	6/6
3. Prep Job	6/4–6/10
4. Shoot Commercial	6/11
5. Screen Dailies	
6. Editorial (Film or *VTR*)	6/12
7. Rough Cut Screening with work tracks	

8. Record and Mix	_____ 6/16
9. Rough Cut and Final Track Screening	_____
10. Screen Slop Print	_____
11. First 35mm Answer Print Screening	_____
12. Corrected 35mm Answer Print Screening	_____
13. First 16mm Answer Print Screening	_____
14. Corrected 16mm Answer Print Screening	_____
15. Quantity Prints	_____
16. Ship Prints	_____
17. Air Date	_____ 7/8

APPROVED
CREATIVE STRATEGY: SOAPS

TONAL OBJECTIVE

The tone of this commercial will be intrusive, dramatic, direct and informational, with strong characterizations to aid memorability.

Advertising must have an announcement tonality. It should portray SOAPS as a delightfully refreshing combination of total cleanliness. The use of SOAPS should promise longer-lasting effectiveness, self-assurance and societal acceptance.

It should appeal to all members of the family.

The AMERICAN SOAP name should be utilized as further re-inforcement for wholesome cleanliness and quality.

The format of the commercial will be classic problem-solution—with the problem established in the beginning.

TARGET

Women 20 to 60 who influence the family's choice of soap. They have average incomes and live in households with children. These women are characterized by their interest in appearance and health. They are interested in their families but they also seek self-assertion and compliments. These are the kind of women who tend to try new household items; they represent the fore-runners of new product purchasers. The commercials will be pleasant, interesting and effective for the entire family as well.

COMPETITIVE FRAMEWORK

Other soaps, including deodorants and soaps to which creams have been added, are well established in homes. There are also medicinal creams which are used as soap.

KEY CONSUMER BENEFIT

The consumer experiences a slight tingle while using SOAPS. This is a most refreshing experience. In addition, SOAPS has a longer-lasting effectiveness. The feeling of cleanliness the day through provides an additional pride of self and a comfortable assurance in society.

<u>SUPPORT</u>

1. SOAPS is made of all natural ingredients.
2. There are no chemical additives; even the scent is supplied by crushed flowers and herbs.
3. There are no abrasives.

<u>MEET AMY GROTON</u>

She's pert and trim and just turned 24 . . . a warm, wonderful girl . . . a modern girl—up-to-the-minute on everything that's happening in this busy world—but a girl with some nice old-fashioned values.

AMY loves being just what she is—curious about life and people—enjoying "today" . . . dreaming a little bit about tomorrow—just a little tentative about the problems she will face later on in life. Then her insistence on her own career and self-assertion must jell with the husband she wants and the children she would raise.

AMY's currently sharing a small apartment with her girl friend, GLADYS, in a medium-size mid-western city about 60 miles from AMY's family home in Centerville. The apartment is cozy and clean and brightly furnished with odds and ends inherited from the families of both girls—and knick-knacks gathered here and there via garage sales. The girls made the draperies and the slipcovers for the sofa and chairs—drafted a couple of boys from a neighboring apartment to help refinish some of the furniture—and in an ambitious moment tried making a set of twin bookcases which GLADYS' father was given the honor of finishing when he visited them one Sunday afternoon. Some of the pretty "furbelows" were courtesy of the house-warming party. (In one of our first commercials, we'd meet AMY and GLADYS just moving into their new apartment; later, we'd see it furnished.) AMY's mother—LYNNE GROTON. Her father—RICHARD GROTON. He works for Centerville's biggest bank. Then there are AMY's sisters. ROBIN, the eldest—about 30 and married with a couple of tots of her own. AUDREY who's 16 . . . and tries to act like AMY—her idol. And then there's WENDY, the baby of the family. She's turning twelve and a little on the tom-boyish side. But WENDY is beginning to get the idea that maybe there's something in pretty dresses and boys and well—just being a girl. AMY has loads of friends in Centerville and in the city. She dates pretty regularly in the city, but local Centerville gossip has it she'll return to marry PETER ANDREWS. He lives just up the street from the Grotons—is now away at law school.

From Centerville High—where AMY was graduated in the upper third of her class and just about first in popularity—she went on to business school. She's still going on with her education by taking some night courses at the city college. After business school, AMY got herself a job as a typist in one of the city's local radio stations. Went on to become secretary and general Girl Friday to the manager of the station, Mr. NEIL WILLIAMS. AMY thinks this job is a dream. She meets a lot of people and something exciting is always happening—a nice way to earn her living.

Speaking of money—AMY must maintain a fashionable but practical wardrobe within her budgetary limit. Her pants, blouses, sweaters, skirts and every day suits are interchangeably coordinated. The formals previously worn during her school days have been re-fashioned to the current mode. For parties and dates, AMY has her choice of wearing one of her special dresses or her dressy pants outfit. There's a nice, fresh, crisp look about AMY . . . A fresh-scrubbed look—a special glow and shine to her whole personality. She's very neat. Not that a hair's never out of place. Just catch AMY going like a whirlwind on those household chores. But AMY thinks that a girl should dress to the occasion. Of course . . . around the apartment . . . visiting friends nearby or back home in Centerville . . . AMY is more casual. But usually you'll meet her when she's nicely dressed. Outside of the apartment . . . according to commercial situations . . . we want to establish a couple of trademarks for AMY—namely the colorful belt or special scarf. For AMY is symbolically to be our SOAPS GIRL. As for jewelry, makeup, et cetera . . . AMY doesn't go in for a lot of doo-dads. Likes a neat necklace her folks gave her when she was 21. You'll find her wearing it on special occasions. Likes it with small earrings. Other than that, she wears a small gold watch and a small ring. As for makeup . . . AMY doesn't need it. Not with her fresh coloring . . . a little lipstick and what she calls "date makeup" when she wants to feel kind of "glamorous." She does her own nails and hair . . . except for a splurge now and then. Doesn't go in for the extreme hair-dos . . . wears hers in a simple but flattering style.

She has a nice figure . . . she's about a medium-size girl. Has a nice, warm, friendly voice—a voice you like listening to.

Talents? Well, she sings a little, plays the piano a little. Turns out a fancy chocolate cake and a special casserole. Takes part in civic affairs . . . does a little "little theatre" work, but mostly *behind* the scenes. Plays tennis . . . wants to learn golf . . . drives a car . . . skis . . . roller skates . . . swims. She just has fun doing things.

WRITER'S PRODUCTION NOTES
SOAPS
"AMY GROTON"
Pretty Soapy—FRCS 9412—SOAPS—:30

OBJECTIVE: To convince the entire family that SOAPS has a unique quality to make them feel refreshed and odor-free . . . because only SOAPS will keep its promise to keep you cool, calm and fresh.

MOOD: Light sell, conversational, natural.

CAST: AMY: See enclosed biography for guidance in casting AMY.
GLADYS: Should be somewhat the gamin type . . . cute, pixie, bright. Should be a bit bouncy. Her hair coloring, size, general build, personality, should be in contrast with AMY.

WARDROBE: Blouse and pants for AMY. Shirt and shorts for GLADYS. These should not be their very best, but their work clothes . . . sport clothes they've had for a while. However, the clothes should not look dirty or sloppy—no torn jeans or such. Flat shoes.

SETTING: AMY's apartment. A three-room, smallish typical bachelor girl's apartment in the city . . . not the exotic studio type . . . just a plain apartment in a building erected in the '30s or thereabouts. It is composed of a living room, bedroom (big enough for twin beds, dressing table, a couple of dressers and perhaps a chair and end table), a bath and a small kitchen. The apartment is not decorated in this commercial; no curtains, pictures, etc., as yet. Instead, we see furniture standing about haphazardly, in all the wrong places . . . many, many packing crates and cartons . . . perhaps a barrel, containing dishes, can be seen in the living room. There are shoeboxes and suitcases in the bedroom . . . plus piles of clothes stacked around. We should get the effect that they are literally wading through the moving-in mess.

DIRECTION: In the opening frames the girls reflect the fact that they are pretty tired from the task of moving in, but happy as a kid with a new toy to have their own place. They should both reflect the fact that they found their temporary quarters, prior to moving into the apartment, *really* ghastly. GLADYS' question in frame #6 should be very casual . . . AMY's emphatic answer, contrasting. She then gropes for ways to illustrate . . . GLADYS' "are you kidding?" of course, refers to the fact that she has been laboring like a truck driver, moving in. AMY's lines concerning the merit of SOAPS must be kept very natural and conversational. GLADYS can play it kind of saucy in #14 and #15.

TITLES: Lettering style for super on opening frame and also on closing frame will be sent to you. Opening title will be a dainty script, like AMY's actual hand-writing.

PRODUCT: SOAPS bars and packages will be sent you.

MUSIC: There will be *no* music at the opening. Musical gliss separating the dramatic episode from the announcer tag—also musical accent on words "cool—calm—fresh."

OPTIONAL CUTS: Frame #7 could be omitted if the spot runs too long.

ANNCR: Easy, intimate, happy.

TELEVISION COMMERCIAL PRODUCTIONS

STUDIO COST SUMMARY

		Date:	
Production Co:	Agency:	Agency job #	
Address:	Client:	Product:	
Telephone No.: Job =			
Production Contact:	Agency prod:	Tel:	
Director:	Agency art dir:	Tel:	
Camerman:	Agency writer:	Tel:	
Set Designer:	Agency Bus. Mgr:	Tel:	
Editor:	Commercial title: No. Length:		
No. pre-prod. days pre-light/rehearse	1.		
No. build strike days Hours:	2.		
No. Studio shoot days Hours:	3.		
No. Location days Hours:	4.		
Location sites:	Agency supplies:		

SUMMARY OF ESTIMATED PRODUCTION COSTS				
1. Pre-production and wrap costs				
2. Shooting crew labor				
3. Studio costs: Build/shoot/strike				
4. Location travel and expenses				
5. Equipment costs				
6. Film stock develop and print: No. feet mm				
7. Props, wardrobe, animals				
8. Payroll taxes, P & W, and misc				
9. Sub total: Direct costs				
0. Director/creative fees				
1. Insurance:				
2. Mark-up: (% of direct costs)				
3. Editorial and finishing per:				
4. Talent costs and expenses				
5. Total production estimate				
6. Weather day				
7.				
8.				

Comments:

FORM TV - 173

A: PRE-PROD'N / WRAP   B: SHOOTING

CREW	ESTIMATED				(Actual)			ESTIMATED				(Actual)		
	Days	Rate	O/T Hrs	Total	Days	Rate	Total	Days	Rate	O/T Hrs	Total	Days	Rate	Total
1. Producer:														
2. Asst. Director:														
3. Dir. Photography:														
4. Camera Operator:														
5. Asst. Cameraman:														
6. Outside Props:														
7. Inside Props:														
a.														
b.														
c.														
d.														
e.														
8. Electricians:														
a.														
b.														
c.														
d.														
e.														
9. Grips:														
a.														
b.														
c.														
d.														
e.														
10. Mixer (or Playback:)														
11. Recordist:														
12. Boom Man:														
13. Make-Up:														
14. Hair:														
15. Stylist:														
16. Wardrobe Attendant:														
17. Script Clerk:														
18. Home Economist:														
19. Scenics:														
20. VTR Man:														
21. EFX Man:														
22. Nurse:														
23. Telepr. & Operator:														
24. Generator Man:														
25. Still Man:														
26. Loc. Contact/Scout:														
27. P. A.														
28. 2nd A. D.														
29. Teamsters														
a)														
b)														
c)														
30.														
	SUB TOTAL A							SUB TOTAL B						

Job Description / Schedule Breakdown

PRE-PRODUCTION & WRAP/MATERIALS & EXPENSES	Estimated	Actual	
31. Auto Rentals (Cars @ $ x days)			
32. Air Fares: No. of people ( ) x Amount per fare ( )			
33. Per Diems: No. of people ( ) x Amount per day ( )			
34. Still Camera Rental & Film			
35. Messengers			
36. Trucking			
37. Deliveries & Taxis			
38. Home Economist Supplies			
39. Telephone & Cable			
40. Art Work			
41. Casting (Days @ $)			
42. Casting Facilities / Equipment			
SUB TOTAL C			

SET CONSTRUCTION (CREW FOR BUILD, STRIKE)	# MAN DAYS	Estimated	Actual	
43. Set Designer Name:				
44. Carpenters				
45. Grips				
46. Outside Props				
47. Inside Props				
48. Scenics				
49. Electricians				
50. Teamsters				
51. Men for Strike (grips, props, elect., misc.)				
52.				
53.				
54.				
SUB TOTAL D				

man days.........................

SET CONSTRUCTION MATERIALS	Estimated	Actual	
55. Props and Set Dressings			
56. Lumber			
57. Paint / Wallpaper			
58. Hardware			
59. Special Effects			
60. Special Outside Construction			
61. Trucking			
62. Messengers / Deliveries			
63.			
SUB TOTAL E			

STUDIO RENTAL & EXPENSES - STAGE:	Estimated	Actual	
64. Rental for Build / Strike (days @ $)			
65. Rental for Pre-Lite Days (days @ $)			
66. Rental for Shoot Days (days @ $)			
67. Rental for Shoot O. T. (Hrs.)			
68. Rental for Build / Strike Days O.T. (Hrs.)			
69. Total Power Charge & Bulbs			
70. Misc. Studio Charges & Service			
71. Meals (Lunches & Dinner for Crew and Talent)			
72.			
73.			
74.			
75.			
SUB TOTAL F			

LOCATION EXPENSES	Estimated	Actual	
76. Location Fees			
77. Guards			
78. Car Rentals			
79. Bus Rentals			
80. Camper / Dressing Room Vehicles			
81. Parking, Tolls, & Gas			
82. Trucking			
83. Other Vehicles A /			
84. Other Vehicles B /			
85. Special Crew Equipt. / Clothing			
86. Air Freight / Customs / Excess Baggage			
87. Air Fares: No. of people ( ) x cost per fare ( )			
88. Per Diems: Total No. man days ( ) x amt. per day ( )			
89. Breakfast: No. of man days ( ) x amt. per person ( )			
90. Lunch: No. of man days ( ) x amt. per person ( )			
91. Dinner: No. of man days ( ) x amt. per person ( )			
92. Gratuities, Tips and Misc. Outside Labor			
93. Cabs and other passenger transportation			
94. Limousines (Celebrity Service)			
95.			
96.			
97.			
98.			
99.			
SUB TOTAL G			

EQUIPMENT RENTAL			
100. Camera Rental Type:			
101. Sound Rental			
102. Lighting Rental			
103. Grip / Dolly Rental			
104. Generator Rental			
105. Crane / Cherry Picker Rental			
106. VTR Rental			
107. Production Supplies			
108.			
109.			
SUB TOTAL H			

FILM RAW STOCK DEVELOP AND PRINT			
110. Purchase of Raw Stock: footage amount ( ) x per foot			
111. Developing and Printing: footage amount ( ) x per foot			
112. Studio for Transfer: No. of hours ( )			
113. 16mm or 35mm Mag Stock: No. of hours ( )			
114. Sync / Screen Dailies			
115.			
SUB TOTAL I			

PROPS AND WARDROBE			
116. Location Props			
117. Costume / Wardrobe Rental & Purchase			
118. Animals & Handlers			
119. Wigs, Mustaches / Special Make-Up			
120. Color Correction			
SUB TOTAL J			

DIRECTOR / CREATIVE FEES:	Estimated	Actual	
121. Prep Days			
122. Travel Days			
123. Shoot Days			
124. Post-production Days			
125.			
SUB TOTAL K			

MISCELLANEOUS COSTS	Estimated	Actual	
126. Total Payroll & P & W Taxes % of total of A, B, D, & K			
127. Air Shipping / Special Carriers			
128. Phones and Cables			
129. Misc. (Petty Cash)			
130. Misc. Trucking & Messengers			
131.			
132.			
133.			
SUB TOTAL L			

TALENT	No.	Rate	Days–Fees	Travel	O.T.	Estimated	No.	Days–Fees	Actual
134. O/C Principals									
135. O/C Principals									
136. O/C Principals									
137. O/C Principals									
138. O/C Principals									
139.									
140.									
141.									
142. General Extras									
143. General Extras									
144. General Extras									
145.									
146.									
147.									
148. Hand Model									
149. Voice Over									
150. Fitting Fees									
151. Audition Fees: No. of talent ( ) x Amount ( )									
152. SUB-TOTAL									
153. Payroll & P & W Taxes									
154. Wardrobe Allowance: No. of talent ( ) x No. of garments ( ) x fee per garment ( ).									
155. Agents' Commissions									
156. SUB-TOTAL									
157. Other									
158. Handling Fee (_____%)									
SUB TOTAL M									

TALENT EXPENSES	Estimated		Actual
159. Per diem: No. of man days ( ) x amount per day ( )			
160. Air fare: No. of people ( ) x amount per fare ( )			
161. Cabs and other transportation			
162.			
163.			
164.			
SUB TOTAL N			

FORM AICP-2 SIMAX PRINTING 320 E. 45 ST. N.Y.C. 10017 (212) 573-9030

EDITORIAL COMPLETION	Estimated	Actual	
165. Editing			
166. Asst. Editor			
167. Coding			
168. Projection			
169. Artwork for supers			
170. Shooting of artwork			
171. Stock footage			
172. Still photographs			
173. Opticals (incl. pre-optical)			
174. Animation			
175. Stock music			
176. Original music			
177. Sound effects			
178. Dubbing studio			
179. Studio for narration - including transfer to mag. No. of hours ( )			
180. Studio for mixing - including transfer to mag. No. of hours ( )			
181. Negative tracks			
182. Answer & corrected prints			
183. Contract items			
184. Film to tape transfer (incl. reprints & masters)			
185. Film to tape transfer - editorial fee			
186.			
187.			
188. Editorial Handling Fee:			
SUB TOTAL O			

VIDEOTAPE PRODUCTION AND COMPLETION	Estimated	Actual	
189. Basic crew (No. of men:)			
190. Additional crew (No. of men:)			
191. Labor overtime			
192.			
193.			
194. VTR/Camera rental			
195. Additional VTR's/Cameras			
196. Equipment overtime			
197. Special equipment (specify)			
198. Special processes (specify)			
199. Trucking			
200. Mobile unit			
201. Stock (rental ☐ purchase ☐ No. of hrs:)			
202. Screening			
203. On-line editing No. VTR hrs:)			
204. Off-line editing (No. of hrs:)			
205. Videotape A/B roll preparation and stock			
206. Audio mix with VT projection			
207. Video air masters			
208. Video printing dupe			
209. 3/4'' videocassette			
210. Tape to fim transfer			
211. Markup			
SUB TOTAL P			

No. of hours in basic day: _____
No. of travel hours: _____
No. of setup/wrap hours: _____
No. of net shoot hours: _____
Crew O.T. rate per hour: _____
Eqpt./stage O.T. rate per hour: _____

Comments:

Index